IS ASSESSMENT FAIR?

Sara Miller McCune founded SAGE Publishing in 1965 to support the dissemination of usable knowledge and educate a global community. SAGE publishes more than 1000 journals and over 800 new books each year, spanning a wide range of subject areas. Our growing selection of library products includes archives, data, case studies and video. SAGE remains majority owned by our founder and after her lifetime will become owned by a charitable trust that secures the company's continued independence.

Los Angeles | London | New Delhi | Singapore | Washington DC | Melbourne

IS ASSESSMENT FAIR?

Isabel Nisbet
& Stuart Shaw

$SAGE

Los Angeles | London | New Delhi
Singapore | Washington DC | Melbourne

Los Angeles | London | New Delhi
Singapore | Washington DC | Melbourne

SAGE Publications Ltd
1 Oliver's Yard
55 City Road
London EC1Y 1SP

SAGE Publications Inc.
2455 Teller Road
Thousand Oaks, California 91320

SAGE Publications India Pvt Ltd
B 1/I 1 Mohan Cooperative Industrial Area
Mathura Road
New Delhi 110 044

SAGE Publications Asia-Pacific Pte Ltd
3 Church Street
#10-04 Samsung Hub
Singapore 049483

Editor: James Clark
Assistant editor: Diana Alves
Production editor: Nicola Carrier
Copyeditor: Sharon Cawood
Proofreader: Derek Markham
Indexer: Silvia Benvenuto
Marketing manager: Lorna Patkai
Cover design: Naomi Robinson
Typeset by: C&M Digitals (P) Ltd, Chennai, India
Printed in the UK

© Isabel Nisbet and Stuart Shaw 2020

First published 2020

Apart from any fair dealing for the purposes of research or private study, or criticism or review, as permitted under the Copyright, Designs and Patents Act, 1988, this publication may be reproduced, stored or transmitted in any form, or by any means, only with the prior permission in writing of the publishers, or in the case of reprographic reproduction, in accordance with the terms of licences issued by the Copyright Licensing Agency. Enquiries concerning reproduction outside those terms should be sent to the publishers.

Library of Congress Control Number: 2020930578

British Library Cataloguing in Publication data

A catalogue record for this book is available from the British Library

ISBN 978-1-5264-7494-0
ISBN 978-1-5264-7492-6 (pbk)

At SAGE we take sustainability seriously. Most of our products are printed in the UK using responsibly sourced papers and boards. When we print overseas we ensure sustainable papers are used as measured by the PREPS grading system. We undertake an annual audit to monitor our sustainability.

Table of Contents

About the Authors   vii
Acknowledgements   ix
Preface   xi
Foreword   xv

1   Introducing fairness   1

2   Fair assessment viewed through the lenses of measurement theory   15

3   Fair assessment viewed through the lenses of professional standards, guidelines and procedures   51

4   Fair assessment viewed through the lenses of the law   73

5   Fair assessment viewed through the lenses of philosophy   97

6   Fair assessment viewed through the lenses of social justice   121

7   Conclusions, challenges and a template for fairness   145

Index   165

About the Authors

Isabel Nisbet's academic training was in philosophy, with tutors including R. S. Downie and R. M. Hare. Her professional career has been in branches of government and regulation in the UK. She has held senior posts in organisations regulating the medical profession and postgraduate medical education, followed by a leading role in the regulation of educational assessments and qualifications. She was the founding CEO of Ofqual, the statutory regulator of qualifications in England. From 2011 to 2014, she worked for Cambridge Assessment in South East Asia, based in Singapore. Isabel serves on the Board of Qualifications Wales and is a governor of two universities in England. She has also been appointed to two committees advising government on ethical issues. She is an affiliated lecturer at the Faculty of Education, University of Cambridge.

Stuart D. Shaw has worked for Cambridge Assessment since January 2001 where he is particularly interested in demonstrating how Cambridge Assessment seeks to meet the demands of validity in its assessments. As Head of Research at Cambridge Assessment International Education, Stuart has a wide range of publications in English second-language assessment and educational research journals. His assessment books include: *Examining Writing: Research and practice in assessing second language writing* (Shaw and Weir, 2007); *The IELTS Writing Assessment Revision Project: Towards a revised rating scale* (Shaw and Falvey, 2008); *Validity in Educational and Psychological Assessment* (Newton and Shaw, 2014); and *Language Rich: Insights from multilingual schools* (Shaw, Imam and Hughes, 2015). Stuart is a Fellow of the Association for Educational Assessment in Europe (AEA-E) and a Fellow of the Chartered Institute of Educational Assessors (CIEA).

Acknowledgements

We are very grateful to the following people for comments on draft chapters:

Ben Colburn

Stephen Cromie

Anthony Dawson

Robin Downie

Lindsay Gee

Jessica Minaeian

Paul Newton

Natalie Prosser

Mary Richardson

Ben Schmidt

Lesley Wiseman

We are also grateful to Fiona Beedle for invaluable assistance in obtaining texts and references.

The content of the book has benefited from the comments of participants in workshops held in 2019 by the International Association of Educational Assessment and the Association of Educational Assessment, Europe.

Preface

This book has been prompted by our increasing awareness that it is timely and necessary to look hard at fairness in assessment. In the corridors of measurement theory, fairness has recently come to be seen as one of the central values of assessment, mounting the podium alongside validity and reliability. At the same time, allegations that assessments are *un*fair are commonplace in social media, the press and the courts. It is rare to find a theoretical assessment concept that commands the attention – and emotional engagement – of young children, students, parents, teachers, test providers, regulators, researchers, journalists and politicians. But fairness is just such a concept.

In parallel, academic thinking about fairness and social justice outside the context of assessment has also been moving forward. Footprints can be found in many academic disciplines – notably, social and political philosophy – and in the language and literature of civil rights movements.

It is clear that ideas about fairness from these different traditions have influenced each other. However, we have been struck by the extent to which debates about fair assessment are at cross-purposes, with the arguing parties meaning different things by 'fair' and being left aggrieved after the argument.

The book has its genesis in research which we undertook independently over a period of two to three years that reflected our different academic and professional backgrounds. We decided to pool our resources at the 43rd Annual International Association for Educational Assessment (IAEA) conference in 2017. We then wrote a critique of the 'Fairness' chapter in the current issue of the *Standards for Educational and Psychological Testing* (AERA, APA and NCME, 2014). But, before the article was published (Nisbet and Shaw, 2019), we realised that the time was ripe for a more extended project, examining assessment fairness from a range of perspectives and applying our thinking to the changing world of assessment in the twenty-first century.

This book therefore examines assessment fairness using different 'lenses' – intellectual traditions and ways of thinking. In the last chapter, we attempt to draw together some conclusions which can be applied in the future to make assessments fairer.

There are two important limitations to this discussion which need to be recognised from the outset. First, much of the material discussed in this book can be described as Anglophone. The source documents used are almost all written in

English, and the cases and examples cited are from English-speaking countries. Chapter 2, which applies lenses from measurement theory, reflects the reality that the overwhelming majority of published works in this area tend to be both psychometric and US-centric in their focus. Chapters 3 and 4 draw on examples from Ireland, Australia and South East Asia, as well as from the USA and the UK. But the legal cases are all from common law systems. And the unpacking of the concept of 'fairness' in Chapters 1 and 4 concentrates on the uses of 'fair' in English, which are different from the nuances of corresponding words in, for example, Spanish or French.

The second limitation is that we have largely concentrated in this book on educational assessment, rather than assessment in vocational or professional contexts. We do touch on issues about fair assessment for selection or promotion, the assessment of competency and 'fitness to practise' assessments in the professions. However, there has not been space here to apply our thinking to these areas in the depth that they deserve. We hope that this book will stimulate further work on fairness in vocational and professional assessments and in the world of work.

We further hope that this book will be of interest to education students, teachers and lecturers, assessment practitioners, researchers and policy-makers. We have not assumed prior knowledge or experience of philosophy or law, and the legal and philosophical chapters include descriptions of some examples which we hope will bring these disciplines to life for the reader, without recourse to law reports or philosophical texts. A secondary, wider audience would be readers with an interest in social and political theory in an applied context, or in public law as applied to educational assessment. Some of the examples we have described will be familiar to these readers, but we hope our thinking about them will be of interest.

Six of the seven chapters of the book end with a few brief accounts of cases 'for further reflection'. These are fictionalised – and by necessity simplified for purposes of discussion – but each of them has a link with real-world issues and dilemmas. We have learned a lot from discussing these with colleagues at workshops and seminars, and we hope that readers will enjoy considering them and discussing them with others.

The multidisciplinary nature of this book, together with the assembly of information from a wide variety of documentary sources, inevitably means that differing styles of expression can be detected in different chapters. However, apparent shifts in voice or style simply testify to the complex network of the stakeholders engaged (either directly or indirectly) in establishing fair assessment.

Many people have helped us with this project. In addition to those named in the 'acknowledgements' section, we wish to thank all the colleagues and students with whom we have discussed some of the issues raised in this book.

Fairness matters to everyone concerned, and when one source of unfairness is identified and tackled, more appear to present themselves. It may never be right to sign off an assessment or test as fair in all senses and all contexts. However, we hope that this book will move the debates forward and provide a framework which readers can use when they ask 'Is this assessment fair?'.

Isabel Nisbet and Stuart Shaw
April, 2020

References

American Educational Research Association (AERA), American Psychological Association (APA) and National Council on Measurement in Education (NCME) (2014) *Standards for Educational and Psychological Testing*. Washington, DC: AERA.

Nisbet, I. and Shaw, S. D. (2019) Fair assessment viewed through the lenses of measurement theory. *Assessment in Education: Principles, Policy & Practice*, 26(5), 612–629. DOI: 10.1080/0969594X.2019.1586643.

Foreword

Examinations are generally more or less accepted as a public good, allowing society to be run along the lines of meritocracy rather than patronage, corruption or other methods that have been tried. To select people for opportunities on the basis of their knowledge and skills must surely be the right way to run a society, for who wants a doctor or a pilot who is not up to the job? And not everyone can be a doctor or a pilot. When fairness of assessments is raised as a topic in academic texts, it has typically been handled in a narrow way. Assessment researchers and practitioners have debated the issues with each other and found better, technical, ways of investigating, handling and proceduralising fairness. Although the assessment field has been engaged with the societal issues of fairness, it has often been caught unawares and we have found ourselves fighting fires rather than at the vanguard. This book is different, in that it raises broad, societal issues connected with assessment fairness. It does so in a scholarly manner and recognises the technical solutions that are available without constraining the discussion to them.

Acceptance of examinations relies on their perceived fairness, at least in a democracy. Since the 1970s, inequality has been rising in society, with some economists arguing that there was only a brief period in history when inequality was reduced. Examinations are used to justify the distribution of resources in society, based on the notion of meritocracy. However, there are various signs of disquiet, with boycott movements related to school testing in several countries around the world such as Australia, Chile, Hong Kong, Spain, the UK and the USA. Big questions about fairness have arisen, such as the impact of testing on students' lives, whether children are tested too young and therefore judged too early and, ultimately, whether the promise of education and testing has been in good faith. Social mobility has not grown. Instead, in many countries young people are saddled with huge debt from a university education that was the result of doing well enough on all of those tests – and that without a graduate job to show for it. Assessment is not the only factor at work here, as opportunities are unevenly distributed in education systems, healthcare and so on throughout our lives. The effects of this are everywhere to be found, including in the make-up of our political representatives and Olympic teams, and even in the creative industries such as stage and screen. Even if it is not the testing itself which is the causal agent of these social issues, it is an important societal mechanism. Meritocracy and assessment are in a co-dependent relationship, justifying each other.

Assessment is an industry, with commercial interests at stake. Notwithstanding, industry insiders have often been open about its fallibility and sought to improve how it operates. This book, written by two well-known insiders, is an example of this. Through several lenses, the book analyses the approaches that have been taken to define and operate fairness in assessment. A key justification of standardised testing that is addressed is the even playing field approach: we all get the same test. What could be more fair? This book tackles this issue for several groups for whom this is clearly unfair. A challenge, which the authors raise, is how to approach assessment in a socially situated manner in a way that maintains fairness. If taken too far, underprivileged children may never gain the emancipatory effects of powerful scientific knowledge, for example. Key strengths of the book are the multidisciplinary approaches taken and the insightful selection of examples, which will become standard reading in many assessment courses.

Frank unfairness in assessment is not hard to come by. Here are some recent examples. A couple of famous actors in the USA were found to be paying bribes for someone else to take the college entrance tests so that their children could get into top universities. In Leon in Spain, two women were found guilty of murdering a politician in a case which involved a fraudulent examination for a civil service job: the only way to get the job was to be given the answers to the test in advance. A Japanese medical school deducted 20% of the marks from women applicants' scores on the entrance examination and added at least 20 points to the men's to ensure that there were more male doctors. Fairness in assessment is clearly important if we want to avoid corruption. This book raises issues about systemic unfairness in ways that have not been seen for some time; they are modernised here, through cases, references to empirical work and in the theoretical framing. The book is thought-provoking, will stimulate debate and hopefully will fire up the field to connect with the big issues it raises.

Professor Jo-Anne Baird, University of Oxford

1
Introducing fairness

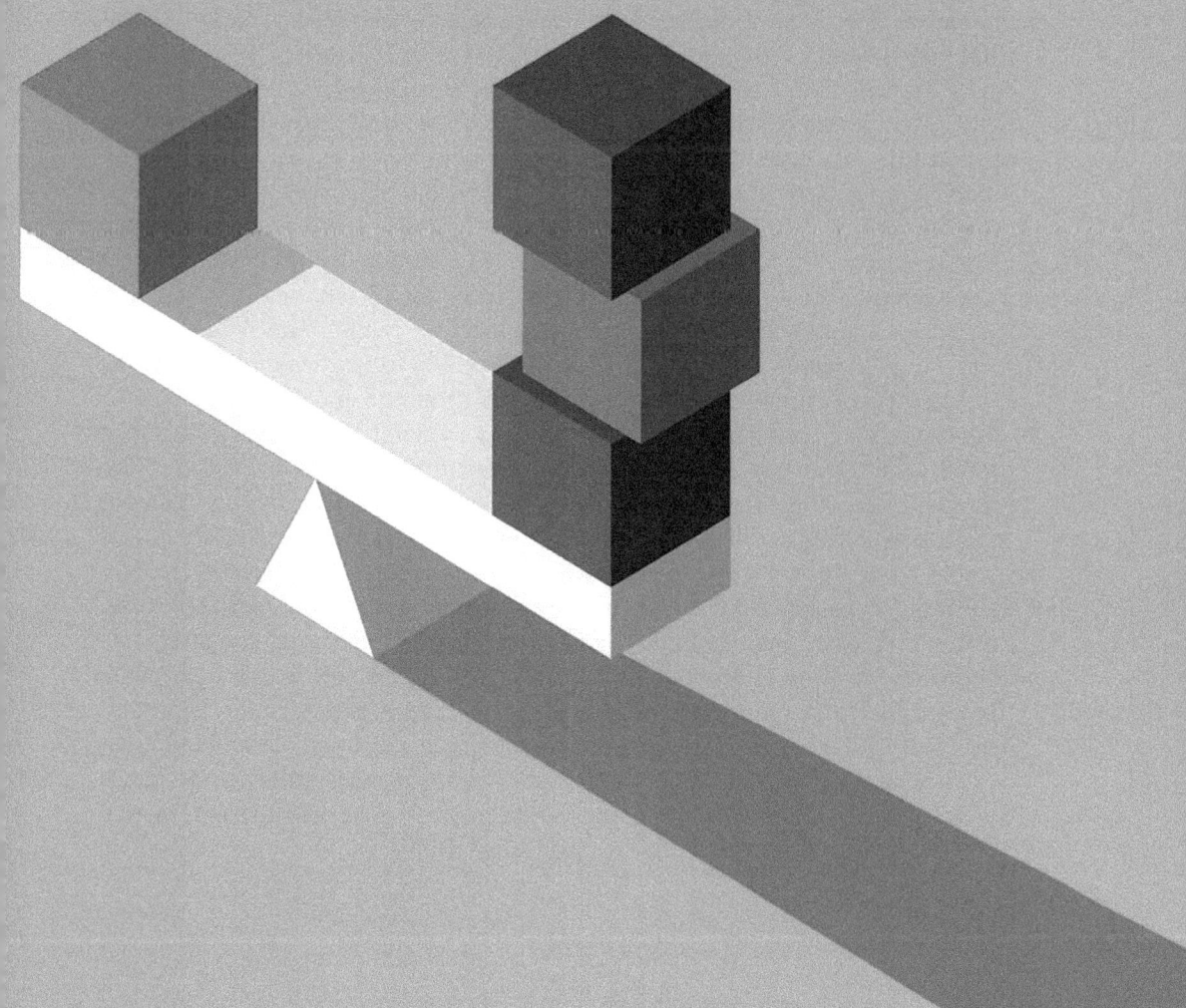

'These men ask for just the same thing, fairness and fairness only. This, so far as in my power, they, and all others, shall have.' (Abraham Lincoln)

'Life is not fair; get used to it.' (Bill Gates)

Purpose of the book

'"That's not fair" is one of my daughter's regular sayings'. So wrote one long-suffering mother on a consent form for an academic psychological study of children's reactions to different scenarios (Evans et al., 2001, p. 212). Sensitivity to unfairness – particularly in the way we are treated ourselves – does seem to manifest itself early in our pre-social development. And that deep-rooted emotional response reappears in some of the comments made on social media by teenagers before and after their exams.[1] However, when the concept of fairness is analysed in the context of social policy, or applied to particular social activities such as educational assessment, it can be difficult to pin down.

On an intuitive level, fairness suggests some level of sameness (all are equal, though we realise that it can be fair to treat people differently) and merit (you get what you deserve). And we associate *un*fairness with bias or inappropriate discrimination. Both in philosophy and in ordinary language, the concept of fairness is linked to concepts of equality and justice, but there are different accounts of the relationships. The idea of treating people equally or in a way that is right or reasonable appears to lie at the very heart of fairness. And unfairness matters – use of the word 'unfair' usually implies that someone has been harmed and has reason to be unhappy. Allegations of unfairness in educational assessments – such as public examinations – are made by candidates (test-takers), parents, teachers, journalists, politicians, employers and the general public. The debate is not confined to academics. The purpose of this book is to unpack and inform the consideration of fairness in assessment, with all these audiences in mind.

In recent years, (un)fairness in testing and assessment has had a growing public profile across the world. In the USA, an organisation called 'FairTest' (the National Center for Fair & Open Testing) 'works to end the misuses and flaws of standardised testing and to ensure that evaluation of students, teachers and schools is fair, open, valid and educationally beneficial'.[2] There have been scandals about cheating by teachers to affect the marking of standardised tests, notably in Atlanta, Georgia in 2011.[3] In China, legislation was passed in 2016 to criminalise cheating by students in the all-important university entrance exam, the 'gaokao'. In praise of this development, a leading Chinese education academic said, 'Safeguarding fairness in the gaokao and education, in general, is the baseline for China to maintain social justice'.[4] Academic writing about educational assessment has also increasingly emphasised fairness to the extent that some commentators (Worrell, 2016, p. 284) have seen the gods of assessment theory as moving from the 'big two' (validity and reliability) to the 'big three'. And more fundamentally, fairness in assessment has been seen as a weapon in support of social, political and ideological objectives, such as civil rights and social mobility, and as a weapon against prejudice, inherited privilege and unfair (sic) discrimination.

But amid this flurry of interest, whether in the public arena or in academia, two things are clear. The first is that many who criticise or praise assessments in terms of [un]fairness are not clear what they mean by 'fair'. The second is that the fairness of assessments has been viewed through a range of different 'lenses' (a metaphor which we shall explore later) – not only those of assessment theorists and practitioners, but also the viewpoints of the courts in different legal traditions, philosophers, social and political theorists, and others. There is a need for analytic ground-clearing to inform this increasingly crowded debate. There is also a need for better understanding of the different lenses applied and a vocabulary to support cross-disciplinary discussion about fairness, including in the public arena.

Defining our terms

Given the title of the book, it seems only fair to the reader that the two concepts referred to – fairness and assessment – should be unpacked at the outset, looking in particular for senses which seem relevant to considering whether educational assessment(s) is/are fair. We shall start with fairness.

Fairness

It is helpful to distinguish a number of senses of fairness – and unfairness – that can be confused in discussions about educational assessment. We shall concern ourselves in this chapter with uses of 'fair' in the English language, though it is important to note that the analysis would be different if applied to corresponding vocabulary in some other languages. We return to this point in the introduction to Chapter 5, which considers fairness viewed through the lenses of philosophy.

The first sense of 'fair' is a *formal* sense, denoting accuracy or the appropriate application of a rule or design. If we breach a formal rule of a game, it is fair for the referee to blow his whistle. In this formal sense, there is no necessary implication that the rule in question is good – just that it has been applied correctly.

The second sense may be labelled an *implied contractual* sense: something is fair if it meets the legitimate expectations of those affected. This was one of the meanings of 'fairness' in the UK court case brought in 2013 by a number of bodies against some of the providers (and their regulator, Ofqual) of an English exam for 16-year-olds taken the previous summer. We discuss this case in Chapter 4. But we note here the account of 'legitimate expectation' in the judgment:

> A legitimate expectation may arise either out of an express promise given on behalf of a public body, or from the existence of a regular practice which a claimant can reasonably expect to continue. (*LB Lewisham and Others v. AQA and Others* (2013) para. 94)

Although the legal bar for 'legitimate expectation' may be higher than that used in non-legal discussions of fairness (Cumming, 2008), the concept is broadly the same. If something about an examination fails to meet those expectations, the candidates or their teachers may have a nasty surprise and accuse the examining body of 'unfairness' in the implied contractual sense.

The third sense is *relational* – treating (relevantly) like cases alike. Almost all assessments involve 'discrimination' of some kind, meaning distinguishing between levels of achievement or between candidates who perform differently in relevant respects. In this sense, the discrimination is fair if it is based on relevant considerations and unfair if it is based on something else, such as the candidate's race or gender. As we shall see, this sense is central to much discussion of assessment fairness and lies at the heart of an emerging consensus in assessment theory. It has also featured in the courts – in the UK case referred to above, it was alleged that candidates who sat part of the exam in June 2012 received lower grades than did candidates of a comparable standard who sat the same part the previous January.

A fourth sense of 'fair', as applied to assessment, can be described as *retributive*. An outcome is regarded as fair in this sense if it is an appropriate reward (or penalty) for what has gone before. This sense goes beyond the first, formal, sense and implies that the outcome is deserved and thus, to that extent, justified. We often talk of students 'getting the grades (or marks/scores) they deserve'. This can be said in a value-neutral way, simply implying that the requirements for the grade have been met, but it more often has evaluative overtones, implying that it is a just reward for the student's hard work.

In addition to these four main senses, there are two more which are brought up in some of the examples we consider in later chapters and which are more recognisable when used negatively to describe an assessment as *unfair*.

One of these – and a fifth sense of '(un)fair' – can be labelled *consequential*. In this sense, an assessment could be accused of unfairness if its outcomes might be used as a basis for unfair or unjust actions in the future. An example of this is the Irish case considered in Chapter 4 (*Cahill v. Minister for Education*[5]) where a student complained that if the accommodations made for her disability were recorded on her certificate, that might lead future employers to discriminate against her. This raises questions of how far into the future it is appropriate to look when considering the fairness of the test itself, and of how strong the causal link between the test and the outcome needs to be to merit such a judgement, but at this stage we shall simply note the usage of '(un)fair' to refer to future consequences.

Correspondingly, there is a sixth, *retrospective*, sense of '(un)fair', which has been used in some discussions of fairness in testing in the USA. In this sense, an assessment may be unfair if its outcomes are the consequence of unfair/ socially unjust actions in the past, such as racial segregation of school education. For example, in the US case of *Debra P. v. Turlington*,[6] described in Chapter 4, the difference in test scores between black candidates and white candidates was seen as a 'vestige' of past discrimination. This usage raises similar questions (though looking backward in time) to those raised about the future by the 'consequential' sense.

Yet another sense has been used increasingly in recent years, as it is linked to the much-cited value of 'respect'. It may be seen as a sub-set of relational fairness, and denotes *equality of esteem*. In this sense, an assessment would be unfair if it could reasonably be seen as disrespectful (or causing legitimate offence) to a sub-group or an individual. For example, the language used in a test question may cause offence to an ethnic group. We say more in Chapter 3 about sources of guidance on words or phrases to avoid for this reason.

Awareness of the distinctions between the senses of 'fair' identified above can illuminate educational controversies. However, as Wittgenstein (1953) has argued, using the metaphor of 'family resemblances', different usages can be loosely linked by overlapping similarities. In our view, the senses which most resonate in discussions about the (un)fairness of assessment are notions of treating like cases alike (*relational* sense) and of legitimate expectations (*implied contractual* sense), and these two notions are themselves loosely linked, if we believe that candidates have a right to expect to be treated similarly to others in relevant respects.

In discussions of educational assessment, there is a danger of assuming that the only sense of fairness that matters is the third, *relational*, sense – treating relevantly like cases alike. But we shall argue in this book that relational fairness may not always be as important as it is thought to be. Granted, it may be particularly apposite to assessments which determine competitive access to limited goods, such as medical school places which have to be limited due to cost. But that paradigm does not apply to all assessments. Let us consider this example: Tom and Mary are both applicants for a local college where there is room for all who are able to complete the course. Tom is allowed extra time for his entrance test because he has a disability, but Mary has to do hers in the time allocated. Both are accepted by the college. Why should it matter to Mary whether or not she was treated exactly comparably to Tom? The questions raised by this apparently simple example are profound ones, and we shall return to them at greater length later.

As we have seen, calling a situation unfair usually implies that it *matters* to someone. This applies to all the senses of 'fair' that we have outlined except (perhaps) the first, purely formal, sense. A faulty or structurally biased statistical survey may be described as inaccurate or unreliable, but it seems odd to describe it as 'unfair' unless people have been harmed by it.

One of the questions about fairness which is often neglected is *Fairness to whom?* Writers on educational assessment often appear to assume that fairness applies only to candidates (or 'test-takers'). Their interests are, of course, very important, but there may also be issues of fairness to candidates' peers (who did not take the test), to users of the assessment outcomes (e.g. employers or universities), to future clients of candidates for a professional qualification or to society at large.

Another implicit assumption which is open to question is that fairness applies to groups rather than individuals. This appears to fly in the face of ordinary language – we quite often say 'That was unfair to John' as well as 'That was unfair to people with dyslexia (or whatever)'.

There may be two reasons for this assumption in the context of assessment. One is that the statistical methodology of some psychometric analysis of unfairness in test outcomes ('differential functioning analysis') requires groups of candidates to be identified, using different criteria, for comparison. Where the group has a very small membership (or is reduced to one), that will present technical (statistical) problems. Another possible reason is the logical point that judgements of unfairness to an individual will normally be justified by some characteristic possessed by the individual (for example, a disability) that is theoretically applicable to others, even if no others shared it when the test was taken. We say more about this in Chapter 2, but in this introductory survey of uses we would point out that a test with one candidate can be fair or unfair in several of the senses which we have distinguished.

Another neglected question is *Fairness of what?* As we shall see, those considering the fairness of an assessment may focus on specific aspects of the assessment, such as the design or the marking scheme. But there is also an underlying distinction between the fairness of a process and the fairness of its outcome – or of the decision to use the process in question. In legal cases, judges may distinguish between 'procedural' and 'substantive' fairness. Procedural fairness is a particular form of relational fairness, or even-handedness, when a dispute or grievance is being dealt with. It is reflected in the centuries-old legal doctrine of *audi alteram partem*: no person should be judged without a fair hearing in which each party is given the opportunity to respond to the evidence against them. We shall discuss this principle in more detail in Chapter 4, but here we should note that, in many countries, grounds for appeal against the fairness of assessment outcomes in national exams or university degrees are confined to procedural fairness and will not consider the substance of examiners' academic judgement.

It is now commonplace to talk of 'felt fairness' in educational contexts. This refers to *perceptions* of fairness or unfairness by the people concerned – for example, by the candidates being assessed. This raises the question of whether felt fairness is the same as fairness. Can a perception of fairness be wrong? Or, if an assessment is perceived as unfair, does that mean it is unfair? We return to this question in Chapter 2, where we shall suggest that there can be cases when a student's judgement of fairness may be based on false beliefs. For example, students may believe that the same individual marker marked all of their question papers (and feel aggrieved that their marker was unduly severe), whereas in reality individual test items were marked by different markers.

Calling something fair or unfair carries emotive force[7] and, as every parent knows, the emotion expressed can be remarkably strong in the case of perceived *un*fairness. The emotion could be genuine or feigned, and in the latter case a statement of 'felt fairness' might be false in the sense of reporting a feeling that was not, in fact, felt. However, in the vast majority of cases, statements about 'felt fairness' of assessments are probably genuine and provide information about the views of people affected by the assessments which deserve attention, even if they are based on false assumptions.

In summary, we have identified a range of senses in which 'fair' is used. All of them can feature in discussions of educational assessment, although the most common are probably the 'relational' sense (treating relevantly like cases alike) – although we argue in this book that this is not always the most important sense – and the 'implied contractual' sense (meeting legitimate expectations). Also, we need to remember the frequently neglected question, 'fair to whom?'.

Assessment

We now turn to unpacking what is meant by 'assessment', with a view to identifying those features which are relevant to judgements about whether [an] assessment is fair. The verb 'to assess' derives from Latin and French roots depicting sitting by or alongside someone ('ad sedere').[8] Modern applications include determining how much tax is owed and estimating the value of a house, but at heart the concept implies *making a judgement based on evidence*. Simply describing the evidence is not assessing it. A common way of assessing is by comparing the observed subject with some kind of measurement scale (e.g. 'John is six feet tall'). A tax inspector will observe evidence about the taxpayer's earnings and compare it against the criteria set out in the tax regulations.

The noun 'assessment' is used in several ways. The first, which we shall normally use in this book, simply denotes the *act of assessing*. We might say, for example, that 'the assessment of the children is done at the end of each term'. In the second sense, 'assessment' refers to the *method or instrument(s) used to assess*. For example, in England the national tests used at key stages of pupils' learning are referred to as 'National Curriculum Assessments'. In their influential report in the 1980s, the Task Group on Assessment and Testing defined 'assessment' as:

> A general term enhancing all *methods* customarily used to appraise performance of an individual pupil or a group (Department of Education and Science and the Welsh Office, 1988: Preface). [Emphasis not in original]

In a related sense, 'assessment' can sometimes refer to a *particular event* when the assessment instrument is applied. Thus, guidance produced by the General Medical Council in the UK for doctors whose performance is being assessed includes an answer to 'What if you cannot attend the assessment?'[9]

Finally, 'assessment' can refer to the *conclusion of the assessment process* or the judgement made. Thus, we talk of receiving our 'tax assessment' and, in the medical context described above, the doctor might say that the 'assessment' was that he or she was fit to practise.

This book is concerned with assessment in educational contexts. By this we mean to include all contexts and institutions in which judgements are made on the knowledge, skills, attitude or performance of individuals or groups based on evidence. This includes – but is not confined to – the assessment of pupils in schools and colleges – and applies to judgements about adults as well as to children of all ages, and to individuals as well as groups. The literature on educational assessment tends to use words associated with school (for example, 'pupil', 'student'), but the thinking may be applicable to other contexts, such as the workplace. A helpful start is provided by Harlen, Gipps, Broadfoot and Nuttall (1992: 217): 'Assessment in education is the process of gathering, interpreting, recording and using information about pupils' responses to an educational task.'

This raises the question of what is meant by an 'educational task', but we might note that the means of getting the information can involve reading written work, listening, looking at a product or artefact, or comparing responses (such as holes punched on a card) with a template. Procedures used for assessment can be formal or informal, and in schools may range from normal regular feedback from the teacher to more structured occasions. Assessment events at the more structured end of the spectrum are often described as 'tests', although the use of 'tests' and 'testing' appears to have wider application in the USA than in the UK.

In this book, we shall generally refer to 'assessment(s)', although, in discussing some of the American writers on this subject, we revert to 'tests', and we shall consider a wide range of contexts in which judgements about people's knowledge, skills or attitude are made based on evidence. A similar issue of terminology arises when we want to describe people who are the subject of assessment. Writers tend to resort to the formal end of the spectrum and talk of 'candidates' (UK) or 'test-takers' (USA). When one of the two terms is required, we shall normally opt for 'candidates', unless we are directly citing an American source.

It is widely observed that educational assessment may be carried out for a range of different purposes (or uses).[10] These typically include:

- formative uses ('assessment *for* learning', providing information to the person assessed and/or to those involved in his/her education to feed into further learning)
- summative uses ('assessment *of* learning', communicating a judgement about the subject's achievement at a defined point)[11]
- evaluative uses (assessment for accountability – for example, as evidence of the effectiveness of an educational institution or the system as a whole)
- diagnostic uses (assessment for targeted intervention).

Harlen et al. (1992) also distinguish a 'certification' use, where the conclusions of the assessment 'summaris[e], for the purposes of selection or qualification, what has been achieved' (pp. 217–218). Arguably, this is a sub-set of 'summative uses', but it is an important reminder of the significance to people's lives of gaining – or failing to gain – a qualification.

Discussions of fairness tend to concentrate on summative rather than formative uses and on the more formal types of assessment, such as school examinations, on the assumption that their outcomes matter more to the subjects than, say, informal feedback from teachers. But we think it is important at this stage to keep open the possibility that informal feedback can also raise questions of fairness. An informal comment by a teacher can open or close opportunities for the recipient. We have met adults who were told (probably wrongly) by their primary teacher that they 'couldn't sing' or were 'tone deaf' and thereby were denied a lifetime of rewarding participation in music. And, in the context of the workplace, studies of racial bias have suggested that social and cultural factors, including remarks made in informal work contexts, can be crucial barriers to progression (McGregor-Smith, 2017).

Another term that is applied to assessments which matter is 'high stakes'. These might include summative assessments taken at the end of schooling, whose outcomes determine entry to college or university or to employment, professional and vocational qualifications that are licences to practise, or tests of proficiency that can open and close doors of opportunity, such as the driving test and knowledge tests for national citizenship. High-stakes assessments are a common stamping-ground for debates about fairness. However, we need to remember that the stakes of an assessment which appeared to be low at the time may be high in retrospect.

Also, the outcomes of an assessment may be low stakes to some but high stakes to others. For example, the results of international tests taken by samples of students, such as the OECD's Programme for International Student Assessment (PISA), may not directly affect the fortunes of the students who are assessed, but could be crucial to the reputations of nations and their governments.

Further distinctions are made between different types of evidence for judgements in assessment. These include reports on projects, written work produced under examination conditions, coursework, portfolios to be read or viewed, performances to be listened to or watched, and constructions or compositions. Issues of fairness can arise with all of these. Also, different types of standard can be used for reference in the assessor's judgement – notably the performance of a cohort (in 'norm-referencing') and a description of performance at a relevant level (in 'criterion-referencing'). Finally, we need to recognise that the assessment process can be seen as covering a sequence of activities, all of which may raise questions of fairness. To quote Harlen (2007: 12): '[Assessment] involve[s] decisions about what evidence to use, the collection of that evidence in a systematic and planned way, the interpretation of the evidence to produce a judgement and the communication and use of that judgement.'

In summary, then, we shall use 'assessment' to describe the act of making judgements based on evidence about the knowledge, skills, attitudes or attributes of individuals or groups. This will include informal as well as formal contexts and formative as well as summative uses, although we shall concentrate on contexts in which the outcomes of the assessment process or processes matter to someone – and hence may raise questions of fairness.

Lenses for examining fairness in assessment

Debate about fairness in assessment can involve a wide range of people, who bring their own expectations, conceptual apparatus and assumptions. We have found the metaphor of 'lenses' useful for describing and distinguishing between different approaches. The Cambridge Dictionary defines 'lens' as 'a curved piece of glass ... or other transparent material, used in cameras, glasses and scientific equipment that makes objects seem closer, larger, smaller etc.'.[12] The observer brings the lens (which was made beforehand) to the observation. The observer looks through the lens and it partly determines what the observer perceives and how the observer describes it. An object that looks big through one lens may look small or slanted through another. It is often difficult or impossible to say that one of the lenses is 'correct', as this may depend on the user and the circumstances.

Some of the 'lenses' brought to discussions of fairness in assessment are intellectual traditions (with their inheritance of assumptions, terminology and priorities), and some are professional groups or sectors of society with their own vocabulary, rules and history. In the list which follows, which is by no means comprehensive, we start with different lenses based on the theory and practice of assessment. We then extend the list to lenses that bring in concepts and assumptions from other disciplines or traditions:

- theoretical writing about educational measurement and assessment
- 'industry standards' – models (and rules) for good assessment practice
- legal approaches
- philosophical approaches
- fairness as a component of social justice.

This book looks at fairness through each of these lenses and considers the implications for fair assessment. When applying each lens, we have started by looking for an established consensus view of fairness as viewed through the lens in question. Where there is no one view, we have identified different approaches, or principles derived from particular examples. We have applied our own judgement to the consensus view or views and considered the relation between fairness and other concepts viewed through the same lens or through others. Throughout the book, we offer practical examples and dilemmas from the world of assessment for readers to consider, using the ideas and approaches developed in each chapter.

Structure of the book

This chapter is concerned with scene-setting and conceptual housekeeping, examining particularly different senses in which 'fairness' and 'assessment' are used. Chapter 2 investigates fairness through the lens of *educational measurement theory*. It traces an emerging consensus view of fairness (defined as an absence of variance based on matters irrelevant to the construct being assessed). We consider the strengths and limitations of this approach and how fairness (so understood) is related to other key concepts in assessment theory, notably validity. Chapter 3 moves from theory to practice and cites examples of principles and guidance on good practice in ensuring assessment fairness and in minimising unfairness.

Chapter 4 applies *legal* lenses to fairness of educational assessment. It describes some leading cases (from different countries and different legal traditions) and derives principles from them which have wider application, but also raise some problems.

In Chapter 5, we turn to *philosophical approaches* to fairness, concentrating on two approaches taken by (Western) philosophers – conceptual analysis and philosophical model-building. We give pride of place to two philosophers in particular – Aristotle, arguably a precursor of conceptual analysis, and John Rawls, whose account of justice as fairness has been so influential.

Chapter 6 views fairness of assessment through the wide-angled lens of *social justice*. It looks at the implications for fair assessment of different accounts of justice in society and education, including the much loved (and much criticised) concept of 'meritocracy' and current accounts of 'educational adequacy' as an approach to fairness.

In Chapter 7, we draw conclusions from the application of the different lenses, and we offer an approach to fairness that we hope will be relevant to the changing context of assessment in the twenty-first century.

As we acknowledge in the Preface, a limitation of this book and its use is that the examples and sources we use are largely Anglophile. With the notable exception of Aristotle, almost all the references at the end of each chapter are to books and articles written in the English language. In Chapters 2 and 3, we refer extensively to American professional publications, such as the *Standards for Educational and Psychological Testing* which dominate the scene in much discussion of educational measurement theory and practice. We are conscious that other traditions and publications in other languages may offer insights which we have missed. But we hope that the descriptions here of fairness viewed through different lenses will give readers food for thought and prompt further work to improve fairness in assessment.

For further reflection

Hitler and Stalin

A history examination for 16-year-olds normally has a question (worth a significant number of marks) about either Hitler or Stalin, but the students do not know which one will come up in their exam. In the event, the question this time is on Stalin:

- Sheila gambles that Hitler will come up and prepares Hitler but not Stalin. Stalin comes up and Sheila does badly.
- Joe gambles that Stalin will come up and prepares Stalin but not Hitler. Stalin comes up and Joe does well.

- Fred bribes a member of staff to let him see the paper before the exam is taken. He sees that the question will be on Stalin, prepares only Stalin and does well.
- Helen conscientiously prepares both Hitler and Stalin. Stalin comes up and Helen does well.

Are all of these candidates fairly assessed? Is the outcome fair?

Changes to an important test

In the national system governing this example, pupils take a national test at the end of their primary school. This helps to inform secondary schools of each pupil's levels of achievement, and may determine the teaching group into which pupils are put for particular subjects when they start secondary school. The test outcomes are also used by national authorities to judge the effectiveness of primary schools. Teachers encourage their pupils to take the test very seriously and devote time to preparing for it. One year the test is much harder than usual. It reduces some of the children to tears and many angry parents write to the newspapers. Teachers complain that they have not had enough time to teach all the content or help the children to practise the tasks that the hard test required. The test providers take account of the difficulty of the test in setting grade boundaries and issue a statement saying that no one has been disadvantaged. Was the harder test fair? What do you mean by 'fair'?

Notes

1. For example, 'Exhausted students "crying in toilets and breaking down in class" over "unfair" new GCSE grading system', *Daily Mirror* (UK tabloid), 27 April 2017.
2. See www.fairtest.org.
3. Widely reported, including 'Systematic cheating is found in Atlanta's school system', *New York Times*, 5 July 2011, accessed at www.nytimes.com/2011/07/06/education/06atlanta.html.
4. Xiong Bingqi, vice-president of the 21st Century Education Research Institute in Beijing, in a statement to the *Global Times*, reported at www.independent.co.uk/student/news/exam-cheating-now-a-criminal-offence-in-china-as-students-face-up-to-7-years-imprisonment-confirms-a7072371.html.
5. [2017] IESC 29.
6. 474 F. Supp. 244 (M.D. Fla. 1979); 644 F. 2d 397 (5th Cir. 1981); 564 F. Supp. 177 (M.D. Fla.1983); 730 F.2d 1405 (11th Cir. 1984).
7. We are not arguing that 'This is [un]fair' is *merely* an expression of emotion, but the point being made here is that a judgement of fairness can and often does carry emotive force.
8. This account draws on the entry for 'assess' in the *Oxford English Dictionary*, accessed in August 2018 at www.oed.com.

9. See www.gmc-uk.org/concerns/information-for-doctors.
10. See, for example, Harlen (2007).
11. In a summative assessment based on modules taken over a period of time – as, for example, in many university contexts and in some national examinations – the summative assessment can bring together the conclusions of assessment at several defined points.
12. See https://dictionary.cambridge.org/dictionary/english/lens?q=Lens

References

Cumming, J. J. (2008) Legal and educational perspectives of equity in assessment. *Assessment in Education, Principles, Policy and Practice*, 15(2), 123–135.

Department of Education and Science and the Welsh Office (1988) *National Curriculum: Task Group on Assessment and Testing – A report.* Available at: www.educationengland.org.uk/documents/pdfs/1988-TGAT-report.pdf (accessed 28/08/19).

Evans, I. M., Galyer, K. T. and Smith, K. J. H. (2001) Children's perceptions of unfair reward and punishment. *The Journal of Genetic Psychology*, 162(2), 212–227.

Harlen, W. (2007) *Assessment of Learning.* London: Sage.

Harlen, W., Gipps, C., Broadfoot, P. and Nuttall, D. (1992) Assessment and the improvement of education. *The Curriculum Journal*, 3(3), 215–230.

LB Lewisham & Others v. AQA, Edexcel, Ofqual and Others (2013) EWHC 211.

McGregor-Smith, R. (2017) *'Race in the Workplace': The McGregor-Smith Review.* London: Department for Business, Energy and Industrial Strategy. Available at: www.gov.uk/government/publications/race-in-the-workplace-the-mcgregor-smith-review (accessed 28/08/19).

Wittgenstein, L. (1953) *Philosophical Investigations* (trans. G. E. M. Anscombe). Oxford: Basil Blackwell.

Worrell, F. (2016) Commentary on 'perspectives on fair assessment'. In N. J. Dorans and L. L. Cook (Eds.), *Fairness in Educational Assessment and Measurement.* New York: Routledge. pp. 283–293.

2
Fair assessment viewed through the lenses of measurement theory

'The most useful definition of fairness for test developers is the extent to which the inferences made on the basis of test scores are valid for different groups of test takers.' (ETS, *ETS Standards for Quality and Fairness*, 2015, p. 19)

'Absolute fairness to every examinee is impossible to attain, if for no other reasons than the facts that tests have imperfect reliability and that validity in any particular context is a matter of degree. But neither is any alternative selection or evaluation mechanism perfectly fair.' (AERA et al., *Standards for Educational and Psychological Testing*, 1999, p. 73)

Introduction

In this chapter, we consider the views of fairness in assessment taken by measurement theorists. Many of the leading writers from this tradition are based in the USA, and publications by the assessment professions there, such as the *Standards for Educational and Psychological Testing*, now in its sixth edition, have assumed canonical status, being cited in judicial decisions and being hugely influential on thinking both within and beyond the USA. The first part of this chapter – where we seek to locate and describe any consensus in accounts of fairness – therefore necessarily draws heavily on American sources. However, we do ask critical questions about them and proceed to extend the discussion to assessment issues in a range of contexts in other countries.

Assessment fairness: consensus, what consensus?

The *Standards for Educational and Psychological Testing* (hereafter *Standards*, in the singular) represents a consensual statement by the North American measurement professions and aims to 'provide criteria for the development and evaluation of tests and testing practices' (AERA et al., 2014, p. 1). However, it is surprisingly abstruse when defining fairness, preferring instead to adopt a somewhat agnostic position where fairness has 'no single technical meaning and is used in many different ways in public discourse' (2014, p. 49). As McArthur (2018) comments: 'There is more likely to be a discussion about whether a particular assessment task is "fair" than a discussion as to what fairness might actually entail' (p. 29).

Whilst fairness is increasingly seen by assessment theorists as being vital for good assessment, it has proved resistant to precise definition in terms of its interpretation and reach.

The development of fairness in testing

For centuries, high-stakes public examinations have been employed as the principal assessment instrument for informing decisions on learning outcomes, admissions and educational progression. The primary purpose of many such examinations has been candidate selection (Glaser and Silver, 1994; Gipps and Stobart, 2009). There are famous examples in the history of selection for the Civil Service, both in early China and in nineteenth-century Britain, where concern about unfairness – such as selection depending on family connections or patronage – led to an entrance examination being introduced. This, it was argued, was fairer, as entry would be achieved through 'merit' (the fourth sense of 'fairness'), displayed in the exam. We shall return to the concept of 'merit' in Chapters 5 and 6.

The new examinations were seen to be fairer than the alternatives in the *relational* sense that like cases (in terms of marks) would be treated alike, regardless of the candidate's background. The reformers might have accepted that there was still an element of unfairness in that it was easier for well-connected candidates to prepare for the exams, but selection by examination was seen as a progressive move in terms of fairness. In both countries, questions were asked later about the construct validity of the exams, which in China required mastery of the 'eight-legged essay' and in Britain could involve papers on Shakespeare and the classics. These requirements were eventually replaced by content which was deemed more relevant to suitability for work in the Civil Service.

In more recent times, developments in testing for educational, clinical, occupational and scientific purposes which occurred during the second half of the nineteenth century and the first half of the twentieth century, particularly in England, Germany, France and the USA,[1] have informed thinking about fairness in assessment. In the USA, the history of the development of standardised testing over the last century and a half has both reflected and influenced thinking about fairness of decisions based on test outcomes. Standardised tests became a part of American education from the mid-1800s and were increasingly seen as a basis for fair decisions. In 1851, Harvard University administered what was probably the first standardised written examination. Three years later, in 1854, Horace Mann (considered the father of standardised testing in the USA) had members of his Board of Education prepare and administer the first large-scale achievement test of English composition to Boston school children. Examiners used the test outcomes to criticise teachers and the quality of learning their students were receiving. Teachers countered, arguing that the written exams did not reflect what had been taught to students. The ensuing dispute still has a strangely familiar ring to it. Over time, the use and range of standardised tests broadened to embrace contexts including education, licensing, employment and credentialing.

The standardised test has not been without its detractors, however (Gould, 1996). Standardised testing has been criticised for being a tool of social control for over a century and has long been associated with racism. IQ testing – one of the earliest forms of standardised testing in the USA – prompted such problematic developments as the Eugenics movement. Whilst modern eugenics now mainly focuses on the elimination of genetic disease, most thinkers do acknowledge some element of genetic inheritance in the areas of knowledge and skill measured by many tests. That raises issues of fairness which we shall consider more fully in Chapters 5 and 6.

Baker and O'Neil (1994) have suggested that 'the reason that the USA developed such a love affair with "objective" tests is that they promised fairness' (p. 24), even at the cost of relevance and fitness for purpose. Even though psychologists questioned the scope for underlying bias, and even though the relevance of the content to the use of the test outcomes was debatable, objective tests looked fair – everyone got the 'same' test.

With a growing and increasingly diverse test-taking population, more questions were being raised about the fairness of test results for sub-groups. Initially, these concerns focused on ethnic and racial groups, but expanded to include gender concerns, individuals with disabilities and those with diverse linguistic and cultural backgrounds. In Chapter 6, we discuss the fairness issues raised by the quest for social justice for these, and other, sub-groups. In this chapter, we acknowledge that those societal issues posed questions for the assessment theorists.

Defining assessment fairness

Assessment theorists have tended to choose between a narrow and a broad approach to characterising fairness. In a *narrow* sense, fairness is perceived as an absence of something, for example as lack of construct irrelevance (Sireci, 2008; Dorans and Cook, 2016) or as the absence of measurement *in*accuracy. A fair test, according to the *Standards* (AERA et al., 2014), 'minimizes the construct-irrelevant variance associated with individual characteristics and testing contexts that otherwise would compromise the validity of scores for some individuals' (p. 219).

The *broad* approach perceives fairness as being fundamentally sociocultural, linked inextricably to social justice (Stobart, 2005; Shaw and Imam, 2013; Kunnan, 2014). Stobart argues that fair assessment must be considered in the context of the curriculum, the educational opportunities of the students and the variety of cultural, economic and political circumstances within which the assessment resides (Stobart, 2005, p. 277). McArthur (2018) agrees: fairness must be 'interpreted and engaged with in complex social situations, in which nuances of context and power are critically important' (p. 21).

Amid these differences of approach, two observations can be made: first, whilst assessment professionals may disagree on whether scores from a particular testing programme are fair, they usually agree that fairness is a fundamental aspect of validity. We shall explore the relationship between fairness and validity later in this chapter. Second, as a fundamental quality in educational assessment, fairness is value-laden and contentious[2] (Cole and Zieky, 2001; Stobart, 2005; Camilli, 2006; Kane, 2010), giving rise to a raft of prickly, as yet unresolved, issues.

Challenges in conceptualising assessment fairness

The comparatively late elevation of fairness to a position of prominence alongside the other two gods of assessment theory (Worrell, 2016) has failed to address some of the more obdurate concerns regarding the scope and conceptualisation of fairness. These include the conceptual relationship to other assessment concepts (such as validity and reliability) and the link with concepts of fairness applied beyond education or assessment.

The fundamental questions raised in Chapter 1, such as 'Fairness of what?' and 'Fairness to whom?', are highly pertinent to accounts of fairness by assessment theorists. The second of these is often overlooked. Professional assessment discourse often assumes that fairness in assessment is fairness to candidates ('test-takers') only. Whilst the interests of the test-taker are very important, they are among a group of potentially affected stakeholders. Issues of fairness may also be important to candidates' peers, including those who took the same test and those who did not take the test; to individuals disadvantaged by conclusions taken from 'derived scores' (e.g. teachers); to users of the assessment outcomes such as employers and university admissions staff; to future clients of candidates for a professional qualification who are being assessed on their professional competence or fitness to practise; or to society at large.

The current *Standards* (2014) does extend considerations of fairness from 'test-takers' (Chapter 8, pp. 131–137) to 'test-users' (Chapter 9, pp. 139–148). Test-users, as described in the *Standards*, seem to include those who commission tests, those who supervise their administration and those who make decisions based on the test scores (AERA et al., 2014, p. 139). A lot is said about their obligations which are relevant to fairness to candidates. For example, test-users should record the validity, reliability and fairness of test-based decisions and testing practices and seek to ensure appropriate interpretation and use of test scores. But the *Standards* says little about what it means for a test to be fair *to* test-users. What can a commissioning authority – or a profession using a fitness-to-practise test – reasonably expect of a test? Although there may well be common ground between the requirements for fairness to test-takers and the requirements for fairness to test-users, both questions should be asked and properly explored. The question of fairness to those other than test-takers is neglected in the assessment literature.

Fairness to individuals or to groups?

A prevailing assumption, acknowledged within the *Standards*, is that unfairness applies only to groups (which exhibit certain demographic characteristics) rather than individuals. There are, perhaps, at least two reasons for this assumption. The first relates to the statistical methodology of some psychometric *a posteriori* test analyses of (un)fairness in test outcomes, for example through the use of differential item functioning (DIF) to look for evidence that test items are functioning in ways that potentially advantage or disadvantage defined groups of test-takers. In fact, much of the technical assessment literature is concerned with identifying possible [un]fairness *after* the test has been taken, through DIF analysis (Zumbo, 2007; Andrich and Hagquist, 2012). According to Wu et al. (2017), over the last 30 years or so, DIF has become 'the standard gate-keeping technique for signaling bias in some characteristic of a test item or testing situation; specifically, characteristics that are not relevant to the test purpose' (p. 2).

DIF is a psychometric concept[3] that involves comparison of the outcomes of the test for groups with similar construct-relevant ability (according to some independent measure), but differentiated by other characteristics, such as gender, ethnicity, language or disability. Differential functioning analyses require groups of candidates to be identified, using different criteria, for comparison with a view to determining whether the test is performing in the same manner for each group. However, where the group has a very small membership (or is reduced to one) this approach will present technical problems.

If some construct of the test is not relevant to the underlying ability of interest, then the test may manifest *bias*. The *ETS Quality and Fairness* guidelines define bias as 'the tendency of an estimation procedure to produce estimates that deviate in a systematic way from the correct value' (ETS, 2015, p. 54).

Bias is evident when a large number of items appear to systematically (dis)advantage specific populations, defined, for example, in terms of gender, ethnicity, linguistic proficiency or socio-economic status, through the use of construct-irrelevant criteria (Kane, 2010). When bias is systematic, it can exaggerate one group's scores and/or lower another group's scores (Shepard et al., 1981). A biased test is potentially harmful to all stakeholders as it distorts test scores, making any inferences based on them less valid. Bias is, therefore, a differential construct-validity issue concerned with the extent to which the assessment task measuring the same construct has similar meaning for different populations.

However, bias should not be thought of as a property of test items (nor a property of a test) but rather, as Wiliam (2008) notes, of conclusions drawn on the basis of test outcomes. In other words, bias is manifest in the conclusions drawn from test items manifesting DIF. In such cases, items differentially performing may be removed from the test in order to avoid unwarranted, biased conclusions.

A key distinction between DIF and bias relates to how the terms are used. Angoff (1993) unpacks the distinction in the following way: DIF is more suited for non-judgemental analyses of test score differences between specific groups, whereas bias is best employed as part of a discussion of wider societal issues. 'Bias', as the term is used by assessment professionals, is a negative term, implying criticism.

Several commentators have maintained that DIF is a *necessary though not sufficient condition* for bias (e.g. Linn and Drasgow, 1987; Zumbo, 1999; McNamara and Roever, 2006). We contend, however, that DIF is neither a necessary nor a sufficient condition. First, it is *not sufficient*. One reason for DIF may indeed be bias. Another might be the existence of real (construct-relevant) differences. And if the construct-relevant differences are real, that raises the question of whether the aspects of the construct that lead to the differences are justified. For example, a rule that for admission to a fairground ride, a child must be able to grasp with both hands, and be taller than 1 metre, might be justified in terms of safety, even though it disadvantages small children. But it could promote questions of whether the condition is more excluding than safety requires and whether there might be accommodations for children with disabilities that would otherwise exclude them. In several countries, height requirements for recruitment to the police have been challenged as being unfair to ethnic groups who tend to be shorter[4] and have often been lowered as the challenge has raised the question of whether modern police officers really need to be tall. DIF can raise questions about possible bias in a test instrument or in a construct, but it does not answer those questions.

In our view, it is also possible, though arguably less likely, for an item to be biased and not manifest DIF. That means that DIF is *not necessary* for bias. One possibility is the presence of competing equal and opposite causes for different performance on the item, after controlling for overall ability. Let us suppose, for example, that students from the USA are relatively stronger in geometry than those from the UK, after controlling for overall ability. A contextual geometry question is based on a UK-only context, which arguably makes the item biased against US students. A DIF analysis may show no issue, however, because item bias is conflated with differential true cohort in this element of the construct.

At best, DIF serves to focus attention on items where there is a meaningful difference in performance, to raise the question of 'why?'. DIF alone cannot tell whether the 'positive' is false or true. Doing that also requires consideration of test purpose. And DIF does not address false negatives, where item bias might be conflated with opposed true group difference.

A difficult issue is whether DIF can flag up 'real' differences between groups in construct-*relevant* abilities, rather than unfair bias in the test. For example, two groups may differ in their language proficiency, and this may be judged relevant to the constructs being assessed. The suggestion of 'real' differences has proved particularly controversial in the context of selection testing for employment, and we discuss this more fully in Chapter 6. However, at this stage we merely reflect that it would be logically difficult to discuss this important question if DIF were regarded as sufficient to establish bias. At least in theory, it must be possible for groups to differ in construct-relevant ways that have not been addressed in the selection of criteria for the DIF analysis.[5]

In response to the 'anomalies' produced by DIF, Angoff (1993) observes that assessment theoreticians and practitioners are 'often confronted by DIF results that they cannot understand; and no amount of deliberation seems to help explain why some perfectly reasonable items have large DIF values' (p. 19).

In reality, it is very difficult to determine the source of DIF, and for this reason DIF analyses serve as a precondition for more refined analysis of the underlying causes of differential functioning. A significant concern with all but the most obvious explanations of DIF is that they are unquestionably speculative and seldom subject to further investigation (Zieky, 2016).

A second possible reason for emphasising *group* fairness is the logical point that judgements of unfairness to an individual will normally be justified by some characteristic possessed by that individual (for example, a disability) that is theoretically applicable to others, even if no other candidates shared it when the test was taken.

A final consideration in relation to individual versus group analysis is that it would be quite possible, in principle, to be fair to a group whilst being unfair to the individuals within the group. For example, in the allocation of top grades in an examination, it would be possible to allocate a fair number to each group whilst distributing them unfairly to the individuals making up a group. The reverse, however, is *not* true: if one is fair to all of the individuals, then we think it follows that one has been fair to the groups that they make up.[6]

In our view, group analysis is useful as it can point up aspects of (un)fairness to individuals which may otherwise be missed. It can also help point to weaknesses in test design – such as the use of terms which are unfamiliar to some ethnic groups. However, we consider it wrong for assessment theorists to restrict the concept of unfairness in assessment to groups. Surely there must be a technical vocabulary which will enable questions of fairness to individuals to be considered. It would seem that considerable attention is focused on fairness to groups because they can be treated statistically. However, substituting what is measurable for what is important is rarely a sensible strategy.

Fairness and test score use

A further area of contention relates to the use of test score outcomes: How wide are the contextual considerations that can be said to affect the fairness of the test itself? For example, the US case of *Debra P. v. Turlington* (1979–1984), which is described and discussed more fully in Chapter 4, concerned a test in which black students performed much worse than white students. One of the considerations in the court judgments was whether historic inequalities of teaching in segregated schools rendered the test unfair. And test outcomes can be interpreted and used after the test is taken in ways that are either technically questionable or socially unjust. An example is the combination of different types of test score in performance indicators (Haertel and Ho, 2016). It is particularly difficult to draw a line around contextual factors affecting the fairness of tests when different organisations are responsible for developing exams, deciding when and how they are to be used, regulating their standards and drawing consequences from their outcomes.

Distinguishing between fairness of the test and fairness in its use is more than a linguistic quibble. Assessment theorists have progressively moved from a narrow view that unfair consequences can only be attributed to the test itself if they can be traced to sources of test invalidity (Messick, 1989, 1995) – to a wider view, linking the concept of 'fairness' to at least foreseeable aspects of the test's use.

We argue later in this book for a 'situated' view of assessments, in which the professionals responsible for setting, marking and using tests need to consider aspects of the context in which the test is taken and the results used. This has implications for the moral and professional responsibility for fairness of those involved in all stages of the assessment process. It also raises questions, which we shall consider later, of how reasonable boundaries to those responsibilities can be drawn. However, we note here that the public has little patience when one state organisation passes the blame to another when something goes wrong. As Cronbach observed back in the 1980s, those who validate tests either before or after the tests are taken have a responsibility to 'review whether a practice has appropriate consequences for individuals and institutions, and particularly to argue against adverse consequences' (Cronbach, 1988, p. 3).

Fairness: links to validity and other core measurement concepts

Relationship with validity

In the Glossary of the *Standards*, fairness is defined as:

> The validity of test score interpretations for intended use(s) for individuals from all relevant subgroups. (AERA et al., 2014, p. 219)

This definition sees fairness as a sub-set, or particular application, of validity. It raises the question of how the two concepts are related. The answer will depend on how validity is understood, as well as on the understanding of fairness (Kane, 2010; Newton and Shaw, 2014).

The two most recent editions of the *Standards* espouse a 'unitary' view of validity in the strong sense proposed by Messick (1989, 1995), that is, construct validity conceived comprehensively. Such an inclusive take on validity seems to subsume fairness. However, recent editions of the *Standards* have given greater prominence to fairness as a concept distinct in itself, meriting a separate chapter. This may leave the reader puzzled about whether fairness is distinct from, or part of, validity.[7]

If validity is conceived of narrowly as a precise measurement concept (Borsboom et al., 2004), concentrating on the 'fitness' of the construct measured and the meaning of the scores to the intended purpose, it provides language which enables tensions between fairness and validity (so construed) to be discussed. It allows for the (logical) possibility that a valid assessment might have elements of unfairness. Such an approach allows tensions between fairness and validity to be debated, and provides a language in which the best assessment possible may have an element of unfairness. That may be helpful for a discussion of fairness, but arguably fails to do justice to the richness of the broader view of validity (Newton and Shaw, 2013, 2014).

At the other end of the scale, if the concept of validity is stretched to cover everything that is good in assessment and if fairness (in accordance with the consensus view) is deemed desirable, then it becomes an analytic truth that fairness in assessment is a sub-category of validity. However, this all-embracing approach has a number of shortcomings. Notably, it leaves us without adequate vocabulary to describe possible tensions between fairness and (other aspects of) validity. An example is the issue (which we discuss later in this chapter) of 'modifications' for sub-populations of test-takers which affect the construct being assessed. The test for the sub-population may not be a valid assessment of the totality of the construct, but arguably it may be described as fair. Where modifications affect the construct being measured, there is a clear challenge to the broad professional consensus notions of the validity of the test as a measurement of the same defined set of constructs for everyone (AERA et al., 2014, p. 52).

Much has been written on the debate between narrow and broad approaches to validity (e.g. Cronbach, 1971; Messick, 1989; Kane, 2006, 2010; Newton and Shaw, 2014). For the purposes of this book, focusing on fairness, we believe that it is crucial to have a conceptual language that enables distinctions to be made between *aspects* of validity (in the broader sense), acknowledging that a test which is valid in one sense may be invalid in another.

One approach, which many writers appear to support, sees fairness as comparable validity for relevant, identifiable populations of test-takers. Accordingly, test scores should have the same meaning and consequences across different population groups and assessment settings (Willingham, 1999), whilst decisions based on the test scores should be appropriate for all groups (Willingham, 1999). According to the *Standards*, a valid test is one in which all anticipated test-takers are afforded 'full opportunity to demonstrate their standing on the construct being measured' (AERA et al., 2014, p. 52). This leaves unanswered the question of whether one person's 'full' opportunity is equal – or comparable – to another's. That question is crucial for fairness, at least in the relational sense.

In Chapter 5, we shall examine John Rawls's distinction between a narrow and a wide sense of 'equality of opportunity': selection can be made fairly in the narrow sense ('appointments based on merit') but in a society which does not provide genuine equality of opportunity (Rawls, 1971). Rawls's insight in making this distinction is relevant to our discussion of fairness in assessment theory: a test which is fair in the sense of having comparable validity for different, identified groups of test-takers may be taken in a context where some test-takers have many more opportunities to develop and show the relevant knowledge and skills than others.

What, then, is the relationship between fairness and validity? Can a test (or a test item) be valid but not fair? Can it be fair but not valid? Logically, the relationship could work several ways, and the reader is invited to bear with us as we briefly visit each of the possibilities:

(i) *Fairness is a necessary and sufficient condition for validity*. This would mean that every test that was fair was also valid. We are not convinced by this view: it seems clear that tests which are fair in some of the senses we identified in Chapter 1 (e.g. formal fairness, meeting legitimate expectations) may not meet the technical requirements of validity. And if fairness is construed as comparable validity for different groups of test-takers, that requirement would be met by a test that was equally invalid for all – for example, by not measuring the construct adequately, although the inadequacy did not benefit any group of test-takers over others.

(ii) *Validity is a necessary and sufficient condition for fairness*. This would mean that every test that is valid is also fair. This is also difficult to accept. Even if validity is construed very broadly (see Newton and Shaw (2014) for a discussion of 'liberal' camps[8]), to cover everything good in assessment, it seems implausible to say that a test that is good in one sense must be good in all the others. For example, as we have seen, a test in which candidates with a disability cannot display all aspects of the constructs being measured might be described as valid but not fair. The same might be said of a test for employment in which the constructs measured are appropriate to the job, but in which different population groups perform differently.[9]

(iii) *Fairness is a necessary but not sufficient condition for validity.* This would mean that in order to be valid, a test must be fair. This view would see fairness as an essential requirement for validity – not just one of a series of options. This seems more promising, although it will not stand up if we can conceive of a test that is valid but not fair. For most of the senses of 'fair' that we have identified in Chapter 1, and for most of the approaches to validity that we have discussed here, we find it difficult to imagine a valid test that is not fair. We do, however, accept that valid tests could fail to meet some of the wider senses of 'fair' that we have discussed – for example, they might not meet 'legitimate expectations' derived from undertakings given about the content of the test, or the outcomes might be unequal because of historic injustices affecting test-takers.

(iv) *Validity is a necessary but not sufficient condition for fairness.* This would mean that in order to be fair, a test must be valid. This seems less plausible – in most interpretations of validity, it is a bigger concept than fairness, and we would want to allow validity to cover other aspects of tests (for example, accurate representation of the construct being tested) which do not necessarily imply fairness.

(v) *Fairness and validity are unrelated to each other: fairness is neither a necessary nor a sufficient condition for validity and validity is neither a necessary nor a sufficient condition for fairness.* We consider that this verdict is plausible when applied to some of the outliers in the senses of fairness identified in Chapter 1. For example, a test could be fair in the formal sense of following a set of procedural rules, even if the rules themselves were unfair (in another sense). And a test that did not measure the construct accurately, but was equally inaccurate for all test-takers, might meet the requirement of relational fairness. But, on the whole, we believe that it is not helpful to see fairness and validity as being completely unrelated. Doing so fails to do justice to the place of the fundamental ideas we associate with fairness in most accounts of validity in the literature.

This discussion is not pointless logic-chopping. Validity and fairness both matter to everyone involved in assessment, and are central to public confidence in tests and their outcomes. It is important to understand the relationship between the two, and doing so can provide a vocabulary to discuss such important issues as accommodations for candidates with disabilities and fair selection for employment. In our view, the description that most helpfully depicts the relationship between fairness (in most, but not all, senses) and validity is (iii) (above): *fairness is a necessary but not sufficient condition for validity.*

Relationship with reliability

Fairness is also closely tied to the measurement concept of *reliability*. The primary concern of reliability 'is to quantify the precision[10] of test scores and other measurements' (Haertel, 2006, p. 65). Reliable test scores are stable over time, repeatable (yielding precise scores), consistent in terms of the content sampling, and free from bias. Whilst differences in variability in scores between sub-groups do not necessarily indicate lack of fairness, they may be a pointer to possible bias and invite further investigation, always remembering that there may be unfairness (or bias) in the definition of the sub-groups concerned, or in the allocation of individuals to sub-groups. In the final analysis, any threat to reliability will call the fairness of the test into question.

Reliability is inextricably linked to bias (Shepard, 1987). For example, construct bias (e.g. 'differential appropriateness of behaviors associated with the construct in different cultures'; Van de Vijver and Tanzer, 2004, p. 124) has been investigated by estimating internal consistency reliabilities for different groups. A test is unbiased with regard to the construct of interest to the extent that its reliabilities are similar from group to group. If the reliabilities are different, then there is possible bias – and possible unfairness.

The aim of estimating reliability is to determine how much of the variability in test scores is due to measurement error and how much is due to variability in 'true scores'.[11] The reliability coefficient,[12] for example, is not based on a single score but defined for test scores obtained for a sample of the candidate population (Anastasi, 1988, p. 132). The *standard error of measurement*[13] – another way of reporting reliability – also depends on the population of test-takers sampled. Reliability indices are sensitive, therefore, to variability in test scores within specific sub-groups.

The *Standards* employs the term *reliability/precision* as a more general notion of consistency of scores for a group of test-takers across instances of the measurement procedure. Evaluation of reliability/precision applies to a particular assessment procedure and depends on the population(s) for which the procedure is being used. Reliability can vary, therefore, from one population to another as certain types of error may impact more greatly upon one population than the other. Consequently:

> to the extent feasible (i.e., if sample sizes are large enough), reliability/precision should be estimated separately for *all relevant subgroups* (e.g., defined in terms of race/ethnicity, gender, language proficiency) in the population. (AERA et al., 2014, p. 37)[14] [Emphasis not in original]

This raises questions of what constitutes a 'relevant' sub-group and of how we should respond if the reliability measures for different groups are different.

What, then, is the relationship between reliability and fairness? Without repeating the rubric of necessary and sufficient relationships that we rehearsed for validity and fairness, we would suggest that there is a necessary relationship between *un*reliability and *un*fairness (at least in some senses of 'unfair'). A test which is unreliable would surely be deemed unfair, in either the relational sense or the retributive sense (getting what is deserved). But the converse is less plausible: a test could be unfair (in many of the senses we have identified) but not necessarily unreliable. For example, there might be aspects of the testing process that caused problems for some groups or individuals – for example, by being disrespectful to them – but did not affect their performance or the test scores. And when we consider the positive concepts of fairness and reliability, it is difficult to describe the relationship. If reliability is represented by a range of possible measures, it is difficult to conceive of a 'tipping point' in the range that necessarily renders the test unfair.

We conclude that reliability and fairness are related, but logically separate. And the more our ideas of fairness take account of the social context in which an assessment is taken, and of the longer-term consequences of the outcomes, the more separate the concepts become. For example, one can imagine a test that was precise and repeatable, but inaccessible to some individuals or groups for reasons that we would consider unfair.

Relationship with other concepts in assessment theory

One of the six distinguishable aspects of construct validity evidence identified by Messick (1995) which function as general validity criteria or standards for all educational and psychological measurement[15] is *generalisability*. According to Messick (1995, p. 745), this refers to 'the extent to which score properties and interpretations generalize to and across population groups, settings, and tasks (Cook and Campbell, 1979; Shulman, 1970)'. Generalisability appears to intersect with reliability in that it refers to the consistency of performance across populations (as well as tasks, occasions and raters) (Feldt and Brennan, 1989). It may also be seen as intersecting with fairness in that a test which fails to satisfy the generalisability criterion may well be unfair.

As we have seen, the consensus view, focusing on relational fairness and the absence of construct-irrelevant bias, invites a close link between fairness, so understood, and *comparability*. A test which does not have comparable outcomes for relevantly similar sub-populations of test-takers will be deemed unfair. However, for reasons discussed above, this view is narrow and limited in its application to all kinds of assessment.

This discussion has illustrated that assessment concepts of validity, reliability, generalisability, comparability and fairness are intertwined and interconnected, and it is difficult to categorise the relationships. However, it is helpful to have a vocabulary that can enable us to consider possible tensions between them, as well as how closely linked they are.

Sources of construct-irrelevant variance

A prime threat to fair and valid interpretations of test scores comes from aspects of the test or testing process that may produce construct-irrelevant variance in scores for an identifiable group of test-takers. Construct-irrelevant variance exists when the 'test contains excess reliable variance that is irrelevant to the interpreted construct' (Messick, 1989, p. 34). This can happen when a test measures too many variables, some of which are irrelevant to the intended construct.

The risk of construct-irrelevant difficulty is heightened when extraneous aspects of the assessment such as linguistic complexity (unfamiliar or inaccessible language) make the assessment irrelevantly difficult for some individuals or groups. Martiniello (2006), exploring linguistic complexity in mathematics questions (in the English language), noted that complex language appeared to increase question difficulty for students who were not proficient in English compared to students of comparable mathematical ability who were English-proficient. Scores on a mathematics test ought to provide an accurate reflection of content area mastery. If a student gets a high score, it should be legitimate to infer that the student has mastery of the content area of interest – mathematics. A high score may also indicate that the student will do well in a further, related course, or in a job in a similar field. If the level of linguistic ability demanded by the test is not part of the intended skill (or skills) being assessed, or the linguistic demands of the test are not kept to a minimum, or the language used in the test is inaccessible to candidates with limited proficiency in that language, then claims of validity and fairness may be subject to challenge. In such cases, it is not known, for example, whether a student's low mathematics test score is indicative of poor content mastery, limited English ability, or a combination of both. In the example given here, construct-irrelevant barriers 'interfere with examinees' ability to demonstrate their standing on the target constructs' (Standard 3.9, AERA et al., 2014, p. 67) and, therefore, seek to undermine fairness. A test question that is linguistically overly complex or contains redundant language is a potential source of bias (Martiniello, 2008). Similar considerations apply to a test that has an excessive reading load, beyond the requirements of the constructs being assessed (Carver, 1994; Nagy and Scott, 2000).

The problem of testing candidates with limited proficiency in the language of the test raises a number of separate issues. As pointed out in the *Standards*, 'potential threats to test validity for examinees with limited English proficiency are different from those for examinees with disabilities' (AERA et al., 2014, p. 49). For example, should a test be administered in the language in which the test-taker is most proficient? Should tests be translated and adapted from one language to another?

Fairness and disability

We have seen that the concepts of validity and fairness are complicated and controversial. The same is true of the term 'disability'.[16] The words 'disability' and 'disabled' have been criticised as being inappropriately negative and pejorative, implicitly depicting a gap between the person described and some paradigm of form or functioning that is thought 'normal' or desirable. The words 'handicap' and 'impairment' are even more prone to this criticism and, probably for that reason, are less used nowadays. An alternative view sees people with different physical, sensory or psychological attributes as simply different, and sees disability as a form of diversity. For example, supporters of this view might argue that people with sensory disabilities (such as blindness) may have a richer sensory life in other ways than those without the so-called 'disability' (Anderson, 1999).

It is not possible to do full justice to this debate here, but we wish to make three points. First, where we use the words 'disabled' or 'disability' in this book, we do not wish to imply a negative judgement, or that one condition is superior to another. Second, we would argue that the debate between positive and negative conceptions of disability is largely irrelevant to the theoretical discussion in this chapter about fairness in assessment. Whether disabilities are seen as an absence of something valuable or as an enriching form of diversity – or just as a fact of life – they raise broadly the same theoretical issues about fairness when a person with a disability is the subject of an assessment. Third, if those commissioning or designing tests display a prejudice against people with disabilities, or impatience with the effort and resources required to provide for them, then such an attitude deserves moral criticism in the strongest terms, even if the prejudice does not directly affect the performance of disabled candidates.[17]

Another controversy about disability is the dispute between 'microists', who advocate special arrangements for people with disabilities, and 'macroists', who advocate an environment which enables those with or without disabilities to take part on equal terms. In architecture, for example, microists might design a separate entrance for wheelchair-users, whilst macroists would design all the entrances to be accessible to all, including those in wheelchairs (Goldsmith, 1997). With regard to assessments, a 'micro' approach would seek out separate, special, arrangements for candidates with disabilities, whilst macroists would aim for as many aspects of the assessment as possible to be equally accessible to all. For example, macroists would make sure that diagrams in an exam paper were readable by all, including those who were colour-blind, whilst a microist might favour a separate version of the exam paper, with differently-coloured diagrams for those with colour-blindness.

We say more in Chapter 3 about good practice in this, and other, regards. But it is relevant to note here that often the (macroist) measures required to make an assessment accessible to all – such as bigger font sizes and clearer/louder audio recordings for listening tests – benefit all candidates, not just those with a relevant disability. The approach which seems to us to maximise fairness would start with a presumption of macroism (making the assessment accessible to as many people as possible) and only resort to separate arrangements for candidates with disabilities when the potential of the macro approach had been exhausted. However, where different arrangements are required for some candidates with disabilities, this can raise theoretical questions about validity and fairness, which we shall consider here.

In many countries, students with disabilities that may affect their performance in educational assessments are entitled to 'accommodations' (adaptations that do not change the score meaning) or 'modifications' (adaptations that do change the score meaning) (AERA et al., 2014, p. 215). Some of these are required by legislation, offering protection to individuals with disabilities similar to that provided to people with protected characteristics under anti-discrimination laws. We discuss some examples of this in Chapter 4.

The issue of what constitutes 'disability' continues to remain a thorny one, however, and the identification of a disability can be difficult for teachers and parents. In one survey, teachers in the UK were asked whether dyslexia as a subject was sufficiently covered during their initial teacher training course. Of those who replied, 72% felt that it was 'not covered well at all' (Knight, 2018).

In a study undertaken by Richardson et al. (2015), teachers of pupils diagnosed with, or at risk of, attention deficit hyperactivity disorder (ADHD) described their professional responsibility to be the classroom as a whole, and expressed reluctance to adapt their teaching to accommodate the individual needs of a pupil displaying ADHD symptoms if this might risk a reduction in learning for the whole class.

Also at risk, it would seem, are children living in low-income families who are less likely to have their psychological symptoms recognised as being a learning difficulty. Underprivileged students are more likely to be labelled as having an emotional and behavioural disorder (McCoy et al., 2012).

Some of the most problematic issues about fairness concern candidates with psychological or intellectual disabilities. The academic discipline known as *neurodiversity* depicts neurological differences as aspects of diversity that should be recognised and respected in the same way as any other human variations in a society valuing diversity. There is a long list of conditions linked to neurodiversity.[18] Some of them come close to denoting deficiencies in cognitive or intellectual skills that underlie the constructs of many academic tests or exams. Barkley, Murphy and Fischer (2008) observed that adults with ADHD perform poorly in spelling, mathematics and comprehension tests. Inattentiveness can also interfere with reading acquisition, resulting in problems with comprehension (Rasmussen et al., 2002). The closer disabilities come to the heartland of the constructs being assessed, the greater the problems raised, both for assessment theory and for fair assessment practice.

Many national, state and institutional rules require evidence that a student's physical, mental, developmental, traumatic or psychological disorder has been assessed by an appropriate health care expert (such as a therapist or psychologist). A description of how the student's functioning is affected in respects relevant to the assessment is regarded as crucial. One assumes that these requirements are to prevent unfairness which would result if the accommodations (such as extra time) were allowed for a candidate who did not have the relevant disability, thus putting the cheating candidate at an unfair advantage compared with other, non-disabled candidates.

Accommodations

The *Standards* uses 'accommodations' to denote 'relatively minor changes to the presentation and/or format of the test, test administration, or response procedures that maintain the original construct and result in scores comparable to those on the original test' (AERA et al., 2014, pp. 58–59). The relevant literature in many countries describes a wealth of accommodations and support strategies for test-takers with physical, sensory and psychological disabilities or learning difficulties. These include using a different medium (such as Braille) to present the tasks, the use of prompts, reinforcements of written instructions in another medium (such as speech) and extra time.

How fair are accommodations for candidates with disabilities? A principal concern must be how we measure who needs what for different assessments. What is reasonable? What diagnostic assessments are being used to check eligibility for accommodations? Are these diagnostic assessments themselves fair? The most challenging theoretical question is: What is the comparator for determining the accommodations required for a candidate? And how should the extent of the accommodation – for example, the percentage of extra time to be allowed – be calculated? We return to these questions in Chapters 5 and 7, but they are important for assessment theory too. To anticipate the conclusions there, we conclude that these calculations should be seen as policy judgements, not mathematical calculations with a 'correct' answer.

In the UK, exam boards distinguish between 'access arrangements' and 'special consideration'.[19] Access arrangements are pre-exam arrangements for candidates with long-term disability or illness. The arrangements allow candidates to access the assessment and remove unnecessary barriers, with the intention of not changing the demands of the assessment. 'Special considerations' are post-exam adjustments to a candidate's mark. They are given to reflect some adverse circumstances, for example temporary illness or bereavement.

The topic of disability and fair assessment is, as we have seen, complex both in theory and in practice. We conclude this section with three observations. First, a practical problem arises from the happy consequence of medical advances in recent decades: in many developed countries, more multiply-disabled babies are surviving[20] and may become candidates for assessments. It is difficult to apply rules for testing accommodations based on categories of disability to multiply-disabled candidates. Second, applying rules based on categories does not always result in substantive fairness for individuals whose disabilities do not closely match the categories. In Chapter 4, we refer to an Australian legal case of a student to whom the rules (for students with his broad category of disability) were fairly applied but the accommodation did not fit the particular needs of that student. Third, there are particular problems in determining what is fair assessment of candidates with psychological disabilities – such as difficulty with verbal reasoning – which are very close to (construct-relevant) intellectual skills which underlie the constructs of much educational assessment. An extreme example of such a problem occurs when the disability appears to be central to, rather than underlying, the construct being assessed, as, for example, in the case of a candidate for a test of critical thinking who has a disability affecting his or her capacity for verbal reasoning.

Modifications

Fairness as absence of construct-irrelevant differences raises the question of how the concept applies to construct-*relevant* differences where, in order to meet the needs of some (but not all) candidates, the construct itself is adapted for a subgroup but not for all. The *Standards* refers to these as 'modifications' (AERA et al., 2014, p. 58). An example of a modification would be exempting a candidate from part of a language assessment which the candidate is unable to perform and subsequently using statistical means to calculate an overall score. Guidance by the English examinations regulator Ofqual (2017) refers to 'a deaf student who cannot take a listening assessment in a modern foreign language qualification' and who is exempted from that part of the assessment.

Recent advances in the use of technology and other aids to communication and physical movement that enable test-takers with disabilities to demonstrate pertinent skills, knowledge an understanding have led, we believe, to a more enhanced understanding of the constructs themselves. Theoreticians and practitioners have been challenged to reconceptualise the traditional assumptions of what types of performance are inherent features of a construct such as language proficiency – must this involve the skill of speaking and/or listening or is it primarily about communication? – or musicianship – can a candidate with a severe hearing impairment display musicality?[21]

However, the theoretical issue remains for any modifications which, despite such challenges, are judged to affect the construct being measured. These clearly offer a prima facie challenge to classic notions of the validity of the test as a measurement of the same defined set of constructs for everyone. Kane's (2013) *Interpretation/Use Argument* (IUA) includes all of the claims based on the test scores. When changes are made to testing materials or procedures to accommodate disabled students, Kane (2010) suggests that the IUA may need to be adapted to reflect accommodations so that the same conclusions for all students are reached. That process needs to be fully supported by appropriate assumptions if the validity argument is to be maintained. Inherent to any changes to the IUA is an assumption that the accommodated and unaccommodated forms of the test remain comparable (Sireci et al., 2005). However, that leaves the question of what should be done if they are not comparable, and where a modification required for fairness significantly changes the construct being measured. In our view, it is a mistake to stretch the concept of comparability to cover such instances: if (and it is an important 'if') a modification is required for fairness and if it is integral to the construct being measured, then comparability may have to be limited for the sake of fairness – some aspects of the test may be comparable and others not.

In the case of both accommodations and modifications, if the relevant rules are followed and the criteria are appropriately applied, then the test will be fair in the first (*accuracy*) sense (as described in Chapter 1). Additionally, it should satisfy the legitimate expectations of the candidates affected (and those without the disability in question). The main issue resides in the *relational sense* – are different arrangements for disabled candidates fair to others without the disability in question? Arguably, this question is more pertinent in the case of modifications, which mean that different candidates are being assessed against different constructs in the same exam. Is it fair, for example, to candidates without impaired hearing who have to sit all parts of a language test – including a speaking element (often regarded as being the most challenging for non-native languages) – if a candidate with impaired hearing is exempted from that part of the assessment? The answer may depend on why it matters to the majority of candidates how the minority in question are assessed (if indeed it does matter).

In summary, there are circumstances in which differences between the constructs assessed by different candidates may be of legitimate concern to some. If candidates are competing for a rationed good (for example, entry to a popular university course), we can conceive of disadvantage to the non-disabled candidates, although the question will remain of whether that apparent disadvantage is justified. Also, but perhaps less persuasively, it could be argued that confidence in the assessment system as a whole may be affected if there is a lack of consistency in the meaning of scores across the whole population of test-takers. But, otherwise, it is not clear that the relational sense of fairness is of particular importance here.

Apprehension regarding these kinds of questions has informed legal and policy challenges to some assessment practices where changes to the construct have been required to be reported in certificates or transcripts.[22] In Ireland, for example, this was debated in the courts in the case of Kim Cahill, who was not assessed on spelling and grammatical aspects of language because of her dyslexia (we discuss this case in Chapter 4).

There may be types of assessment where the safety and welfare of others militates against construct-relevant modifications for some candidates, and an overall judgement of the public good may conclude that adjustments should not be allowed in such cases. An example would be refusing to allow modification of a medical competency test for a candidate with a disability judged by the professional regulator to put patients at risk.[23] In such a case, arguments for the public good may override arguments for the private good. It would be helpful if the theoretical literature could address such tensions.

Fair assessment as perceived by the student

As we observed in Chapter 1, it is common nowadays to talk of 'felt fairness' in educational contexts. This refers to perceptions of fairness or unfairness by the people concerned, including candidates being assessed. Students hold complicated, multidimensional and sometimes contradictory notions of fairness, being more inclined to identify instances of unfairness as opposed to fairness (Sambell et al., 1997; Orr, 2010). Taras (2002) contends that 'students perhaps have the right to demand coherent and logical educational processes that are not detrimental to their learning' (p. 501). Flint and Johnson (2011) identify four criteria that legitimise fair assessment from the perspective of the student: assessment should provide 'a level playing field' for all students (perceived relational fairness); students should receive feedback that validates their effort; students should experience variety in the relevant assessment tasks they are given; and students should be taught by empathetic, skilled and compassionate staff (pp. 9–10). These accounts of perceptions of fairness cover several of the senses of 'fair' which we have distinguished. Perhaps the strongest influence is the 'legitimate expectations' sense, violated when the assessment is a nasty shock.

The National Student Survey (NSS), an annual survey of all final-year undergraduate degree students in participating universities in England, Scotland, Wales and Northern Ireland, asks students to provide feedback on their course in a nationally recognised format. The survey addresses the issue of perceived student fairness explicitly: 'Marking and assessment have been fair'. Students are asked to respond to this statement (as with all other statements) using a 1–5 Likert scale, indicating the strength of their agreement with the statement (5 = definitely agree; 3 = neither agree nor disagree; 1 = definitely disagree). The percentage of responses to the fairness statement ticking 'mostly agree' or 'definitely agree' is normally lower for this question than for most of the others.

Can a perception of (un)fairness be wrong? We think that there can be cases where a student's judgement of fairness may be based on false beliefs. For example, where several examiners (perhaps with different personalities and styles) are involved in tests of the same practical skills, students may assume that they will be inconsistent (relational unfairness), but be unaware of standardisation processes that are operated before the final mark is determined. And concerns about relational unfairness may be based on false assumptions (or rumours) about how others have been treated. Candidates might suspect that a marker had favoured candidates from the same race as the marker, but subsequent statistical analysis might find no evidence of such bias. However, even in these circumstances, the fact that students perceive (un)fairness can hamper the achievement of the educational goals for the student. Listening to, and responding to, students' concerns may improve their experience and learning outcomes.

Fair assessment in the classroom

Most of the discussion so far has focused on systematic, pre-planned formal assessments whose primary goal is to evaluate the progress of students in a specific instructional programme for which the assessment is designed. However, issues of fairness are also relevant to less formal evaluations in the classroom or place of learning. The assessment of student learning might be used formatively to inform teachers and students about progress on learning intentions and to inform and direct subsequent learning and teaching, or used summatively to help measure overall curriculum and programme effectiveness and for future planning.

The contemporary view of classroom assessment is one which emphasises the elicitation of students' knowledge, skills and understanding, and the formative purpose of assessment as part of the learning process (Black and Wiliam, 1998). Clearly, the size and range of the classroom assessment itself can vary, as can the degree of formality of the assessment.

Tierney (2013) characterises fairness in the classroom in two senses: the *ethics of teaching*, and *assessment practices*. Fairness in classroom assessment is heightened through accurate evaluations of student achievement and the perception of fairness on the part of the student and the teacher (as well as other relevant stakeholders). Tierney (2016, p. 5) notes that: 'For classroom assessment to genuinely and openly serve learning, high levels of trust and respect must be nurtured, not only between teachers and students but also between classroom peers.'

Some of the relevant literature reveals a number of practices, strategies and conditions for ensuring fairer classroom assessment practice. A common thread is that students are best served when they are provided with the most effective opportunities to learn (as well as opportunities to demonstrate learning). As Camilli (2006, p. 247) points out: 'The kinds of practices and activities that ensure testing is fair are also those that provide a solid foundation for attaining learning goals.'

Camilli (2006, p. 247) also asserts that 'fairness is inherent in, rather than external to, effective classroom instruction'. Assessment is fair when teachers have developed appropriate learning goals/targets, provided competent content and given instruction to match those goals and content (Santrock, 2004). It is not immediately clear why good practice of the kind described by Santrock is required specifically for fairness, but, arguably, assessment on matters covered by such a structured approach to teaching would meet pupils' legitimate expectations (*contractual* fairness) and maximise the opportunities for each student to progress (a form of *relational* fairness).

In what ways do the core technical measurement concepts of validity and reliability relate to classroom assessments? Theories of validity and reliability have largely been developed in situations of 'assessment of learning' rather than 'assessment for learning' paradigms (Earl, 2003). Given the wide variety of classroom contexts and the diversity of teaching practices, theoreticians have argued that traditional conceptions of validity and reliability need to be re-thought when applied to assessment in the classroom (Brookhart, 2003; Shepard, 2003; Smith, 2003; Parkes and Giron, 2006; Parkes, 2007; Bonner, 2013; Tierney, 2013).

Validity is based on the purpose(s) of an assessment and how well the interpretations and uses of the assessment outcomes serve each of the intended purposes. The principal purpose of formative assessment, for example, is to motivate learning (Stobart, 2012). Its validity is in how well it meets its purpose. Thus, in a classroom context, formative assessment is valid if it contributes to the advancement of student learning. Moss (2003, p. 19) notes that 'validity in classroom assessment – where the focus is on enhancing students' learning – is primarily about consequences'; in other words, how well inferences drawn from classroom assessments inform pedagogic decisions and assist in advancing students along a trajectory of increasing ability. In the classroom context, then, validity is concerned with whether learning takes place as a consequence of classroom assessment. It follows that an evaluation of the validity of classroom assessment requires an understanding of the nature of learning, and of what it means for learning to progress:[24]

> Psychometric methodologies for determining reliability are largely grounded in ... the consistency of scores obtained by the same persons when re-examined with the same test on different occasions, or with different sets of equivalent items, or under variable examining conditions. (Anastasi, 1988, p. 109)

For public examinations, reliability methodologies require replication before an estimate of their reliability can be made – often in the form of a reliability coefficient (Brennan, 2001). In a classroom setting, however, theoretical consistency across repeated tests may not be practicable or educationally justified.

McMillan (2014) suggests that the reliability of a classroom assessment is a function of both error measurement and instructional decision-making, with a principal focus on decisions after the assessment has been administered. Appropriate psychometric methods for measuring reliability in everyday classroom settings have yet to be developed, though Parkes and Giron (2006) have suggested teacher-constructed reliability arguments (much like validation arguments) through which the accuracy and dependability of a classroom assessment can be supported by evidence (mainly narrative) as an appropriate source of sufficient information of classroom reliability (see also Smith, 2003, p. 30).

From this brief review, it is clear that the concepts of validity and reliability need to be re-thought in the context of assessment in the classroom (Brookhart, 2003). We suggest that the same is true of ongoing assessment in the workplace or other learning situations. More work is required on this, but a direction of travel is that validity refers to the purpose of the assessment – informing the student's learning (or work-related skills). Reliability may have a different meaning in classroom contexts – and a different method of measuring it may be needed – but, arguably, at least some aspects of it are still important. Wayward or unjustified feedback to learners can be harmful and render an assessment invalid by sending the student's future learning in the wrong direction.

What does this mean for fairness? Do fairness and unfairness matter as much in the classroom context as in high-stakes summative examinations? We would argue that fairness (in most of the senses that we have identified) does apply to classroom contexts and should not be confined to so-called 'high-stakes' assessments. An exception may be fairness as the formal sense of following rules and designs, which may be less important. Also, some senses of fairness (for example, *relational* fairness) may be less important than others in some classroom contexts, and the consequences of unfairness may be less significant than others in some classroom situations. However, it would be foolish to underestimate the impact on students of unjustified or biased feedback in the classroom. The authors have met friends and colleagues who have cited, with great bitterness or regret, 'unfair' feedback that they received from teachers several decades before.

Fair assessment in higher education

Thus far, our discussion has largely focused on assessment in schools, including assessment in school classrooms. But the same fairness issues are also raised and discussed in the context of further and higher education. In many colleges and universities, continual assessment and the modular structure of degrees mean that assessment is often a way of life, and the distinction between classroom assessment and high-stakes summative assessment becomes less important: every assessment matters. Of course, practice varies from institution to institution and the ubiquity of assessment is controversial (Price et al., 2011). However, there is an increasing insistence that university assessments should be fair. In the UK, for example, the *Quality Assurance Agency for Higher Education* (QAA) (2012, p. 7) asserts that 'assessments should be conducted with rigour, probity and fairness'. However, as we have seen, feedback in surveys such as the UK's National Student Survey tend to show poor levels of student satisfaction regarding the fairness of their assessments. Assessment is frequent and expected to be fair, but does not feel fair.

Concern about unfairness by universities to sub-groups (such as ethnic minorities and students from socially disadvantaged backgrounds) typically has two reference points: to students' opportunities to get into university ('fair access') and to differential attainment, in terms of class of degree, once the student has got there. On the first of these, universities in England are required to produce an 'Access and Participation Plan' which is considered by the Regulator's 'Director for Fair Access and Participation'.[25] This aims to widen equality of opportunity to enter university, for example through outreach activities with local schools and colleges. However, the issue raises questions of fairness about all the assessments used – the school exam grades obtained by the disadvantaged students and the judgement exercised by the university in setting its 'tariffs' (qualification requirements) for entry. We discuss these matters further in Chapter 5. John Rawls's distinction between the narrower concept of 'careers open to all the talents' and more genuine opportunities for all is highly relevant to the university access agenda.

With regard to attainment, many countries report a persisting gap between levels of attainment achieved by university students of different ethnicities and socio-economic backgrounds. In the UK, for example, 'the gap between the likelihood of White students and students from Black, Asian or minority ethnic (BAME) backgrounds getting a first- or upper-second-class degree was 13% among 2017–18 graduates' (UUK and NUS, 2019, p. 1). The English Office for Students (2018, p. 4) has required universities to 'eliminate the unexplained gap in degree outcomes (1sts or 2:1s) between white students and black students by 2024–25, and to eliminate the absolute gap (the gap caused by both structural and unexplained factors) by 2030–31'. If the performance of

BAME students improves, but that of white students also improves, then that requirement will not be met. However, if differential assistance were given to black students and denied to white students in order to narrow the gap, that would raise issues of fairness.

So-called 'grade drift' in undergraduate degrees is much discussed. In the UK, for example, in 1996/97 just over half of undergraduates received a first-class or an upper-second class honours degree (Baker, 2018; HESA, 2019[26]). In 2016/17, this number had risen to three-quarters. The number of students earning a first-class honours degree rose from 8% to 26% in the same period.

There is much speculation about reasons for this trend (e.g. Bachan, 2018), but the relevance for fairness is not clear. It might be argued that the trend is relationally unfair to students in the 8% that got a first-class degree in 1996, compared with the 26% who had the same outcome in 2017. But it is not clear why this difference should matter to the 1996 graduate – why should he/she feel that it is unfair that many more students received first-class degrees in 2017? It is highly unlikely that the two generations of graduates will be applying for the same jobs on the basis of their degree. It could be argued that the esteem and perceived value of the historic degree will have been reduced, and that this might cause distress to the 1996 graduate, but this seems to us a weak basis for a judgement of unfairness. Sudden changes in requirements from one year to the next would be a different matter, and could raise issues of relational fairness to a cohort who might well be competing for the same opportunities and to their future employers who might misinterpret the information they receive about the student's achievement.

Another area potentially affecting students' perceptions of fairness and their relationships with lecturers is the impact of anonymous marking (Pitt and Winstone, 2018). Although anonymous marking is unlikely to eradicate all sources of bias during marking, it has been argued that it can encourage students' confidence in the assessment process (Falchikov and Goldfinch, 2000); minimise discrimination on grounds of race, age and other personal features (Dennis and Newstead, 1994); and protect higher education staff from potential allegations of prejudice (Fleming, 1999). Conversely, it is argued that anonymous marking may reduce trust in the assessment process and could dehumanise teaching and weaken the instructional function of formative feedback by minimising the role of dialogue in feedback from assessments (Price et al., 2010). Overall, there is little empirical evidence that the practice of anonymous marking reduces the gap in attainment between different groups of students. In a study across four first-year undergraduate subjects (n = 442), where the coursework module was marked anonymously and three other modules were marked non-anonymously, Pitt and Winstone (2018) found no significant difference in perceptions of fairness.

Some of the fairness issues reported in the higher education literature echo those already discussed in the previous section on classroom assessment. Several studies indicate that university students tend to associate fair assessment with respectful interactions between students and their teachers (Gordon and Fay, 2010). If respect should be diminished in any way, students often perceive themselves being left with the idea that they are merely a 'cog in the assessment machine', nothing more than 'passive subjects' (Boud, 2007, p. 17), ultimately 'to be measured and classified' (Boud, 2007, p. 17). Students sometimes perceive their part in the assessment process as simply fulfilling a purpose of assessment designed to assess the teaching of their lecturers rather than their own learning.

Emphasis on student 'voice' and student perceptions of assessment fairness is starting to figure more prominently in the literature (e.g. Entwistle, 1991; Sambell et al., 1997; Orr, 2010; McArthur and Huxham, 2011; Carvalho, 2013; McArthur, 2016). In Chapter 1, we distinguish between fairness and perceived, or 'felt', fairness. Greater student engagement in university assessment should, in theory, improve perceived fairness and, if students help mould assessment processes that widen the scope for all to demonstrate their knowledge and skill, that may improve fairness in several of the senses we have identified. But there is a long way to go in this quest, as students continue to express dissatisfaction with fairness, and their understanding of assessment is reported as being limited (MacArthur, 2018, p. 196).

Conclusion

This chapter has applied the lenses of measurement theory to fairness in assessment.

The mainstream view held by educational and psychological measurement and assessment experts is that fairness is the absence of construct-irrelevant variance in assessment outcomes. We rejected the consensual view that fairness in assessment applies only to groups: in our view, the concepts we have identified can also apply to individuals. Most theorists see fairness as a fundamental aspect of validity. We explored possible accounts of the relationship between fairness (so understood) and validity, and concluded that fairness (in most but not all of the senses we have identified) was a necessary but not sufficient condition for validity. However, a lot depends on what we mean by validity. Even after more than 70 years of sustained and seminal scholarship, there is still no conclusively correct way to use the term (Newton and Shaw, 2016). We proceeded to consider the relationship with reliability and comparability, and found a web of contingent relationships. What is undoubtedly true is that each term represents a distinct emphasis whilst each offers complementary perspectives on test score interpretations and uses.

The major concern of validity is score meaning: consistency of score meaning across test-taker groups – and, we would add, individuals – is central to deriving similarly valid interpretations across the multiple populations to which the test is administered.

We then considered fairness to assessment candidates with disabilities, highlighting the difficulty of modifications to an assessment for a disabled candidate which changes the construct being measured. In conclusion, we accepted that there might have to be a trade-off between fairness and some aspects of reliability.

Finally, we considered assessment fairness in the contexts of classroom assessment (which require a re-think of validity and reliability, as well as of fairness) and higher education. We concluded that fairness is relevant to these contexts, and should not be seen as confined to so-called 'high-stakes' summative assessments. The concept of 'felt fairness', based on the perceptions of students, was very important in these contexts.

Fairness is an increasingly prominent concept in theoretical approaches to assessment in all the contexts we have considered. The interrelationships between fairness and other values of good assessment are complex and merit further work, taking into account the different situations of assessment, not just analyses of scores. It is good to minimise construct-irrelevant variance between groups – but there is more to fairness than that.

For further reflection

Sue's extra time

Sue's parents produce a report from a private psychologist saying that Sue has dyslexia. The exam rules say that candidates with dyslexia can get up to 25% extra time. Sue is allowed an additional 30 minutes for a 2-hour exam. After the exam, many of Sue's classmates complain on Twitter that it was difficult to complete the exam in 2 hours. Was it fair for Sue to have extra time? What do you mean by 'fair'? Are there any factors which would lead you to say that it was *un*fair?

Differential entry requirements for university

Research in the UK suggests that 'persistently disadvantaged students' (defined as those who claim free school meals, under UK welfare law, for over 80% of their time at school) are some two years behind their peers by the time they leave secondary school. To give these students a fair chance to get a place on a competitive university course, one university decides that for courses with an entry requirement of three 'A' grades at A level (a pre-university qualification used in parts of the UK and internationally), the requirement for persistently disadvantaged students should be three 'C' grades. Students who just missed out on the three 'A's complain when they see students with lower A level achievements than theirs being accepted, and their parents write to the newspapers alleging 'outrageous unfairness'. Is the university's practice fair? Or are the 'outraged' critics right in calling the practice unfair?

Disrespect to indigenous populations?

In a country with a minority indigenous population, an item on a high school test requires students to perform calculations about the dimensions of a well-known landmark which has a special place in indigenous culture, and is regarded by them as having religious significance. Critics of the test say that this is unfair to the indigenous candidates, and after the test is taken the test organisation carries out DIF analysis to see if there was construct-irrelevant variance in the outcomes. The analysis does not suggest any construct-irrelevant difference of outcome – the indigenous candidates did not do well, but that outcome was consistent with their (low) performance in similar tests. Was the item unfair?

Notes

1. Newton and Shaw (2014) provide an in-depth historical overview of accounts during this period in terms of the prevailing scientific, philosophical and socio-cultural winds of the time.
2. The fairness of high-stakes examinations is periodically subject to intense public and media scrutiny in the UK. Newspaper headlines such as: 'Student protest against "unfair" GCSE maths question goes viral'; 'Teacher "bias" gives better marks to favourite pupils, research reveals'; and 'Exhausted students "crying in toilets and breaking down in class" over "unfair" new grading system' are but three of countless headlines not untypical of media allegations following seasonal examinations in the UK.
3. See Zumbo (2007) for an overview of the state of theorising and praxis of DIF in general and a reflection on three generations of DIF analyses in particular.
4. See, for example, www.nytimes.com/1973/07/23/archives/height-requirement-for-police-officers-may-be-eliminated.html.
5. We are grateful to Stephen Cromie for his contribution to this discussion.
6. We are grateful to Anthony Dawson for this point.
7. In the words of the *ETS Fairness Guidelines* (2015: 4): 'The division into separate chapters may be misleading in certain respects. Fairness, for example, is a pervasive concern, and standards related to fairness could appropriately occur in many chapters. Placing most of the fairness-related standards in a single chapter is not meant to imply that they are isolated from other aspects of testing.'

8. 'Liberal' is used here to denote those who are prepared to extend validity to the overall evaluation of testing policy, covering measurement aims, decision-making aims, and secondary policy aims; from both a scientific perspective and an ethical one.
9. This is the issue of 'disparate impact' in selection for employment, which we discuss further in Chapters 3 and 4.
10. Precision refers to the closeness of two or more measurements to each other. Accuracy refers to the closeness of a measured value to a standard, 'true' or known value.
11. In Classical Test Theory, a person's true score is the score obtained if there were no errors in measurement. 'True score' is defined as 'the expected value of the observed scores, where the expectation is taken over an infinitely long run of independent repeated observations' (Borsboom and Mellenbergh, 2002, p. 507). Scores on a test can be affected by a variety of factors that are not a part of the constructs the test is designed to measure (such as fatigue or different examiners). As a consequence, test scores are never perfectly reliable, and this lack of reliability leads to measurement error.
12. The *reliability coefficient* is a 'unit-free indicator that reflects the degree to which-scores are free of random measurement error' (AERA et al., 2014, p. 222).
13. The standard error of measurement is defined as 'the standard deviation of an individual's observed scores from repeated administrations of a test (or parallel forms of a test) under identical conditions' (AERA et al., 2014, pp. 223–224).
14. This is because 'reliability or generalizability coefficients derived from scores of a nationally representative sample may differ significantly from those obtained from a more homogenous sample drawn from one gender, one ethnic group, or one community' (AERA et al., 2014, p. 37).
15. Content; Substantive processes; Score structure; Generalizability; External relationships; and Consequences of testing.
16. See, for example, Oliver (1996).
17. Such a reprehensible attitude is sometimes called 'ableism' (see J. P. Sterba, 'Ableism', in T. Honderich (Ed.), *The Oxford Companion to Philosophy*, Oxford University Press, Oxford, 2nd edition, 2005).
18. Conditions linked to neurodiversity include attention deficit hyperactivity disorder (ADHD), autism spectrum disorder (ASD)/autism spectrum conditions (ASC), developmental coordination disorder (DCD) or dyspraxia, dyscalculia, dyslexia, developmental language disorders (DLD) (including non-verbal learning disorder), Tic disorders (such as Tourette's syndrome) and hyperactivity disorder.
19. See www.jcq.org.uk/exams-office/access-arrangements-and-special-consideration. There is a third category, 'reasonable adjustments', to reflect the circumstances of individual candidates covered by disability legislation, which we do not discuss here.
20. For a contemporary overview of the condition of the world's children, see UNICEF (2013).
21. The latter question was considered by the admissions panel of the Royal Academy of Music in London when auditioning the young Evelyn Glennie, now Dame Evelyn Glennie, the virtuoso percussionist, who is deaf. See, for example, www.rhinegold.co.uk/music_teacher/listen-dame-evelyn-glennie.

22. This practice has been referred to in the UK as 'certificate indications' and in other countries (including Ireland) as 'certificate annotations'.
23. Although it is important not to prejudge this – see the account of the position in the UK in Snashall (2009).
24. See, for example, Shephard (2000) and Stobart (2012).
25. The guidance on this from the UK's Office for Students was accessed in November 2019 at www.officeforstudents.org.uk/media/0bcce522-df4b-4517-a4fd-101c2468444a/regulatory-notice-1-access-and-participation-plan-guidance.pdf.
26. According to data from the Higher Education Statistics Agency (HESA), more than a quarter of graduates (26%) were awarded a first-class degree in 2018, up from 18% in 2012/13. Retrieved 02/08/19 from www.hesa.ac.uk/news/17-01-2019/sb252-higher-education-student-statistics.

References

American Educational Research Association (AERA), American Psychological Association (APA) and National Council on Measurement in Education (NCME) (1999) *Standards for Educational and Psychological Testing*. Washington, DC: AERA.

American Educational Research Association (AERA), American Psychological Association (APA) and National Council on Measurement in Education (NCME) (2014) *Standards for Educational and Psychological Testing*. Washington, DC: AERA.

Anastasi, A. (1988) *Psychological Testing* (6th edn). New York: Macmillan.

Anderson, E. S. (1999) What is the point of equality? *Ethics*, 109(2), 287–337.

Andrich, D. and Hagquist, C. (2012) Real and artificial differential item functioning. *Journal of Educational and Behavioral Statistics*, 37(3), 387–416.

Angoff, W. (1993) Perspective on differential item functioning methodology. In P. W. Holland and H. Wainer (Eds.), *Differential Item Functioning*. Hillsdale, NJ: Lawrence Erlbaum. pp. 3–24.

Bachan, R. (2018) The drivers of degree classifications. UKSCQA-commissioned analysis. Available at: www.universitiesuk.ac.uk/policy-and-analysis/reports/Documents/2018/drivers-of-degree-classifications.pdf (retrieved 22/07/19).

Baker, E. L. and O'Neil Jr, H. F. (1994) Performance assessment and equity: A view from the USA. *Assessment in Education: Principles, Policy & Practice*, 1(1), 11–26.

Baker, S. (2018) Is grade inflation a worldwide trend? *Times Higher Education World University Rankings*, 28 June. Available at: www.timeshighereducation.com/features/grade-inflation-worldwide-trend (retrieved 23/07/19).

Barkley, R. A., Murphy, K. R. and Fischer, M. (2008) *ADHD in Adults: What the science says*. New York: Guilford Press.

Black, P. and Wiliam, D. (1998) Assessment and classroom learning. *Assessment in Education: Principles, Policy, and Practice*, 5(1), 7–74.

Bonner, S. M. (2013) Validity in classroom assessment: Purposes, properties, and principles. In J. H. McMillan (Ed.), *Sage Handbook of Research on Classroom Assessment*. Los Angeles, CA: Sage. pp. 87–106.

Borsboom, D. and Mellenbergh, G. J. (2002) True scores, latent variables, and constructs: A comment on Schmidt and Hunter. *Intelligence*, 30, 505–514.

Borsboom, D., Mellenbergh, G. J. and van Heerden, J. (2004) The concept of validity. *Psychological Review*, 111, 1061–1071.

Boud, D. (2007) Reframing assessment as if learning were important. In D. Boud and N. Falchikov (Eds.), *Rethinking Assessment in Higher Education*. Abingdon: Routledge. pp. 14–25.

Brennan, R. L. (2001) *Generalizabilty Theory*. New York: Springer-Verlag.

Brookhart, S. M. (2003) Developing measurement theory for classroom assessment purposes and uses. *Educational Measurement: Issues and Practice*, 22(4), 5–12.

Camilli, G. (2006) Test fairness. In R. Brennan (Ed.), *Educational Measurement* (4th edn). Westport, CT: American Council on Education/Praeger. pp. 221–256.

Carvalho, A. (2013) Students' perceptions of fairness in peer assessment: Evidence from a problem-based learning course. *Teaching in Higher Education*, 18(5), 491–505.

Carver, R. P. (1994) Percentage of unknown vocabulary words in text as a function of the relative difficulty of the text: Implications for instruction. *Journal of Reading Behavior*, 26, 413–437.

Cole, N. S. and Zieky, M. J. (2001) The new faces of fairness. *Journal of Educational Measurement*, 38(4), 369–382.

Cook, T. D. and Campbell, D. T. (1979) *Quasi-experimentation: Design and analysis issues for field settings*. Boston, MA: Houghton Mifflin Co.

Cronbach, L. J. (1971) Test validation. In R. L. Thorndike (Ed.), *Educational Measurement* (2nd edn). Washington, DC: American Council on Education. pp. 443–507.

Cronbach, L. J. (1988) Five perspectives on validity argument. In H. Wainer and H. I. Braun (Eds.), *Test Validity*. Hillsdale, NJ: Lawrence Erlbaum. pp. 3–17.

Debra P. v. Turlington (1983) 644F. 2d 397, 5th Cir. (1981) 564 F. Supp. 177 (M.D. Fla.).

Dennis, I. and Newstead, S. E. (1994) The strange case of the disappearing sex bias. *Assessment & Evaluation in Higher Education*, 19(1), 49–56.

Dorans, N. J. and Cook, L. L. (2016) Introduction. In N. J. Dorans and L. L. Cook (Eds.), *Fairness in Educational Assessment and Measurement*. New York: Routledge. pp. 1–6.

Earl, L. M. (2003) *Assessment as Learning: Using classroom assessment to maximize student learning*. Thousand Oaks, CA: Corwin Press.

Educational Testing Service (ETS) (2015) *ETS Standards for Quality and Fairness*. Princeton, NJ: ETS.

Entwistle, N. (1991) Approaches to learning and perceptions of the learning environment: Introduction to the special issue. *Higher Education*, 22, 201–204.

Falchikov, N. and Goldfinch, J. (2000) Student peer assessment in higher education: A meta-analysis comparing peer and teacher marks. *Review of Educational Research*, 70(3), 287–322.

Feldt, L. S. and Brennan, R. L. (1989) Reliability. In R. L. Linn (Ed.), *Educational Measurement* (3rd edn). New York: Macmillan. pp. 105–146.

Fleming, N. D. (1999) Biases in marking students' written work: Quality? In S. Brown and A. Glasner (Eds.), *Assessment Matters in Higher Education: Choosing and using diverse approaches*. Buckingham: Open University Press. pp. 83–92.

Flint, N. R. and Johnson, B. (2011) *Towards Fairer University Assessment: Recognising the concerns of students*. Abingdon: Routledge.

Gipps, C. and Stobart, G. (2009) Fairness in assessment. In C. Wyatt-Smith and J. Cumming (Eds.), *Educational Assessment in the 21st Century: Connecting theory and practice*. London: Springer. pp. 105–118.

Glaser, R. and Silver, E. (1994) Assessment, testing, and instruction: Retrospect and prospect. In L. Darling-Hammond (Ed.), *Review of Research in Education*. Washington, DC: American Educational Research Association. pp. 393–419.

Goldsmith, S. (1997) *Designing for the Disabled: The new paradigm*. Abingdon: Routledge.

Gordon, M. E. and Fay, C. H. (2010) The effects of grading and teaching practices on students' perceptions of grading fairness. *College Teaching*, 58(3), 93–98.

Gould, S. J. (1996) *The Mismeasure of Man* (revised and expanded edn). New York: Norton.

Haertel, E. H. (2006) Reliability. In R. L. Brennan (Ed.), *Educational Measurement* (4th edn). Washington, DC: American Council on Education/Praeger. pp. 65–110.

Haertel, E. and Ho, A. (2016) Fairness using derived scores. In N. J. Dorans and L. L. Cook (Eds.), *Fairness in Educational Assessment and Measurement*. New York: Routledge. pp. 217–239.

Higher Education Statistics Agency (HESA) (2019) *UK, 2017/18*. Cheltenham: HESA. Available at: www.hesa.ac.uk/news/17-01-2019/sb252-higher-education-student-statistics (retrieved 02/08/19).

Kane, M. T. (2006) Validation. In R. L. Brennan (Ed.), *Educational Measurement* (4th edn). Washington, DC: American Council on Education/Praeger. pp. 17–64.

Kane, M. (2010) Validity and fairness. *Language Testing*, 27(2), 177–182.

Kane, M. T. (2013) Validating the interpretations and uses of test scores. *Journal of Educational Measurement*, 50(1), 1–73.

Knight, C. (2018) What is dyslexia? An exploration of the relationship between teachers' understandings of dyslexia and their training experiences. *Dyslexia*, pp. 1–13. https://doi.org/10.1002/dys.1593.

Kunnan, A. J. (2014) Fairness and justice in language assessment. In *The Companion to Language Assessment*. New York: Wiley. pp. 1–17.

Linn, R. L. and Drasgow, F. (1987) Implications of the Golden Rule settlement for test construction. *Educational Measurement Issues Practice*, 6(2), 13–17.

Martiniello, M. (2006) *Sources of Differential Item Functioning for English Learners in Word Math Problems*. Paper presented at the annual meeting of the Northeastern Educational Research Association, New York, October.

Martiniello, M. (2008) Language and the performance of English-language learners in math word problems. *Harvard Educational Review*, 78(2), 333–368.

McArthur, J. (2016) Assessment for social justice: The role of assessment in achieving social justice. *Assessment & Evaluation in Higher Education*, 41(7), 967–981.

McArthur, J. (2018) *Assessment for Social Justice: Perspectives and practices within higher education*. London: Bloomsbury.

McArthur, J. and Huxham, M. (2011) *Sharing Control: A partnership approach to curriculum design and delivery – ESCalate*. Higher Education Academy Education Subject Centre. Available at: www-New1.Heacademy.ac.uk/Assets/Documents/Studentengagement/Edinburgh-2011-Student-Engagement2.doc.Maruyama.

McCoy, S., Banks, J. and Shevlin, M. (2012) School matters: How context influences the identification of different types of special educational needs. *Irish Educational Studies*, 32(2), 119–138.

McMillan, J. H. (2014) *Classroom Assessment: Principles and practice for effective standards-based instruction* (6th edn). Upper Saddle, NJ: Pearson.

McNamara, T. and Roever, C. (2006) *Language Testing: The social dimension*. Malden, MA: Wiley.

Messick, S. (1989) Validity. In R. Linn (Ed.), *Educational Measurement* (3rd edn). Washington, DC: American Council on Education. pp. 13–100.

Messick, S. (1995) Standards of validity and the validity of standards in performance assessment. *Educational Measurement: Issues and Practice*, 14(4), 5–8.

Moss, P. A. (2003) Reconceptualizing validity for classroom assessment. *Educational Measurement: Issues and Practice*, 22(4), 13–25.

Nagy, W. and Scott, J. (2000) Vocabulary processes. In M. Kamil, P. Mosenthal, P. D. Pearson and R. Barr (Eds.), *Handbook of Reading Research*. Mahwah, NJ: Lawrence Erlbaum. pp. 269–284.

Newton, P. E. and Shaw, S. D. (2013) Standards for talking and thinking about validity. *Psychological Methods*, 18(3), 301–319.

Newton, P. E. and Shaw, S. D. (2014) *Validity in Educational and Psychological Assessments*. London: Sage.

Newton, P. E. and Shaw, S. (2016) Disagreement over the best way to use the word 'validity' and options for reaching consensus. *Assessment in Education: Principles, Policy & Practice*, 23(2), 178–197.

Office for Students (2018) *A new approach to regulating access and participation in English Higher Education: Consultation outcomes*. Reference OfS 2018.53. 13 December 2018.

Ofqual (2017) *Specifications in Relation to the Reasonable Adjustment of General Qualifications*. Available at: www.gov.uk/government/publications/specifications-inrelation-to-the-reasonable-adjustment-of-general-qualifications.

Oliver, M. (1996) Understanding disability: From theory to practice. *The Journal of Sociology & Social Welfare*, 23(3), Article 24. Available at: https://scholarworks.wmich.edu/jssw/vol23/iss3/24.

Orr, S. (2010) Collaborating or fight for the marks? Students' experiences of group work assessment in the creative arts. *Assessment & Evaluation in Higher Education*, 35(3), 301–313.

Parkes, J. (2007) Reliability as argument. *Educational Measurement: Issues and Practice*, 26(4), 2–10.

Parkes, J. and Giron, J. (2006) *Reliability Arguments in Classrooms*. Paper presented at the Annual Meeting of the National Council on Measurement in Education, San Francisco, CA.

Pitt, E. and Winstone, N. (2018) The impact of anonymous marking on students' perceptions of fairness, feedback and relationships with lecturers. *Assessment & Evaluation in Higher Education*, 43(7), 1183–1193.

Price, M., Carroll, J., O'Donovan, B. and Rust, C. (2011) 'If I was going there I wouldn't start from here': A critical commentary on current assessment practice. *Assessment and Evaluation in Higher Education*, 36(4), 479–492.

Price, M., Handley, K., Millar, J. and O'Donovan, B. (2010) Feedback: All that effort, but what is the effect? *Assessment & Evaluation in Higher Education*, 35(3), 277–289.

Quality Assurance Agency for Higher Education (QAA) (2012) *UK Quality Code for Higher Education*. Part B: Assuring and Enhancing Academic Quality. Chapter B5: Student Engagement. Gloucester: QAA.

Rasmussen, E. R., Neuman, R. J., Heath, A. C., Levy, F., Hay, D. A. and Todd, R. D. (2002) Replication of the latent class structure of attention-deficit/hyperactivity disorder (ADHD) subtypes in a sample of Australian twins. *Journal of Child Psychiatry*, 43, 1018–1028.

Rawls, J. (1971) *A Theory of Justice*. Cambridge, MA: Belknap Press.

Richardson, R., Moore, D. A., Gwernan-Jones, R., Thompson-Coon, J., Ukoumunne, O., Rogers, M., Whear, R., Newlove-Delgado, T. V., Logan, S., Morris, C., Taylor, E., Cooper, C., Stein, K., Garside, R. and Ford, T. J. (2015) Non-pharmacological interventions for attention-deficit/hyperactivity disorder (ADHD) delivered in school settings: Systematic reviews of quantitative and qualitative research. *Health Technology Assessment*, 19(45). National Institute for Health Research.

Sambell, K., McDowell, L. and Brown, S. (1997) 'But is it fair?': An exploratory study of student perceptions of the consequential validity of assessment. *Studies in Educational Evaluation*, 23(4), 349–371.

Santrock, J. W. (2004) *Educational Psychology* (2nd edn). New York: McGraw-Hill.

Shaw, S. D. and Imam, H. (2013) Assessment of international students through the medium of English: Ensuring validity and fairness in content-based examinations. *Language Assessment Quarterly*, 10(4), 452–475.

Shepard, L. A. (1987) The case of bias in tests of achievement and scholastic aptitude. In S. Modgil and C. Modgil (Eds.), *Arthur Jensen: Consensus and controversy*. London: Falmer Press.

Shepard, L. A. (2003) Intermediate steps to knowing what students know. *Measurement: Interdisciplinary Research and Perspectives*, 1, 171–177.

Shepard, L. A., Camilli, G. and Averill, M. (1981) Comparison of procedures for detecting test-item bias with both internal and external ability criteria. *Journal of Educational Statistics*, 6, 317–377.

Shulman, L. S. (1970) Reconstruction of educational research. *Review of Educational Research*, 40, 371–396.

Sireci, S. G. (2008) Validity issues in accommodating reading tests. *Journal of Educators and Education*, 23, 81–110. (Centre for Educational Assessment Research Report No. 515. Amherst, MA: School of Education, University of Massachusetts, Amherst.)

Sireci, S., Scarpati, S. and Li, S. (2005) Test accommodations for students with disabilities: An analysis of the interaction hypothesis. *Review of Educational Research*, 75, 457–490.

Smith, J. K. (2003) Reconsidering reliability in classroom assessment and grading. *Educational Measurement: Issues and Practice*, 22(4), 26–33.

Snashall, D. (2009) Doctors with disabilities: Licensed to practise? *Clinical Medicine*, 9(4), 315–319.

Sterba, J. P. (2005) Ableism. In T. Honderich (Ed.), *The Oxford Companion to Philosophy* (2nd edn). Oxford: Oxford University Press.

Stobart, G. (2005) Fairness in multicultural assessment systems. *Assessment in Education*, 12(3), 275–287.

Stobart, G. (2012) Validity in formative assessment. In J. Gardner (Ed.), *Assessment and Learning*. London: Sage. pp. 233–242.

Taras, M. (2002) Using assessment for learning and learning from assessment. *Assessment & Evaluation in Higher Education*, 27(6), 501–510.

Tierney, R. D. (2013) Fairness in classroom assessments. In J. H. McMillan (Ed.), *SAGE Handbook of Research on Classroom Assessment*. Thousand Oaks, CA: Sage. pp. 125–144.

Tierney, R. D. (2016) Fairness in educational assessment. In M. A. Peters (Ed.), *Encyclopedia of Educational Philosophy and Theory*. Singapore: Springer Science+Business Media.

UUK & NUS (2019) *Black, Asian and Minority Ethnic Student Attainment at UK Universities: Closing the gap*. May. London: UUK & NUS. Available at: www.universitiesuk.ac.uk/policy-and-analysis/reports/Documents/2019/bame-student-attainment-uk-universities-closing-the-gap.pdf.

United Nations Children's Fund (UNICEF) (2013) *State of the World's Children*. New York: UNICEF.

Van de Vijver, F. and Tanzer, N. K. (2004) Bias and equivalence in cross-cultural assessment: An overview. *European Review of Applied Psychology*, 54(2), 119–135.

Wiliam, D. (2008) Quality in assessment. In S. Swaffield and M. Williams (Eds.), *Unlocking Assessment: Understanding for reflection and application*. London: David Fulton. pp. 123–137.

Willingham, W. W. (1999) A systemic view of test fairness. In S. Messick (Ed.), *Assessment in Higher Education: Issues in access, quality, student development, and public policy*. Mahwah, NJ: Lawrence Erlbaum. pp. 213–242.

Worrell, F. (2016) Commentary on perspectives in fair assessment. In N. J. Dorans and L. L. Cook (Eds.), *Fairness in Educational Assessment and Measurement*. New York and London: Routledge, pp. 283–293.

Wu, A. D., Liu, Y., Stone, E. J., Zou, D. and Zumbo, B. D. (2017) Is difference in measurement outcome between groups differential responding, bias or disparity? A methodology for detecting bias and impact from an attributional stance. *Frontiers in Education*, 2(39), 1–12.

Zieky, M. J. (2016) Developing fair tests. In S. Lane, M. R. Raymond and T. M. Haladyna (Eds.), *Handbook of Test Development* (2nd edn). New York: Routledge.

Zumbo, B. D. (1999) *A Handbook on the Theory and Methods of Differential Item Functioning (DIF)*. Ottawa, ON: National Defence Headquarters.

Zumbo, B. D. (2007) Three generations of DIF analyses: Considering where it has been, where it is now, and where it is going. *Language Assessment Quarterly*, 4(2), 223–233.

3
Fair assessment viewed through the lenses of professional standards, guidelines and procedures

'This document provides guidance on how good qualification and assessment design can give all learners the fairest possible opportunities to show what they know, understand and can do.' (Qualifications Wales/CCEA (Regulation), 2019, Introduction)

'Impartial processes do not guarantee just outcomes.' (Stowell, 2004, p. 497)

'So much of the lived realities of assessment, and students' future lives, are lost if we just consider due process.' (McArthur, 2018, p. 195)

A developing consensus on best practice for fairness

The fair assessment literature over the last 70 years has been punctuated by a number of key publications, including seminal scholarly papers and a proliferation of technical standards, codes of practice and guidelines. The testing professions have produced guidelines for test developers and practitioners, with a view to providing tests that are fair to all test-takers (Standard 3.2, AERA et al., 2014, p. 64).

In Chapter 2, we identified and discussed a developing consensus among assessment theorists regarding fairness in assessment. Briefly, fairness is seen as applying to identified groups of test-takers (often, this is simply assumed and not explicit) and a fair test is one whose outcomes do not show construct-irrelevant variance between those groups. As Messick (1989, 1998) would suggest, this provides comparable validity for relevant, identifiable populations of interest. In Chapter 2, we argued that this is far from complete as an account of fairness in assessment (see also Nisbet and Shaw, 2019). However, it is not surprising that most of the guidance on best practice for fairness published by test organisations and education academics is derived from the consensual view and concentrates on identifying 'sources of irrelevant variance' (Standard 4.13, AERA et al., 2014, p. 90) and avoiding them.[1] Although the understanding of fairness informing some of the publications discussed in this chapter is limited, that does not detract from their applied value. Many contain a great deal of practical wisdom and readers are strongly encouraged to investigate those that apply to the assessments of interest to them.

Hierarchies of guidance

Many organisations and authorities – ranging from the courts to the local point of service, such as a school or college – consider complaints about unfairness. Often, they will start by asking whether rules or guidance extant at the time were breached. The practitioner may well be daunted by the plethora of advice available, and it can be helpful to classify guidance on good practice using a hierarchy, starting with the most authoritative:

- *The law*: a range of legal requirements and principles are discussed in Chapter 4, but briefly, statute law in the form of primary legislation should be seen as top of the league, representing requirements, not just guidance for consideration. In a federal state, federal law will trump state law. In common law jurisdictions, the law may be interpreted authoritatively by court decisions and many countries spell out more detailed requirements in secondary legislation[2] made under the authority of primary legislation.
- *Rules or guidance authorised by law*: this could include requirements made by a regulatory body established and empowered by law, such as the statutory regulators of qualifications in England and Wales (Ofqual and Qualifications Wales). We say more about their requirements later in this chapter.
- *Authoritative professional guidance*: such guidance can reasonably be regarded as representing the accepted consensual views of relevant professions (rather than the outlying views of a few writers), often drawn up by national or international professional associations. A classic example of such guidance is the North American *Standards* (AERA et al., 2014), which we discuss extensively in this book.
- *Requirements or advice provided by relevant organisations*: those applicable to fairness in assessment include publications by organisations providing tests, either produced by a single provider[3] or in collaboration with others.[4]

These categories are by no means watertight, and some sources of guidance fall between the cracks. For example, some publications by statutory bodies are intended only as guidance rather than having the force of regulation, although their guidance gains credibility and perceived authority by being produced under the auspices of a statutory organisation. And some textbooks and guidelines by particular organisations become recognised by custom and practice as representing the 'state of the art'.

We discuss the first of these categories (the law) in Chapter 4. The point to emphasise here is that where statute law makes an explicit requirement, for example about tests or qualifications, then normally[5] that requirement has a higher force than other requirements or advice. This is particularly important for the many countries with statute law prohibiting discrimination on the grounds of named 'protected' characteristics, such as race, colour, religion, sex, national origin or disability. We discuss such legislation more fully in Chapter 4. However, it is important to note here that unfairness against those with characteristics explicitly named and protected by law carries the risk of successful legal challenge to a greater degree than unfairness against other groups, although the same principles arguably apply to all. It is essential for those designing and producing tests to know the law that applies to them. And those offering international assessments and qualifications need to keep in touch with the relevant legislation in countries where their assessments are taken. This aspect of good practice may seem self-evident but nevertheless is worth repeating.

Rules or guidance authorised by law

Historically, education legislation has both encouraged and contributed to the growth of educational testing, particularly in the USA (Wigdor and Garner, 1982). The majority of current American guidance on test fairness has its genesis in the Civil Rights Movement in the USA during the 1960s. Prior to 1960, issues of test fairness had received little thoughtful attention in the educational and psychological testing literature (Kane, 2013). However, the 1960s and '70s saw a proliferation of sets of specific guidelines to test developers and users and reference texts on important topics in measurement (Ebel, 1966; Cole and Moss, 1989; Cascio et al., 2010), notably guidance on fair assessment.

The years following enactment of the Civil Rights Act also saw a number of high-profile cases, which, among other things, established new terms in the vocabulary of assessment fairness and guidelines which carried the authority of their parent legislation. One of the most conspicuous was *Griggs v. Duke Power Co.* (1971).[6]

Duke Power Company was a public utility in North and South Carolina. Importantly, its clients included federal government agencies which meant it was subject to an Executive Order prohibiting employment discrimination. Throughout the 1950s and up to 1965, Duke Power's Dan River Steam Station, Draper (North Carolina) had a policy that African American workers were only allowed to work in the Labour Department (which had the lowest-paid positions in the five departments). In 1965, one year after the enactment of Title VII of the Civil Rights Act,[7] Duke Power used educational requirements (a high school diploma) plus two employment tests as a condition for transfer to better-paid positions in different departments. This had the effect of limiting its black employees to the lowest-paid jobs.

Championed by Willie Griggs, 13 black employees contended that these requirements for transferring departments did not constitute an accurate measure of a person's ability to perform a particular job role. They contended that setting the requirements was no more than an attempt by the company to obviate laws forbidding workplace discrimination. Given the inferior segregated education available to African Americans in North Carolina, a disproportionate number of blacks were rendered ineligible for certain employee opportunities including promotion or transfer.

The Supreme Court ruled unanimously that the aptitude tests – which were broad and not specifically related to the job for which the tests were required – had a *disparate impact* on ethnic minority groups. As a consequence, Duke Power's employee transfer procedure was found to be in violation of Title VII of the Civil

Rights Act. The educational requirements for selection had been 'adopted "without meaningful study" relating them to performance' (Guion, 1998, p. 190). The message from the Court 'was that Title VII covers "the consequences of employment practices, not simply the motivation of employers," and that a "manifest relationship" between the challenged practice and the "employment in question" must be proven if adverse impact is shown' (Gutman, 2005, p. 28).

This and other cases in the 1970s[8] eventually led to the production by the Equal Opportunities Commission of the Uniform Guidelines on Employee Selection Procedures (EEOC et al., 1979). For reasons which we discuss in Chapter 4, the Uniform Guidelines are controversial. However, they are a leading example of guidance legitimated by statute.

In the 1970s and 1980s, particularly in the USA, the influence of court decisions on thinking about best practice for fair testing was considerable. For example, the case of *Larry P. v. Riles* (1979)[9] scrutinised the assessment of children for placement in classes for the 'educationally mentally retarded' (EMR). Following the case, the California State Department of Education prohibited the use of standardised tests for identifying students for placement in EMR classes. In other cases, the courts defended the fairness of tests which had been criticised as unfair. For example, in *Pase v. Hannon* (1980),[10] some of the IQ tests used in Illinois were ruled 'not to discriminate against black children' (p. 883). This judgment was widely held to be based on a flawed inspection of the test items by the court judge. And, in *Bakke v. The Regents of the University of California* (1978),[11] the Supreme Court found it legal to make decisions on admissions based not solely on academic qualifications but also on race, as a means to promote institutional diversity.

In the first decades of the twenty-first century, some parts of the UK established by statute law regulatory bodies with powers to set requirements to be met by organisations registered with them to provide examinations, qualifications and other educational assessments. The idea of having a statutory regulator of exams and qualifications, at arm's length from government but operating in the framework of government policy, paralleled similar developments in regulation of other sectors in the UK. Ofqual is the statutory regulator of qualifications, examinations and assessments in England. Its role and its powers are set out in legislation (the Apprenticeship, Skills, Children and Learning Act 2009). The parallel organisation in Wales, Qualifications Wales,[12] has a similar but not identical role.

The legal authority of statutory regulators such as Ofqual derives from their governing legislation, and is limited to the areas in which the law entitles them to operate. Their pronouncements can have different kinds of authority: conditions for registration by providers of qualifications, for example, have regulatory force and can be backed up by penalties, whilst other statements or publications are intended more as guidance for consideration.

What is the relevance of regulation to fairness in assessment? The legislation establishing Ofqual gave it five high-level objectives, two of which are 'the qualifications standards objective' and 'the public confidence objective'. The qualifications standards objective aims 'to secure that:

(a) regulated qualifications give a reliable indication of knowledge, skills and understanding, and
(b) regulated qualifications indicate —
   (i) a consistent level of attainment (including over time) between comparable regulated qualifications, and
   (ii) a consistent level of attainment (but not over time) between regulated qualifications and comparable qualifications (including those awarded outside the United Kingdom) which are not [regulated by Ofqual]'.[13]

Arguably, the emphasis on reliability and comparability reflects a relational view of fairness in assessment, with great importance placed on all candidates being assessed by the same standards. It also reflects an underlying concern about standards – the standards of achievement required to achieve a mark or grade. One of the drivers behind the legislation to establish a regulator was a concern that standards were falling – hence the reference to comparability 'over time' in regulated qualifications – and ministers were keen for such controversies to be settled by a regulator at arm's length from government.[14] In our view, this debate intersects with, but is not identical to, the debate on fairness. As we have argued earlier, it is not obvious why it is 'fair' for standards required in a qualification to be the same five years later.[15]

Publications by Ofqual tend to reflect the consensus view of fairness in assessment as the absence of construct-irrelevant variance or bias. For example, *The Regulatory Framework for National Assessments: National Curriculum and Early Years Foundation Stage* (Ofqual, 2011) includes a list of criteria to be applied to the development and application of national assessments, including: 'The assessment should minimise bias, differentiating only on the basis of each learner's ability to meet National Curriculum requirements' (Section 5.39, p. 16). And in an Annex, 'minimising bias' is stated to be 'about ensuring that an assessment does not produce unreasonably adverse outcomes for particular groups of learners' (Annex 1, p. 29).

It may be difficult for regulators to set rules which reflect other senses of 'fairness' than the relational sense. For example, requiring qualifications to meet legitimate expectations begs the question of what these legitimate expectations are. However, statutory and regulatory organisations may, and do, issue wider practical advice which lacks regulatory force but gains respect and authority because it comes from the regulator and is relevant to fairness. A UK example highly relevant to this book is a volume full of practical advice for fairness in aspects of test design, development and administration entitled *Fair Access by Design* (Qualifications Wales and CCEA (Regulation), 2019). This includes checklists of points to be considered by those involved in various stages of the assessment process. It covers the design and wording of assessment tasks and prompts reflection about factors which might cause access problems or offence. Many of these, such as avoiding over-complicated wording, using a readable font size and making diagrams clear are aspects of good tests that benefit all candidates, not just sub-groups with particular needs. Guidance of this kind can bring to the attention of test developers lessons from experience that they may not have encountered before, such as the following (from a section headed 'Diversity'):

> Practices and behaviours accepted by some groups may offend others. For example, gambling 'odds' might seem to offer a real-life context for mathematical problems, but learners with certain beliefs could find such a reference distasteful.
>
> In addition, learners from particular cultures may be confused by an apparently familiar term such as 'dice', which they may associate with food preparation ('dice the vegetables') rather than with gambling or chance. (Qualifications Wales and CCEA (Regulation), 2019, p. 21)

Authoritative professional guidance

National professional associations typically work to draw together and publish a consensual professional view of good practice, to which those inside and outside their profession may refer. If mainstream professional opinion develops or changes, then guidance and codes of practice change with them. Although such publications do not have the force of law, they will normally be considered with respect in disputes or where professional practice has been challenged. Educational assessment has increasingly developed as a 'profession' in this sense and a number of professional publications have assumed authoritative status not only in the country of authorship but also internationally. A leading example in the USA is the *Standards for Educational and Psychological Testing*, which has represented a broad professional consensus for over 70 years.

The history of professional standards for the publication and use of tests has its origins in the work of the American Psychological Association (APA) in the late nineteenth century (Novick, 1981, cited in Linn, 1989). The now familiar, much vaunted *Standards* made its initial appearance in the mid-1950s. Its successive editions – six at the time of writing this book – have reflected a hard-won consensus between three powerful sponsoring organisations – the American Educational Research Association (AERA), the American Psychological Association (APA) and the National Council on Measurement in Education (NCME). This may help to explain why the *Standards* has stood the test of time so well.[16]

The vision of fairness developed through the *Standards* sees fairness and validity as inseparable, recognising 'measurement bias as a central threat to fairness in testing' (AERA et al., 2014, p. 49; see also comment on Standard 3.0, AERA et al., 2014, p. 63). The *Standards* applies the foundational principle of fairness to every step in the testing process.

The overriding message promulgated through successive versions of the *Standards* (either implicitly or explicitly) is that fairness is a fundamental right of all individuals and sub-groups in the test population: 'The first view of fairness in testing ... establishes the principle of fair and equitable treatment of all test takers during the testing process' (AERA et al., 2014, pp. 50–51). However, how fairness is understood in theory and practice, and the detailed wordings of particular standards, have evolved over the years.

Whilst issues of fairness are woven into the fabric of the texts of the early editions of the *Standards*, albeit implicitly, the earliest explicit references to fairness appeared in the 1974 edition which referred to the detrimental effect of introducing irrelevant test content: 'Some unfairness may be built into a test, for example, requiring an inordinately high level of verbal ability to comprehend the instructions for a nonverbal test' (APA et al., 1974, p. 2).

In the same year (1974), the National Institute of Education (NIE) established an advisory committee to commission a number of papers on aspects of sex discrimination in inventories of interests used for selection. These papers were used as the background for a conference whose primary goal was to produce NIE *Guidelines on Sex Bias and Sex Fairness in Career Interest Inventories*. Consequently, the *Guidelines* advanced a working definition of sex bias:

> Within the context of career guidance, sex bias is defined as any factor that might influence a person to limit – or might cause others to limit – his or her considerations of a career solely on the basis of gender. (NIE, July, 1974, p. 1)

This definition articulates a fundamental concern that career alternatives should not be limited by bias or stereotyped sex roles in the workplace. Importantly, the *Guidelines* represented a more specific definition of many aspects of sex fairness in interest inventories and related interpretive, technical and promotional materials than had hitherto been available.

The fourth edition of the *Standards* (APA et al., 1985) was the first to contain an integrated section dedicated to fairness issues, though it appeared under the guise of the general heading *Standards for Particular Applications*, and was subdivided into *Testing Linguistic Minorities* (Standards 13.1–13.7) and *Testing People Who Have Handicapping Conditions* (Standards 14.1–14.8).

The focus of the *Testing Linguistic Minorities* standards was on the challenges of dual-language tests and their psychometric properties across translated versions, the importance of language proficiency testing and tests that may assist in appropriate educational programme placement, particularly in relation to the then growing population of students in US schools who had not been given sufficient opportunities to learn the English used in school. It also referred to the culture-specific behaviour – sometimes judged negative or unexpected – of students, with the risk of invalid interpretations being potentially detrimental to the individual being tested.

The section relating to *Testing People Who Have Handicapping Conditions* focused on test modifications. Specific illustrations of how modifications for visually and hearing impaired individuals are implemented were proposed. Other suggestions included methods used to help individuals, who cannot otherwise record their answers, record a response (e.g. using a tape recorder, a typewriter or a braille-writer) as well as the provision of additional time for reading braille, using a recorder or reading regular print. Interestingly, the authors of the 1985 *Standards* highlighted the paucity of available research for determining how much time individuals with handicapping conditions actually require, noting that, at that time, few empirical studies of the effects of special accommodations on the resulting test scores or on their validity and reliability had been conducted. This may reflect the difficulty, which we discuss later in this book, of calculating the level of achievement aimed for in determining requirements for extra time. The point was also made that many of the suggested modifications necessitate that the tests be administered individually rather than to groups of test-takers.

The authors of the 1985 *Standards* also broached ethical tensions relating to the provision of non-standard tests, particularly when their modifications appear to address a different construct from the one being measured in the standard test. The authors posed the question of whether changes in the medium of expression affect cognitive functioning and the meaning of responses (APA et al., 1985, p. 78).

A specific intention of the fifth edition of the *Standards* (AERA et al., 1999) was 'to emphasise the importance of fairness in all aspects of testing and assessment to serve as a context for the technical standards' (AERA et al., 1999, p. 73). Other chapters in the same edition either explicitly or implicitly addressed fairness in relation to the roles and responsibilities of test-takers, the testing of test-takers with diverse linguistic backgrounds, and the testing of those with disabilities.

As we observed in Chapter 2, the current edition of the *Standards* (2014) gives fairness its own prominent chapter early in the text, following on from the chapters on validity and reliability. It unpacks the concept of fairness in assessment as applied to different aspects of test design, development and use (AERA et al., 2014, pp. 50–54). It also seeks to establish principles of good practice for fair assessment, and we shall consider some of these here.

The principle of *accessibility* aims that 'all test-takers should have an unobstructed opportunity to demonstrate their standing on the construct(s) being measured' (AERA et al., 2014, p. 49). A test that is fair will reflect the same constructs for all test-takers and scores have the same meaning for all individuals in the intended population. Accessibility takes this principle one step further and requires that careful thought be given to what construct(s) the test is intended to measure. For example, if a reading comprehension test includes decoding words printed on paper as part of the construct, the use of a screen reader would invalidate scores of test-takers who use this accommodation. A testing situation designed according to principles of accessibility, will facilitate:

> all test-takers in the intended population, to the extent feasible, to show their status on the target construct(s) without being unduly advantaged or disadvantaged by individual characteristics (e.g., characteristics related to age, disability, race/ethnicity, gender or language) that are irrelevant to the construct(s) the test is intended to measure. (AERA et al., 2014, p. 52)

Another important principle introduced in the 2014 edition was *universal design*: 'an approach to test design that seeks to maximize accessibility for all intended examinees' (AERA et al., 2014, p. 50). The thinking here is very similar to that informing the UK regulators' guidance on 'Fair access by design', which we discussed earlier in this chapter. Universal design requires that test developers have a clear knowledge of the constructs the test is designed to measure; a clear understanding of the purpose of the test; who the 'intended examinees' are (including sub-groups who may raise accessibility issues); who the users of the test outcomes will be; and how those outcomes are likely to be used. The objective of universal design principles (e.g. precisely defined constructs; simple, clear and intuitive instructions and procedures; maximum readability and comprehensibility; maximum legibility; accessible, non-biased items) is to improve access to assessments for *all* students, regardless of construct-irrelevant characteristics (AERA et al., 2014, p. 50). Almost all of the good practice required by 'universal design' benefits all test-takers, not just a minority with identified characteristics.

The principles of *accessibility* and *universal design* are linked in that:

> Universal design processes strive to minimise access challenges by taking into account test characteristics that may impede access to the construct for certain test takers, such as the choice of content, test tasks, response procedures, and testing procedures. (AERA et al., 2014, p. 58)

It is clear that the principles for fairness set out in the *Standards* reflect the consensual theoretical view of fairness – as the absence of construct-irrelevant variance – which we have discussed in Chapter 2. In addition to our criticisms of the limitations of this view, there have also been criticisms – for example by Cizek (2016) and Newton (2016) – of the limitations of the *Standards* as a framework for validation. Both have argued that existing guidance cannot be described as sufficiently accessible or practical to enable an assessment professional who works in the development or management of qualifications to conduct a validation study easily. The *Standards* offers little prescription or guidance regarding specific types of fairness evidence and how to gather it. This has implications for evidence in relation to attention to fairness, equitable participation and access. There remains an ongoing requirement to refine sources of fairness evidence to accommodate analysis of group differences, differential item functioning, and statistical analysis of test bias. In our view, these criticisms suggest that the *Standards* has not had the last word on assessment fairness, in theory or practice. Saying that, however, the *Standards* is consistent with welcoming the prominence of fairness and the examples of good practice for fairness in the 2014 edition.

The professional thinking reflected in successive editions of the *Standards* has been influential well beyond the USA.[17] The same can be said of codes of practice for fair testing produced by, for example, the Joint Committee on Testing Practices (JCTP, 2002/2004) and the Smarter Balanced Assessment Consortium (2012). In addition, some international organisations have aimed to provide advice on assessment that is designed to be interpreted by individual countries in the light of their circumstances and country-specific guidance.

The International Guidelines for Test Use (ITC, 2013), developed by the International Test Commission (ITC), offer an international perspective on areas of consensus on what constitutes 'good practice' in test use, without being prescriptive about how these guidelines should be implemented. The guidelines are intended to provide a valuable source document for national professional psychological associations and other organisations associated with testing. Drawing on a number of national test standards and codes of practice, the guidelines have been particularly influenced by the North American *Standards*, as well as by the work of the Australian, Canadian and British Psychological Societies.

The principal objective of the ITC *Guidelines* is to set out what competent test-users should be able to do. They should be able to use tests appropriately, professionally and in an ethical manner. The *Guidelines* approach test use from two differing perspectives, suggesting that a competent test-user will (a) take responsibility for ethical test use and (b) follow good practice in the use of tests. They suggest best practice in both these areas of competence, each of which has close links to aspects of fairness in assessment, as discussed here. We particularly welcome the ITC's emphasis on the ethical use of test outcomes.

Good practice for classroom assessment

The *Standards* and other, similar volumes of professional guidelines are intended for professionals who develop tests and for those who interpret or evaluate the technical quality of test results – among them educators. Plake and Wise (2014) note that whilst 'classroom teachers would benefit from reading the Standards'

(p. 6), the technical language they encounter is not altogether accessible, especially if they are unfamiliar with psychometric formulations of fundamental measurement concepts. There is value, therefore, in translating relevant portions of the fairness *Standards* into standards for classroom assessment practice (Ferrara, 2014).

Classroom assessments encompass all of the strategies and techniques that a classroom teacher might use to collect information from students about their progress. The quality of classroom decisions will depend on the quality of the information garnered from the assessment used in the classroom. More precise inferences drawn from the outcomes of 'fair' classroom assessments will better inform teachers about the achievement of their students and will help facilitate more accurate decision-making about student progress.

The *Principles for Fair Assessment Practices for Education in Canada* (Joint Advisory Committee, 1993) and the *Joint Committee on Standards for Educational Evaluation* (JCSEE, 1994/2003) embrace the need to stress explicitly and clearly the purpose, assessment criteria and assessment outcomes of any classroom assessment. The JCSEE has also published a document entitled *Classroom Assessment Standards for Pre K-12 Teachers: Joint Committee on Standards for Educational Evaluation* (Klinger et al., 2015). The *Classroom Assessment Standards* contain a set of standards and related guidelines which are endorsed by professional organisations as being indicative of consistent and accurate classroom assessment practices.

The guidance offered by the *Classroom Assessment Standards* is intended to guide teachers at the outset of test planning and any instruction occurring alongside (or leading up to) an assessment. It covers, for example:

- assessment purpose (including decisions to be influenced by assessment outcomes)
- learning targets or expectations
- assessment method (given the purpose and learning targets)
- communication (how best to communicate outcomes and to whom), and
- student involvement.

The JCSEE claims that guidance of this kind can positively benefit students' continuous learning. Successful implementation of each standard is contingent on the professional judgement of the teacher within a specific educational context to identify which standards are most appropriate for each classroom assessment situation. Each standard has the potential for teachers to engage in valuable discussions within the context of their school setting.

Regardless of the purpose of the classroom assessment, it is assumed that adherence to standards like the JCSEE will help ensure that the information obtained from a classroom assessment and the interpretation of that information is accurate, allowing for follow-up activities designed to support continuous evidence-based learning.

What is the relevance of this kind of guidance to fairness? In our view, the wide scope of the JCSEE's guidance – covering, for example, communication and assessment methods – takes account of some wider concepts of fairness than those we find in testing professional publications. In particular, it reflects the importance of the 'legitimate expectations' sense of fairness, where the purpose and outcomes of a fair test are understood by the candidate.

Teachers may not hold consistent beliefs about what is fair and unfair in student assessment. In a study focusing on ethical behaviour and examining educators' ethical judgements in relation to assessment, Green, Johnson, Kim and Pope (2007) presented teachers with various scenarios and asked them to indicate whether the student evaluation practice depicted was ethical or unethical. Results showed weak agreement among teachers on more than half of the scenarios. Authors of the study concluded that ethical guidelines for fair assessment are clearly needed for teachers and other educators. We agree.

We have argued in this book that the concept of fairness is applicable to classroom assessment and not confined to 'high-stakes' summative tests. More needs to be done to spell out best practice for fair assessment in the classroom. The same can be said for (fair) assessment in workplace settings.

Local and organisational guidance on fair assessment

Last, but not least, in the hierarchy of guidance on good practice is local guidance provided by testing organisations and other educational bodies. Readers of this book who work with or for organisations providing or administering tests are strongly recommended to consider the published and unpublished guidance of their own organisation – and to share good practice with professional colleagues.

For example, Zieky (2016), drawing on the guidance produced by the testing organisation ETS, identifies some 'general principles' for fairness which include, but go beyond, the consensual view of fairness as being about the absence of construct-irrelevant bias:

- 'Include whatever is necessary for valid measurement
- Show respect for all test-takers
- Give different groups of test-takers an equal chance for a validly interpreted score
- Avoid construct-irrelevant material that may lead people to believe that the test is unfair or inappropriate'. (p. 24)

Zieky (2016) also gives examples of 'physical sources of construct-irrelevant variance'. These are useful prompts for test designers who might not have realised that they could be problematic – an example is 'novel response formats such as dragging and dropping words in a table when the same construct could be measured by simpler items' (p. 24).

Some local guidance may seem strange to readers from a different organisation or culture. Zieky (2016) gives a list of 'acceptable and unacceptable terms for groups', in which 'deaf' and 'visually impaired' are acceptable but 'hearing impaired' is not (p. 22). The obvious response for readers from other cultures is to ask the relevant question of their own situation – what terms would the likely candidates for their tests find offensive? And designers of international tests and qualifications have a particular responsibility to be aware of guidance on fairness and unfairness as perceived in the countries where their tests are used. Where it is not possible to accommodate all of these views, fairness will require careful and sensitive communication with test-users in situations where problems might be unavoidable.

Procedural fairness

Much of the laws, regulations and guidance we have considered is about having procedures in place in order that test-takers are assessed fairly. There are rules for administering examinations and their security; standardisation and monitoring procedural guidelines designed to ensure the reliability of marking; detailed guidance on syllabuses (their rationale and development); processes required for producing question papers, items and mark schemes; and codes of practice for establishing and maintaining standards.

Fair assessment procedures, as instantiated in the kinds of guidance documentation described here, are largely predicated on the principle of procedural due process. Simply stated, due process refers to the carrying out of the law according to established rules and principles. The rules and principles are 'for the protection and enforcement of private rights, including notice and the right to a fair hearing before a tribunal with the power to decide the case' (Garner, 2001, p. 223).[18] Embedded within the concept of procedural due process is the notion that fair assessment procedures and rules should be applied to all test-takers in largely the same way (whilst also acknowledging that there may be a need to modify procedures in order to accommodate test-takers with special needs or requirements; see Kane, 2010).

In the USA, due process has become a constitutional right. The 5th Amendment of the Constitution of the United States includes an expanded version of the due process concept. The 14th Amendment also contains a due process clause, ensuring that all persons have the protection of the law irrespective of their race.[19]

The right to a fair procedure is also enshrined in the European Convention on Human Rights (Article 6(1)) (Council of Europe, 1950).

There are clear implications for how procedural due process relates to fairness, as defined in professional standards and guidelines. In order to maintain procedural fairness, it is necessary to ensure that the correct procedures for identifying and minimising construct-irrelevant bias (the mainstream consensus view of fairness) are followed in decision-making processes.

We contend that procedural fairness is a *necessary though not sufficient requirement* for fair assessment.[20] Procedural adherence alone can raise the potential for prescriptive, unreflective practice. Guidance procedures and rules for fair test construction, administration and marking, no matter how impartially crafted, can engender 'taken for granted cultures and practices' (Stowell, 2004, p. 496) if left unchecked. Fairness needs to reflect the spirit as well as the letter of the implementation of procedural guidance. An example from the personal experience of one of the authors was a regulatory requirement in the UK for meetings of committees establishing grade boundaries for national examinations to 'refer to sample scripts', as one of several means of ensuring consistency and fairness. In practice, this became no more than a ritual to satisfy the regulator.

In our view, many of the procedures, guidelines and processes which are described in this chapter do not take sufficient account of the experiences, perceptions and expectations of candidates (test-takers). They need to be assured that all procedural requirements for their assessment have been met (fairness in the formal sense), and also that the procedures do not disadvantage them (or anyone else) unfairly. They will also complain of unfairness if a test differs from their reasonable expectations, and further examination of examples of this may help to identify good practice for fairness in the 'legitimate expectations' sense. Candidates' reactions to their test may be relevant to its validity (and reliability) as well as to an understanding of its perceived fairness.

Greater student engagement with assessment practices, adopting a more inclusive, proactive role in shaping practices and procedures, should be encouraged (Entwistle, 1991; Orr, 2010; McArthur and Huxham, 2011; Carvalho, 2013; McArthur, 2016). Carless (2009) advances the notion that students need to assume a mediating function in negotiating matters relating to fairness.

Honest negotiation aligned to genuine interaction between all affected parties in the construction of assessment practices is crucial to the credibility and persuasive power of the processes, rules and regulations that underpin assessment. The authority and trustworthiness of an assessment procedure will be significantly enriched by identifying the needs and values of all affected parties, acknowledging and taking seriously their concerns, wishes and sensitivities. Fair procedural guidance is the product of 'social constructs': 'the decision as to what does or does not get included in an assessment rule of procedure is itself a social construction reflecting many values and assumptions' (McArthur, 2018, p. 45).

Values and assumptions are rarely universally shared. False assumptions as to what constitutes good practice may lead to procedural uncertainty and prescriptivism. Test-taker engagement in establishing what is fair, will help to ensure that these test-takers are more knowledgeable about how assessment works and the various purposes and uses of those assessments. Research undertaken with higher education students demonstrates a sophisticated understanding of assessment fairness, revealing a multi-faceted concept (Orr, 2010).[21] We believe that test-takers engaging in the formulation of assessment policy and practice through direct consultation with educational policy-makers will go some way to incorporating their perceptions, as the work of Leitch et al. (2007) attests.

Fair assessment standards, guidelines and procedures must reflect 'the lived realities of assessment, and students' future lives' (McArthur, 2018, p. 195) if assessments are to be deemed fair for all test-takers.

Conclusion

In this chapter, we describe a hierarchy of sources of guidance on good practice for assessment fairness – the law; rules or guidance authorised by law; authoritative professional guidance; and local guidance by organisations (including test providers). Most of it is grounded in the consensual theoretical view of fairness in assessment as the absence of construct-irrelevant variance, although some goes beyond that and covers communication and fairness of use. Much of the guidance that we have referred to reflects generations of experience and is full of practical wisdom which deserves to be more widely read and used. In our view, more work needs to be done on the practical implications of wider aspects of fairness, both in summative tests and exams and in assessment carried out in the classroom or workplace; and due process alone is not sufficient for fair assessment.

The good practice described here has its limitations, but we can make significant progress along the road to fairness if assessment professionals at all levels are familiar with the rules and guidance that apply to the tests they provide or use, and benefit from the wisdom of those who have gone before.

For further reflection

Selection for an opera course at a music conservatoire

A music college has to choose among a large number of hopeful applicants for its prestigious opera course. It draws up a shortlist based on listening to performances recorded on audio CD, and Sandra, who has an outstanding soprano voice, is one of the best. However, after the live auditions, on stage at the college, Sandra is told that she has not been selected. The rejection letter is polite but vague, and when Sandra's parents press for an explanation, the selectors explain that her genetic obesity and unattractive appearance would make opera companies reluctant to cast her. They offer her a place on a different course, but Sandra's heart is set on opera and she complains that she has been treated unfairly. Is she right?

The test in applied mathematics

A national education administration commissions a new test to assess the ability of 16-year-olds to apply mathematics to real-life situations. The administration thinks that doing so will improve fairness as the new test will be more interesting and appealing to students who do not perform well in abstract mathematical tasks, such as manipulating equations, and thus enable them to demonstrate their mathematical skills. The administration takes best advice in making sure that the examples of real-life situations used are familiar to most students and that the tasks are clearly worded. Practice tests are sent to schools for preparation before the first tests are taken 'for real'. Teachers report that students from some ethnic minorities find the new-style questions harder than do students from the majority ethnic population, even in instances where the teacher thought that the mathematical skills of the two groups were broadly similar. After the first year of running the new test, the administrators commission a DIF analysis by ethnic group, which finds that the results for some ethnic minority groups are significantly lower than those of comparator groups. What should the administration do? Is the new test fair?

Notes

1. Zieky (2016) contends that the most successful guidelines are those that help the test developer avoid or eliminate bias that differentially affects various groups of test-takers (p. 84). Drawing mainly on the ETS Guidelines for Fairness Review of Assessments (Educational Testing Service, 2009), Zieky unpacks the guidance that focuses on the identification and reduction (and/or removal) of cognitive, affective and physical sources of construct-irrelevant variance.
2. Forms of secondary legislation vary from country to country. For example, in the UK, over 3,000 'Statutory Instruments' are produced every year.
3. For example, the *ETS Standards for Quality and Fairness* (ETS, 2014).
4. For example, in the UK, the eight largest organisations awarding qualifications form the 'Joint Council on Qualifications' (JCQ) which claims to 'provide ... a single voice for its members on issues of examination administration' (see www.jcq.org.uk). Its publications include detailed guidance relevant to fairness, for example on the practicalities of accommodations for candidates with disabilities (JCQ, 2019).

5. This statement may be modified in countries with a written constitution or legislation on human rights which is established as pre-eminent.
6. *Griggs v. Duke Power Co.* (1971) 401 U.S. 424.
7. Title VII makes it unlawful to deprive any individual of employment opportunities or otherwise adversely affect his status as an employee, because of such an individual's race, colour, religion, sex or national origin (Section 703(a) (2)).
8. Such as *Albemarle Paper Co. v. Moody* (1975) 422 U.S. 405.
9. 495 F. Supp. 926 N.D. Calif. 1979.
10. 506 F. Supp. 831 N.D. Ill. 1980.
11. 432, U.S. 265, 1978.
12. Established by the Qualifications Wales Act 2015.
13. Apprenticeships, Skills, Children & Learning Act 2009, S128(2). S128 (2) (a) (ii) – relating to comparability with other qualifications – was inserted by S22 of the Education Act 2011.
14. Hansard, 23 February 2009, cols 26–27.
15. We recognise that there may be arguments for this objective based on other values than fairness, e.g. public confidence, or educational benefits such as enabling high achievement to be recognised.
16. The first edition of the *Standards* (1954), entitled 'Technical recommendations for psychological tests and diagnostic techniques', was sponsored by the American Psychological Association, American Educational Research Association, and National Council on Measurements Used in Education. The National Council on Measurements Used in Education became the National Council on Measurements in Education in later editions.
17. A related content analysis of another highly influential document, *Educational Measurement* (sponsored by the National Council on Measurement in Education and the American Council on Education), reveals a similar developing consensus.
18. See www.merriam-webster.com/dictionary/due%20process (accessed 11/07/19).
19. The US Supreme Court also recognises a second category of due process. *Substantial* due process is a judicial requirement that enacted laws may not contain provisions that result in the unfair, arbitrary or unreasonable treatment of an individual. The remit of substantial due process is much wider than that for procedural due process, potentially including issues embraced by other definitions in the Standards (e.g. validity of individual test score interpretations for the intended uses).
20. See Kane (2010) for a discussion of procedural and substantive due process in relation to the 1999 Standards.
21. Students also perceive assessments as having the potential to hamper the quality of their learning.

References

Albemarle Paper Co. v. Moody (1975) 422 US 405.
American Psychological Association (APA), American Educational Research Association (AERA) and National Council on Measurements Used in Education (NCME) (1954)

Technical recommendations for psychological tests and diagnostic techniques. *Psychological Bulletin*, 51(2), Supplement.

American Psychological Association (APA), American Educational Research Association (AERA) National Council on Measurement in Education (NCME) (1974) *Standards for Educational and Psychological Tests*. Washington, DC: APA.

American Psychological Association (APA), American Educational Research Association (AERA) and National Council on Measurement in Education (NCME) (1985) *Standards for Educational and Psychological Testing*. Washington, DC: APA.

American Educational Research Association (AERA), American Psychological Association (APA) and National Council on Measurement in Education (NCME) (1999) *Standards for Educational and Psychological Testing*. Washington, DC: AERA.

American Educational Research Association (AERA), American Psychological Association (APA) and National Council on Measurement in Education (NCME) (2014) *Standards for Educational and Psychological Testing*. Washington, DC: AERA.

Apprenticeships, Skills, Children & Learning Act 2009 (2009) Chapter 22. London: TSO.

Bakke v. The Regents of the University of California (1978) 432 U.S. 265.

Carless, D. (2009) Trust, distrust and their impact on assessment reform. *Assessment & Evaluation in Higher Education*, 34(1), 79–89.

Cascio, W., Jacobs, R. and Silva, J. (2010) Validity, utility, and adverse impact: Practical implications from 30 years of data. In J. Outtz (Ed.), *Adverse Impact: Implications for organizational staffing and high stakes selection*. New York: Routledge. pp. 271–288.

Carvalho, A. (2013) Students' perceptions of fairness in peer assessment: Evidence from a problem-based learning course. *Teaching in Higher Education*, 18(5), 491–505.

Cizek, G. J. (2016) Validating test score meaning and defending test score use: Different aims, different methods. *Assessment in Education: Principles, Policies & Practice*, 23(2), 212–225.

Cole, N. S. and Moss, P. A. (1989) Bias in test use. In R. L. Linn (Ed.), *Educational Measurement* (3rd edn). New York: American Council on Education/Macmillan. pp. 201–219.

Council of Europe (1950) European Convention for the Protection of Human Rights and Fundamental Freedoms, as amended by Protocols Nos. *11 and 14*, 4 November 1950, ETS 5. Available at: www.refworld.org/docid/3ae6b3b04.html (accessed 21/10/19).

Ebel, R. (1966) *The social consequences of educational testing*. In A. Anastasi (Ed.), *Testing Problems in Perspective: Twenty-fifth anniversary volume of topical readings from the invitational conference in testing problems*. Washington, DC: American Council on Education. pp. 18–28.

Educational Testing Service (ETS) (2009) *ETS Guidelines for Fairness Review of Assessments*. Princeton, NJ: ETS.

Educational Testing Service (ETS) (2014) *ETS Standards for Quality and Fairness*. Princeton, NJ: ETS.

Entwistle, N. (1991) Approaches to learning and perceptions of the learning environment: Introduction to the special issue. *Higher Education*, 22, 201–204.

Equal Employment Opportunity Commission (EEOC), Civil Service Commission, Department of Labor, & Department of Justice (1979) Adoption by four agencies of Uniform Guidelines on employee selection procedures. *Federal Register*, 43, 38290–38315.

Ferrara, S. (2014) Formative assessment and test security: The revised standards are mostly fine; our practices are not (invited commentary). *Educational Measurement: Issues and Practice*, 33(4), 25–28.

Garner, B. (Ed.) (2001) *Black's Law Dictionary* (2nd pocket edn). St Paul, MN: West Publishing Group.

Green, S. K., Johnson, R. L., Kim, D. H. and Pope, N. S. (2007) Ethics in classroom assessment practices: Issues and attitudes. *Teaching and Teacher Education*, 23(7), 999–1011.

Griggs v. Duke Power Co. (1971) 401 U.S. 424.

Guion, R. M. (1998) *Assessment, Measurement, and Prediction for Personnel Decisions*. Mahwah, NJ: Lawrence Erlbaum.

Gutman, A. (2005) Adverse impact: Judicial, regulatory, and statutory authority. In F. L. Landy (Ed.), *Employment Discrimination Litigation*. San Francisco, CA: Jossey-Bass. pp. 20–46.

International Test Commission (ITC) (2013) ITC Guidelines on Test Use, 8 October, Version 1.2. Final version document reference: ITC-G-TU-20131008.

Joint Advisory Committee (JAC) (1993) *Principles for Fair Assessment Practices for Education in Canada*. Edmonton, AB: JAC.

Joint Committee on Standards for Educational Evaluation (JCSEE) (1994/2003) *The Program Evaluation Standards: How to assess evaluations of educational programs*. Newbury Park, CA: Sage.

Joint Committee on Testing Practices (JCTP) (2002/2004) *The Code of Fair Testing Practices in Education*. Washington, DC: JCTP.

Joint Council on Qualifications (JCQ) (2019) *Adjustments for Candidates with Disabilities and Learning Difficulties: Access arrangements and reasonable adjustments*. Available at: www.jcq.org.uk/exams-office/access-arrangements-and-special-consideration/regulations-and-guidance/access-arrangements-and-reasonable-adjustments-2019-20 (accessed 01/10/19).

Kane, M. (2010) Validity and fairness. *Language Testing*, 27(2), 177–182.

Kane, M. T. (2013) Validating the interpretations and uses of test scores. *Journal of Educational Measurement*, 50(1), 1–73.

Klinger, D., McDivitt, P., Howard, B., Rogers, T., Munoz, M. and Wylie, C. (2015) *Classroom Assessment Standards for PreK-12 Teachers*. Joint Committee on Standards for Educational Evaluation (JCSEE).

Larry P. v. Riles (1979) 495 F. Supp. 926 (N.D. Calif.).

Leitch, J., Gardner, J., Mitchell, S., Lundy, L., Odena, O., Galanouli, D. and Clough, P. (2007) *Consulting Pupils on the Assessment of their Learning (CPAL) Research Report*. Available at: www.cpal.qub.ac.uk.

Linn, R. L. (1989) Current perspectives and future directions. In R. Linn (Ed.), *Educational Measurement* (3rd edn). Washington, DC: American Council on Education. pp. 1–10.

McArthur, J. (2016) Assessment for social justice: The role of assessment in achieving social justice. *Assessment & Evaluation in Higher Education*, 41(7), 967–981.

McArthur, J. (2018) *Assessment for Social Justice: Perspectives and practices within higher education*. London: Bloomsbury.

McArthur, J. and Huxham, M. (2011) *Sharing Control: A partnership approach to curriculum design and delivery – ESCalate*. Higher Education Academy Education Subject Centre.

Available at: www-New1.Heacademy.ac.uk/Assets/Documents/Studentengagement/Edinburgh-2011-Student-Engagement2.doc.Maruyama.

Messick, S. (1989) Validity. In R. Linn (Ed.), *Educational Measurement* (3rd edn). Washington, DC: American Council on Education. pp. 13–100.

Messick, S. (1998) *Consequences of Test Interpretation and Use: The fusion of validity and values in psychological assessment*. ETS Research Report No. RR-98-48. Princeton, NJ: Educational Testing Service. Paper presented at the International Congress of Applied Psychology, San Francisco, CA, August.

National Institute of Education (NIE) (1974) *Guidelines for Assessment of Sex Bias and Sex Fairness in Career Interest Inventories*. July. Washington, DC: Department of Health and Welfare, National Institute of Education.

Newton, P. E. (2016) Macro- and micro-validation: Beyond the 'five sources' framework for classifying validation evidence and analysis. *Practical Assessment, Research & Evaluation*, 21(12). Available at: http://pareonline.net/getvn.asp?v=21&n=12 (accessed 28/07/17).

Nisbet, I. and Shaw, S. D. (2019) Fair assessment viewed through the lenses of measurement theory. *Assessment in Education: Principles, Policy & Practice*, 26(5), 612–629.

Novick, M. R. (1981) Federal guidelines and professional standards. *American Psychologist*, 36, 1035–1046.

Ofqual (2011) *Regulatory Framework for National Assessments: National curriculum and early years foundation stage assessments*. Updated March 2018. Ofqual/18/6354/3.

Orr, S. (2010) Collaborating or fight for the marks? Students' experiences of group work assessment in the creative arts. *Assessment & Evaluation in Higher Education*, 35(3), 301–313.

Pase v. Hannon (1980) 506 F. Supp. 831 (N.D. Ill.).

Plake, B. S. and Wise, L. L. (2014) What is the role and importance of the revised AERA, APA and NCME standards for educational and psychological testing? *Educational Measurement: Issues and Practice*, 33(4), 4 12.

Qualifications Wales/CCEA (2015) *CCEA (Accreditation) and Welsh Government: Fair access by design – Guidance for awarding organisations on designing high-quality and inclusive qualifications*. Guidance document no. 174/2015, June.

Qualifications Wales & CCEA (Regulation) (2019) *Fair Access by Design: Guidance for awarding organisations on designing high-quality and inclusive qualifications*, July. Available at: www.qualificationswales.org/media/4739/fair-access-by-design.pdf (accessed 01/10/19).

Smarter Balanced Assessment Consortium (SBAC) (2012) *Bias and Sensitivity Guidelines*. Olympia, WA: SBAC.

Stowell, M. (2004) Equity, justice and standards: Assessment decision making in higher education. *Assessment & Evaluation in Higher Education*, 29(4), 495–510.

Wigdor, A. K. and Garner, W. R. (Eds.) (1982) *Ability Testing: Uses, consequences and controversies, Pt. 1*. Report of the committee. Washington, DC: National Academy Press.

Zieky, M. J. (2016) Fairness in test design and development. In N. J. Dorans and L. L. Cook (Eds.), *Fairness in Educational Assessment and Measurement*. New York: Routledge. pp. 9–31.

4
Fair assessment viewed through the lenses of the law

'[The qualifications regulator] was engaged in an exercise of damage limitation. Whichever way it chose to resolve the problem, there was going to be an element of unfairness.' (*LB Lewisham & Others v. AQA, Edexcel, Ofqual & Others* (2013) EWHC, 211, para. 153)

'Unfairness is often alleged when groups or individuals are differentially denied something of value or subjected to an undesirable outcome as a result of their test scores.' (Phillips, 2016, p. 239)

Introduction

We are all subject to the law, and those who deliver and administer assessments are no exception. There are many different legal lenses, depending on each country's legal system, the type of law invoked in particular cases and the social context when leading cases are determined. In this chapter, we start by describing the different kinds of legal lenses applied to fairness in assessment. We then consider typical settings in which the courts have considered the fairness of assessments and identify some common themes, asking the same questions as in other chapters.

We have picked out four cases in particular – one from each of the USA, the UK, Australia and Ireland – and described them in 'case studies' which should give readers a feel for the background and some of the issues involved without recourse to law reports. But there are two limitations to the discussion in this chapter which it is best to declare at the beginning. First, the cases to which we refer are from common law jurisdictions such as the UK and the USA, rather than civil law systems such as that in France. Second, even though the countries we refer to have broadly similar kinds of legal system, examples in one country do not bind others. However, we believe that the principles informing legal approaches to fair assessment are of interest beyond their immediate environment. Assessment professionals need to know the specific legislation, regulations and guidelines which courts in their country may apply to their activities; but we can also learn wider lessons from developments in other countries.

The different legal lenses applied to assessment

Some countries have written constitutions, recent or long-standing, and assessments that are felt to be unfair may be challenged as unconstitutional. The Founding Fathers who wrote the US Constitution had no experience of public education, let alone of public exams, but principles derived from the Constitution have been active in many of the cases cited in this chapter. As we shall see, applying constitutional principles may involve approaches which seem strange to educationalists in other countries – for example, seeing a diploma or qualification as a 'property', of which citizens may not be deprived without 'due process of law'.

As well as interpreting constitutions (where these exist), in common law jurisdictions, judges interpret and apply statutes and other provisions, such as regulations or Statutory Instruments. Statute law is created by national or state legislatures, and legislation affecting education and assessment may include statements of principle or may be more specific – for example, setting out the duties and powers of statutory bodies such as regulators or inspectors or imposing requirements in defined situations. And legislation on human rights and civil rights – typically derived from international charters such as the United Nations' Universal Declaration of Human Rights (UNGA, 1948) and/or the European Convention on Human Rights (Council of Europe, 1953) – may be the basis for challenges to assessment in education. Title 6 of the US Civil Rights Act 1964 prohibits discrimination based on race, colour or national origin in programmes which receive federal financial assistance. These publicly funded programmes may include educational assessments.

Many countries have statute law forbidding discrimination on the grounds of named 'protected characteristics' such as sex, disability, ethnicity and religion. The specific categories may differ from country to country and even by state within the same country. Actions under such legislation are limited to the characteristics listed: if, for example, a test was thought to be unfairly disadvantaging poor students, but socio-economic status was not included in the list of protected characteristics by anti-discrimination legislation, that legislation could not be the basis for legal challenge, however unfair the test was felt to be.[1]

Candidates for assessments may be the subject of legislation conferring positive rights on them as well as legislation stating detailed conditions which their assessment must meet. For example, a student with a disability in the USA might cite a positive right to a 'free and appropriate education in the least restrictive environment' (Individuals with Disabilities Education Act 1990, para. 1412(a)(5) [US Govt, 1990]) or the specific duty on his/her examiners to provide test material that does not 'reflect … the student's impaired sensory, manual or speaking skills (except where those skills are the factors that the test purports to measure)' (Rehabilitation Act 1973, s504 [US EEOC, 1973]).

In common law jurisdictions, judges in higher courts make decisions which bind junior courts in the same country, although subsequent courts may decide that the relevant circumstances have changed, and the authoritative view may develop over time. Countries differ in the attention they pay to case law from other jurisdictions, but at most it is only persuasive.

Two categories of challenge deserve particular mention here. The first is an allegation of *negligence*. In ordinary language, a person or an organisation is negligent if they are careless or thoughtless. In law, negligence is a breach of a duty of care which causes harm. There are several conditions which must be met for an action to be negligent in law. These are largely derived from the colourful UK case of *Donoghue v. Stevenson* (1932),[2] in which the unfortunate Mrs Donoghue drank from a bottle of ginger beer only to find that it contained a dead snail. First, there must be a duty owed; second, the breach must cause loss; and third, the action (or lack of action) needs to be below the standard expected of a reasonably competent equivalent person.[3] 'Reasonable competence' in this context refers not to the competence of any member of the public but to a degree of professional knowledge or skill that could reasonably be expected in the circumstances.

In principle, it is not difficult to see how these standards might be applied to organisations providing tests which matter to students. In the USA, there have been many legal challenges relating to the marking of standardised tests which have led to court judgments or costly out-of-court settlements (Rhoades and Madaus, 2003). In one case, the court judged that the test developer's methodology for calculating cut scores was 'so riddled with errors that it could only be described as capricious and arbitrary'.[4] Whether or not the judgment explicitly uses the language of 'unfairness', it is easy to see that poor practice of this kind may unfairly harm students (for example, by requiring them to resit a test which they were incorrectly marked as failing).

The second highly relevant category of common law challenge is *judicial review*. We describe here how such challenges work in England and Wales, but similar features are found in other systems cited in this chapter. A judicial review is generally a review of how a decision was made by a public body, not (normally) of the merits of the decision itself. The 'public institutions' subject to review include universities and the (private) awarding organisations that run national exams in England (at least for some of their functions),[5] as well as national statutory bodies. The broad headings for challenge through judicial review[6] include illegality (such as a public body acting beyond its statutory powers), 'unreasonableness', procedural failings and denial of 'legitimate expectations' – a phrase which has already featured in our analysis of senses of 'fairness' in Chapter 1. The bar for 'reasonableness' (often called 'Wednesbury unreasonableness' after a judgment in the 1940s[7]) is notoriously high: an action by a public body can only be judged 'unreasonable' if no reasonable person acting reasonably could have done the same. Arguably, some actions which fail to follow the best practices described in Chapter 3 of this book might not be sufficiently unreasonable to be caught by this criterion.

Judicial review by the courts is normally seen as appropriate only if other remedies have been explored first. For example, university students who want to complain about their grades or about disciplinary action taken against them cannot go to the courts without first exploring the university's appeal procedures and any routes for further appeal, such as the UK's Office of the Independent Adjudicator.[8] In an Australian case involving an aggrieved student's complaint against the University of New South Wales (discussed in Cumming and Dickson, 2007), the judge gave an informative account of the focus of the lens of judicial review:

> [The Court] does not sit as a Court of factual review over decisions of ... [university] committees ... [but] it can ... intervene in accordance with accepted administrative law principles, for example, where the Committee has not been properly constituted, where it failed to follow proper procedure, where it acted in a way constituting a denial of natural justice, where it otherwise reached a decision that was contrary to law, or where its decision was such that no reasonable committee, acting with a due appreciation of its responsibility, could have arrived at it.[9]

And, of course, assessments can be the backdrop for breaches of other laws – criminal acts (such as theft of test materials), fraud, cheating or bullying and harassment at work. Staff in assessment organisations, schools or colleges may be protected by 'whistleblowing' legislation[10] if they report concerns. Assessment may also be the subject of commercial disputes between testing organisations, some of which may have implications for fairness. Phillips refers to the use of copyright law to prevent some companies offering preparation courses from getting access to secure test items (Phillips, 2016, p. 255).

In summary, there are many legal lenses applied by constitutional law and common law and principles governing their application. We shall now consider some typical settings in which assessments are subject to legal challenge.

Settings for the application of legal lenses to assessment fairness

In the USA, legal scrutiny has been applied to the fairness of *test requirements for graduation from high school*. The high school diploma is very important for students as it is a requirement for most jobs and for progression in education. The most famous case of this kind in recent times is described in Case Study 4.1.

Case Study 4.1: USA

Was it fair to make passing a new test a requirement for obtaining a high school diploma without knowing that all students had been taught the content of the test? Was the introduction of the new test particularly unfair to black students?

Debra P. v. Turlington (1979–1984)[11]

In the 1970s, the state of Florida wanted to improve educational standards. In 1976 it passed state legislation that added a new test to the requirements for obtaining a diploma on leaving high school. In addition to completing their courses (as before), students had to pass a functional literacy test (with a long title, abbreviated to 'SSAT II'). When the new test was introduced, black students fared much worse than white students. In the first sitting (in Fall, 1977), 78% of black students failed, compared with 25% of white students, and in the first two years of the test (including opportunities to resit), the failure rate among black students was approximately 10 times that among white students. The case went to court four times, starting with a legal challenge brought by a group of students[12] and their families and supporters against a list of senior administrators of the Florida State Board of Education.[13] They claimed that the introduction of the new test was in breach of the 14th Amendment of the US Constitution[14] and of US civil rights legislation.

The District Court in 1979 accepted evidence from experts that the new test had 'content and construct validity', but concluded that its hasty introduction, denying students and teachers adequate time to prepare, violated the 'due process' and 'equal protection' clauses of the 14th Amendment and was 'fundamentally unfair'.[15] The Court also found that students who failed the test were harmfully stigmatised as 'functionally illiterate'. The judgment referred to the history of segregation of schools in Florida and the educational disadvantage in black schools. It concluded that the new test reflected 'vestiges' of past injustice and perpetuated the effects of past discrimination. The state was not allowed to make graduation dependent on passing SSAT II for four years (until 1982) to allow time for more preparation and to 'purge the taint of past segregation'.[16]

Both parties appealed. In 1981 the Circuit Court upheld some parts of the original judgment but found that SSAT II lacked 'curricular validity' because there was insufficient proof that the content of the test 'covered material actually studied in the classrooms of the state'[17]. It also judged that students were denied a legitimate expectation that if they attended school and met the requirements of their courses, they would obtain a diploma. The case was sent back to the District Court to receive evidence that the test had curricular validity and that its 'racially discriminatory impact' was not a vestige of past discrimination.

In 1983 the District Court received evidence about the 'instructional validity' (the term that they used) of SSAT II from detailed surveys of practice in schools throughout Florida, including surveys of students and teachers. The Court found that students had an adequate opportunity to learn the skills tested by SSAT II, that they had five chances to pass SSAT before the end of their 12th grade as well as opportunities for remediation, and that SSAT II was 'instructionally valid and therefore

> constitutional'.[18] They also concluded that making the test a requirement for graduation in 1982 would not perpetuate past discrimination.
>
> These findings were broadly upheld by the Circuit Court in 1984. The judgment accepted educational advice that 4–6 years' notice was required for introducing a new mandatory test such as SSAT II. The Court considered that, with proper preparation, the requirement to pass a functional literacy test might have a motivational force on both students and teachers and thus reduce the effects of past educational inequalities in Florida. The Court ruled that, starting with the 'class of 1983', students who did not pass SSAT II could be denied their high school diploma.

This case invoked several of the senses of 'fairness' that we have distinguished. Perhaps the most obvious is the *relational* sense – that black students were not treated the same as white students. Attempts to show bias in the test items themselves were unsuccessful, but there was a clear differential impact in the test outcomes. The approach taken by the court – and reinforced in a later case (*GI Forum v. Texas Education Agency*, 2000)[19] – was that this in itself was not enough to show unfairness, but prompted further enquiry. That principle was reflected in the 2014 edition of the *Standards*: '[G]roup differences in testing outcomes should trigger heightened scrutiny ... However, group differences in outcomes do not in themselves indicate that a [test] is biased or unfair' (AERA et al., 2014, p. 54).

The case also touched on the 'legitimate expectations' sense of fairness, which was alleged to be violated by the introduction of a new requirement for the diploma. If taken to extremes, that argument could be used against any changes to requirements for high-stakes tests, but in *Debra P.* it reinforced the case for adequate notice of and preparation for the changes. Also, the initial District Court judgment touched on the 'stigma' sense of unfairness, referring to the effects of being branded 'functionally illiterate'.

Lastly, the case of Debra P. used the 'retrospective' sense of fairness, finding, at least initially, that the poor record of black students was a 'vestige' of past unfairness (in the historically segregated public school system in Florida). Although the defendants in the case were not blamed for the events of the past, they were seen to have a responsibility not to perpetuate the effects of those events. The Circuit Court took the view that, with adequate preparation time, the 'sanction' of the functional literacy test might motivate teachers and students to improve outcomes for black students, although some might question the view of assessment as a 'sanction' and no evidence was offered for this view of motivation.

The most telling legacy of *Debra P.* was the account of 'curriculum validity', which was morphed by the District Court into 'instructional validity' – rightly so, as the question at issue was not what students should have been taught, but what they were actually taught. The implied argument (from the Circuit Court) linking fairness to instructional validity seems to have gone something like: (1) disparate impact can only be allowed to be fair if the test is valid (or where no equally or more valid alternative can be suggested[20]); (2) the test in *Debra P.* had disparate impact; (3) the test in *Debra P.* was not shown to have curriculum (later, instructional) validity; and (4) until there was evidence that all students were taught the content of the test, it could not be regarded as fair.

Testing organisations or authorities might argue that they are not responsible for teaching practice in schools, and that the tests they produce should not be branded as unfair because of the actions of others. Against that, both the classroom experience and the requirement to pass the test have a collective impact on the student, and some would say that testing authorities must at least identify what needs to be taught in preparation for the test. The 2014 edition of the *Standards* discusses instructional validity in terms of 'opportunity to learn'. Standard 3.19 is confined to 'settings where the same authority is responsible for both provision of curriculum and high-stakes decisions based on testing of examinees' curriculum mastery' (p. 72). In those settings, the *Standards* requires that 'examinees should not suffer permanent negative consequences if evidence indicates that they have not had the opportunity to learn the test content' (p. 72). In Australia, the National Curriculum and Assessment Authority excused itself from the 'equity issues connected with ideas of Opportunity to Learn' on the grounds that 'ACACA agencies are responsible for assessment, not for how schools operate' (ACACA, 1995, p. 1), but it is an open question whether such a clear division of accountabilities will be accepted in future.

Another common setting for legal challenges to assessment fairness is *testing accommodations for candidates with disabilities or special needs*. As we have seen, most countries have specific anti-discrimination legislation which forbids discrimination on the grounds of defined characteristics. Cumming and Dickson (2007) describe the hierarchy of legal requirements in Australia: four separate Federal Acts,[21] state legislation including prohibition of discrimination in education, and Codes of Practice.

The law typically distinguishes between direct and indirect discrimination: a finding of direct discrimination in assessment would require that a candidate with a protected characteristic was treated less favourably than others in circumstances which were otherwise not materially different. Indirect discrimination occurs where 'practices applicable to all have a discriminatory effect on people with a protected attribute' (Cumming and Dickson, 2007, p. 205).[22] An illustration of the concept of indirect discrimination is the Australian case of *Bishop v. Sports Massage Training School* (2000),[23] where a student with dyslexia narrowly failed a written exam and suffered 'a delay in his career and a significant loss of self-esteem' (p. 1). A less straightforward Australian case is described in Case Study 4.2.

Case Study 4.2: Australia

Was it unfair for a student with attention deficit disorder (ADD) not to be allowed extra time when sitting his higher school certificate (HSC) examination?

BI v. Board of Studies (2000)[24]

This case went before the Supreme Court of New South Wales Administrative Law Division. BI was a minor, aged 17, and he, through his tutor, was seeking judicial review of a decision by the Board of Studies of New South Wales ('the Board'). BI had been diagnosed by his doctor as suffering from 'mild attention deficit disorder' (ADD), and he applied for 'special examination provisions' for his HSC examinations in 2000. The categories of special provision available included rest breaks and extra time, and BI's school applied for him to be granted both. However, the Board allowed him rest breaks but denied him extra time. The plaintiff alleged that the Board's special provision policy was flawed, and that, even if it was not flawed, it was applied too inflexibly to BI.

BI's doctor described him as having 'poor concentration and sequencing skills' and stated that 'without extra time he would be unable to demonstrate his knowledge'. The Board published guidance on eligibility for special provisions, and this was revised in 1999. For the first time, the 1999 edition included provision for ADD students. An appendix to the guidance included a table of special provisions, with 'possible provisions' for ADD students listed as 'rest breaks, medication', whilst extra time was possible for students with functional difficulties in reading or writing. Since the 1980s, the Board had been advised by a 'Special Examination Provisions Panel', which included specialists in learning difficulty.

Applicants for special examination provisions are required to sit two tests – a 'reading mastery test' and a timed essay – to inform the Board's decision. BI completed both within the time stipulated and he performed well in both tests.

BI's school twice appealed against the refusal of extra time. In support, his doctor wrote: '[BI] has great difficulty starting to work and works at a very slow pace ... Rest breaks only mean that he has more episodes during the exam when he has to get started again and this makes things even more difficult for him.'

The Board's policy was that 'the special examination provision of extra time allows students to reach a functional level in terms both of reading and production of work'. The Board argued that its guidance about ADD students was consistent with that policy, and stated that if a student with ADD also had functional limitations, he/she could be considered for extra time. However, it accepted the advice from the experts it consulted that this did not apply to BI.

The Board was concerned not to give BI an unfair advantage. When cross-examined, its Director of Examinations and Certification said: 'My concern was not to provide extra time for a student where that need had not been demonstrated as that would advantage him against the rest of the students sitting the examination.'

The judgment examined in some detail the processes taken by the Board in devising the guidelines and considering the appeals made on behalf of BI, including obtaining specialist expert advice. It concluded that the guidelines were consistent with policy and not flawed, and that they were not inflexibly applied in the case of BI. BI lost his case and costs were awarded against him.

It is notable in this case that the court referred to the Board's guidelines, and was concerned in particular with the processes by which they were drawn up and then applied to BI's case. Where there is an established process to be followed, the courts will often concentrate on it rather than on the substance of the action being challenged. Cumming and Dickson (2007, p. 207) suggest that if BI's case had been heard before 1999, when the guidelines first covered students with ADD, it would have been reviewed on its individual merits and BI might have won.

In this case, the Board was concerned that giving BI extra time might give him an unfair advantage over others (without his disability). This is a recurring theme in judgments about educational tests. In the US case of *Doe v. National Board of Medical Examiners* (1999), where Doe had been granted extra time because of his multiple sclerosis, the defendants 'speculated that if non-disabled test-takers were also given extra time, the resulting decrease in anxiety for some might have a positive effect on their test scores' (Phillips, 2016, p. 247).

When accommodations are made for candidates with a disability, the issue arises of whether the fact that the test was different for the disabled candidate should be disclosed to others, for example through an annotation or 'flag' on the candidate's certificate. This contentious issue has been viewed through legal lenses and one such case (from Ireland) is described in Case Study 4.3.

Case Study 4.3: Ireland

Was it unfair to annotate the Leaving Certificate of a candidate with a disability to report that she was exempt from parts of some exams?

Cahill v. the Minister for Education and Science (2017)[25]

Kim Cahill (KC) sat the Leaving Certificate exam in 2001 and was granted a 'reasonable accommodation' by the Department of Education and Science[26] ('the Department') because of her dyslexia. KC was exempted from being examined on spelling in English, French and Irish and her certificate included an annotation stating that she had not been examined in core elements of these exams. KC alleged that the annotation stigmatised her and said that receiving her certificate was one of the most embarrassing moments of her life.[27] She also argued that the annotation could put her at risk of unfair treatment by employers in future.

KC won her case in the Equality Tribunal, which awarded her €6000 compensation and directed the Department to issue a Leaving Certificate free of the annotation and to investigate the feasibility of a system of accommodations tailored to the needs of each individual student. The Minister for Education and Science ('the Minister') successfully appealed to the Circuit Court, and KC subsequently appealed to the High Court, which upheld the Circuit Court decision.

> The case went to the Supreme Court in May 2017, where KC was supported by lawyers from the Irish Human Rights and Equality Commission. The Supreme Court upheld the High Court's decision (generally[28] in favour of the Minister), described the Irish accommodations system as 'generous'[29] compared with practice in other countries and took into account the Department's wish to maintain the integrity of the examination system. The Court also stated that the interest of a third party, such as an employer considering KC's capacity for a job, were relevant.
>
> During the long period when this case was before the courts, the State Examinations Commission in Ireland did not issue Leaving Certificates but used other means to record the outcomes of the examination.

Kim Cahill and her supporters were alleging unfairness in the sense of stigma from information about the accommodation. They also argued that information about the accommodation could prompt unfair discrimination against her in the future, for example by employers. Interestingly, the Supreme Court asked the question, 'Fairness to whom?' (see Chapter 2) and suggested that employers had a right to know about the accommodation and not to be 'misled'.

Similar issues were raised in *Doe v. National Board of Medical Examiners* (1999), where the annotation was that Doe's test was undertaken 'under non-standard conditions' (Phillips, 2016, p. 246), and there appears to have been a concern that those made aware of that fact might jump to the conclusion that he had a learning disability.[30] Although the Doe judgment did not 'prohibit' annotations, the trend in the USA has been to discontinue them, following the case of *Breimhorst v. ETS* (2000)[31] which concerned annotations recording special conditions in the Graduate Management Admissions Test (GMAT). Breimhorst had no hands; he used a track ball instead of a mouse for a computerised test and was granted extra time. ETS settled the case out of court by agreeing to discontinue annotating scores obtained with extra time in a range of admissions tests, and the College Board convened an expert panel to consider doing the same for the SAT tests used for college admission. In a majority opinion, the expert panel recommended stopping annotation of SAT scores, and gradually other organisations have followed suit. This sequence of events started with a legal challenge, but was overtaken by non-legal decisions, and some commentators have criticised this as putting social policy objectives before 'the validity of test score interpretations'.[32]

A further – and very different – setting for the legal lens to be applied to fairness in assessment concerns is the marking methodology used in a particular exam – for example, *the setting of grade boundaries and cut scores*. Generally, the courts will be unwilling to substitute their views for the academic judgement of examiners in setting standards and judging whether they have been met in particular cases. Judges in most countries would agree with the Australian judgment in the case of *Walsh v. University of Sydney* (2007): 'It is for a university to establish ... the academic standard to be achieved as demonstrated by assignments or other coursework. Decisions about such matters are inherently unsuited to judicial review.'[33]

However, the courts have addressed detailed technical matters around marking methodology. A notable example is a UK case about grade boundaries in one sitting of a national examination. The long judgment is summarised in Case Study 4.4.

Case Study 4.4: United Kingdom

In a modular exam, was it unfair for candidates who sat modules in June 2012 to be graded more strictly than those who sat them the previous January?

LB Lewisham & Others v. AQA, Edexcel, Ofqual & Others (2013)[34]

A group of some 150 claimants (pupils, teachers, schools and local authorities) sought a judicial review of the actions of a number of bodies responsible for a national exam (General Certificate of Secondary Education (GCSE) English, mostly taken by 16-year-olds). In England, Wales and Northern Ireland, GCSEs are offered by 'awarding organisations' (AOs), with more than one AO often offering the same qualification under the supervision of a statutory regulator ('Ofqual') which is tasked with ensuring that standards are maintained and regulated qualifications command public confidence. In this case, the complaint was against two of the AOs (with a third cited as an interested party) and Ofqual.

The complaint related to the first awards, in summer 2012, of a new version of the qualification. It had a modular structure, and candidates could take modules at different times during the course. Some candidates were assessed for modules in January 2012 and were told the grades they had achieved. Larger numbers of students took modules in June 2012 and there was a perception that the June modules were graded more severely than the modules taken in January. In particular, there was a 'widespread and deeply held grievance over the way in which the boundary between Grade C and Grade D was fixed ... in June 2012'.[35] This was important for students, as achieving a Grade C was a requirement for many later education options. It was also important for schools, which were held accountable (among other things) for the numbers of students achieving Grade C.

The grounds of complaint included the following: (a) that the grades awarded in June were inconsistent with those awarded in January for the same modules, thus 'infring[ing] the most elementary concept of fairness, which requires that like cases are treated alike';[36] and (b) that the AOs and Ofqual 'failed to give effect to the legitimate expectation ... that grading standards would be the same irrespective of when the assessment was completed'.[37]

> All parties broadly agreed that, on the whole, the grading of the January modules was more generous than that of the June modules. The latter was informed by fuller statistical and other information[38] and Ofqual considered that the (more severe) June grades were more accurate and reliable than the January grades. The court found that Ofqual 'could not remedy any unfairness between the January and June cohorts without creating further unfairness elsewhere'[39] – for example, to candidates in previous or subsequent years – or allowing standards to fall in the long term. On (b) (legitimate expectations), the court noted that Ofqual's published Code of Practice said that grade boundaries could change. There had not been a 'clear and unequivocal assurance' of consistency, which was the high bar for establishing an unlawful failure to meet a legitimate expectation.[40] In any case, it could be lawful not to honour an expectation if doing so was against the public interest.
>
> The judgment concluded that 'it was the structure of the qualification itself which [was] the source of such unfairness as [was] demonstrated in this case, and not any unlawful action by Ofqual or the AOs'.[41]

Although the judgment supported the actions of the regulator and the awarding organisations, the controversy over the case arguably brought discredit on the system as a whole. It was also the subject of a political row between England and Wales, with Welsh ministers requiring the papers of Welsh candidates to be re-graded.[42]

The main sense of fairness invoked was *relational* – the allegation that the June candidates were graded more harshly than the January candidates. The difference in standards was acknowledged by all parties, but the court accepted Ofqual's argument that the problem was that the January candidates were marked too generously, and that if the June marks were made equally generous, it would create relational unfairness with candidates in other years – or require standards to be lowered long term. The court asked the question 'fair to whom?', and concluded that the structure of the examination meant that, in the circumstances, no matter what decision was made someone would be disadvantaged. This left Ofqual to take the least damaging course, justified further by the 'powerful and legitimate public interest' in Ofqual 'maintaining the currency of the qualification'.[43]

This case also showed that the concept of 'legitimate expectation' is construed more strictly in England than was implied in its use in the US *Debra P.* case. Citing two English (non-educational) precedents,[44] Elias LJ noted that the source of a legitimate expectation might be an 'express promise' given by a public body, or a 'regular practice which the claimant can reasonably expect to continue'. However, the assurance given must be 'clear and unequivocal' and the regular practice 'unambiguous, widespread and well-recognised'.[45] Elias LJ did not think that either requirement was met in the case of teachers' belief that grading standards would be the same in successive sittings of the exam. The legal bar here was set at a high level, and one can imagine cases where broader expectations could be disappointed, though there would be poor prospects of successful legal challenge in the English courts.

The final setting for legal challenges to fairness in assessment which we shall describe here is *selection for employment or licensure for a profession*. Legal lenses have been applied to this in a range of cases in the USA, and the position reflected in current guidance is the subject of academic debate. The problem being addressed occurs if a protected group (classified, for example, by ethnicity or gender) is markedly less successful in a test than other candidates. Such 'disparate impact' of a recruitment test can be challenged as an 'unlawful employment practice' under Title VII of the Civil Rights Act 1964. As we have seen, disparate impact has not been seen as of itself implying that the test was unfair, but has been seen as raising the question of whether there is an alternative test, with equal or greater validity, which would have a less disparate outcome. For example, a test for a job requiring manual skills might have greater validity – as well as reduced disparate impact – if it required candidates to show their manual skills rather than writing about them. This approach was taken by US courts following the leading case of *Griggs v. Duke Power Co.* in 1971,[46] which we discuss in Chapter 3. The later Civil Rights Act of 1991 took the significant step of moving the burden of proof (assessing the possibility of a valid alternative) from the plaintiff to the defendant. This potentially puts a burden on employers, with the costly and difficult task of evaluating the validity of (possibly non-existent) alternative tests.

The application of legal lenses to licensure tests in the USA was distorted for a while due to the disputed legacy of what has become known as the 'Golden Rule' case.[47] This was a challenge to the Illinois Insurance Department and the testing organisation Educational Testing Service (ETS) on behalf of five applicants who failed a new licensure test devised by ETS. The new test resulted in a wider difference between the percentage of white and black candidates who were selected, breaching the norm (known as 'the 80% rule') that disparate impact is shown when the selection rate for a specified group is less than four-fifths of that of the most successful group. ETS settled out of court in 1984 and made a commitment to including only test items where the difference between groups in the percentage of candidates correct was less than 15% and there was a success rate of at least 40% among both groups in each content category. This was understandably controversial among psychometricians (Phillips, 2016, pp. 239–266) – for a start, the categories compared were not required to be comparable in any construct-relevant sense – and ETS subsequently pulled back from much of this position (Anrig, 1988).

A parallel debate has taken place among occupational psychologists about the 'Universal Guidelines', which we discuss in Chapter 3. These were consolidated in 1978 after a long period when successive guidelines were produced. In line with thinking in *Griggs v. Duke Power* and some aspects of the Golden Rule case, the Uniform Guidelines require a two-stage process. First, if the proportion of protected status candidates who succeed is less than 80% of the proportion of the majority group who succeed, then there is disparate impact. In that case, the employer must show that the test is more valid than an alternative with less disparate impact. This has prompted some fierce exchanges between supporters and detractors (see Brink and Crenshaw, 2011; McDaniel et al., 2011a, b). Of the arguments used by the critics of the Uniform Guidelines, one is of particular interest to us. It has been called 'the diversity/validity dilemma'[48] and argues that differences in performance are not necessarily a product of bias in the test but can reflect 'real' differences between candidates in job-related attributes.

This can become a very sensitive issue, with those who take this view criticised as racist or prejudiced. In their defence, however, it may be argued that an 'objective' test can show the need for remedial action in a way that an assessment that 'masks' deficiencies cannot (Phillips, 2016, p. 241). On the other side, some of the assumptions made in the past about the fairness of selection tests seem highly questionable now. This passage comes from a written memorandum by a senior UK civil servant in 1979:

> Because we fall over backwards to fill our posts by fair and open competition, we can only assume that, since the ethnic minority groups do not fare as well in our competitions as do people of European descent, the ethnic minority groups do not possess the qualities which we require, on average, to as high a degree as their British-born counterparts. (quoted in Southern, 2018, p. 13)

In summary, the application of legal lenses to testing for employment selection has had a bumpy ride, with requirements in the USA derived from legislation to reduce inequalities in society, but resulting in evidential burdens on employers and an important theoretical debate about whether a test can be fair if the results accurately reflect unfairness in society.

Some common themes when legal lenses are applied

One recurring theme from the variety of settings we have considered is that *the bar for successful legal challenge is generally very high*. An action by a public body would have to be extremely unreasonable to meet the 'Wednesbury' criterion for unreasonableness. Generally speaking, challenges to public bodies acting within their legal powers are unlikely to be successful. Kamvounias and Varnham (2010) review legal challenges to university decisions affecting students in Australia, and conclude that where the university's processes have been followed, a challenge under common law is unlikely to succeed. Felicity Mitchell, reviewing attempts to subject the UK's Office of the Independent Adjudicator (OIA) to judicial review, comes to a similar conclusion (Mitchell, 2015). Of course, the rules applied by the university concerned might be open to criticism as unfair – or at least as susceptible to improvement to make them fairer – and the judgments made by the OIA in the cases it considers might be questioned, but those are judgments made using other lenses.

Another recurring theme in the cases we have considered is a *focus on processes followed rather than on the merits of a decision or action*. In the case of BI, for example (Case Study 4.2), the court looked carefully at the process followed by the Board of Studies, both in drawing up its guidance on ADD sufferers and also in applying that guidance to the case of BI. The 14th Amendment of the US Constitution refers to 'due process of law'.

In the US context, Kane (2010) distinguishes what he calls 'substantive due process' (where the procedures applied are 'reasonable in general and in the context in which they are applied', p. 178) from a broader concept of 'substantive fairness', which requires that 'score interpretation and any test-based decision rule [should] be reasonable and appropriate, and in particular [should] be equally appropriate for all test-takers (at least roughly)' (pp. 178–179; see Chapter 3). He suggests that the judgement of reasonableness in 'substantive fairness' should be the conclusion of a 'prudent and cautious person' (Camilli, 2013, p. 117), not just the conclusion of a 'scientific' analysis. Kane's wider concept goes further than the courts would do, and much further than 'Wednesbury unreasonableness'.

Courts typically apply a form of relational fairness to due process, requiring even-handedness between the parties in dispute, with the relevant information disclosed to complainants.[49] Kamvounias and Varnham (2010) comment that in cases where university judgements are challenged, the courts will 'insist on a high standard of procedural fairness and will intervene if this has been denied to a student, even if university decision-makers have followed internal rules' (p. 180), although they note that the only remedy in that case would be to send the case back to the university.

The flip side of the legal concentration on process is that *the legal lens will not be applied to academic judgement*. The courts will not substitute their views for that of an examiner or academics determining the level of knowledge or skill required or the marking of an individual student's work. This position is clearly set out in the judgment of a UK case brought by a university student:

We cannot put ourselves in the position of the examiners in order to re-mark work or pass comments on the marks given to the student. However, we can look at whether the higher education provider has correctly followed its own procedures, and whether there was any unfairness or bias in the decision-making process the provider followed.[50]

What do we think of the way legal lenses have been applied to assessment?

We have seen that legal lenses are selectively applied and that the standards they apply may be very permissive in some respects (for example, passing as 'reasonable' practices that we might criticise on moral or professional grounds), but demanding in other respects (for example, expecting even-handed 'due process' from educational bodies in considering appeals). We need to understand these limitations and not assume that practices which have withstood legal challenge are necessarily morally right or best professional practice.

We raise here three conceptual questions relating to the examples discussed in this chapter. The first concerns cases where accommodations are made for students with disabilities. In judging what is (relationally) fair in such cases, there is an implicit comparator against which the disabled candidate is to be equated. In the BI case, for example (Case Study 4.2), the court was anxious not to give BI an 'unfair advantage' and, as Cumming and Dickson (2007) comment, 'it would appear that to determine what is fair … students with disabilities may receive accommodations that allow them to achieve a "normal" standard, not accommodations which would allow them to fully demonstrate superior achievement' (p. 208). It seems that the legal approach to accommodations is more difficult to apply to highly gifted students – what standard should they be brought up to?

The second question is also pertinent to legal judgments about accommodations which are not made available to a disabled candidate or test items or conditions which are judged to be unfair. There appears to be a proposition assumed: that under alternative test conditions, or with different test items, an individual or a group of individuals would have achieved a better result. But this is a counterfactual claim (see Camilli, 2013, p. 104) and is very difficult to substantiate – how do we know that in different circumstances (which did not happen) there would have been a different outcome? It would be very difficult to test this by research, and in some cases (e.g. of unfair use of disrespectfully worded test items) a research project would be ethically dubious. So there are epistemological problems underpinning some of the approaches taken by this lens. We shall consider these further in the final chapter.

The third question is prompted by the case of *Debra P.* (see Case Study 4.1). The concept of 'instructional validity' applied in that case requires proof that students were actually taught the content of the test. But the test in question covered generalised skills of verbal and numerical reasoning, and it must be difficult to demonstrate precisely when these were taught, as they underpin many branches of teaching and learning. One assumes that, in the case of *Debra P.*, the 'instruction' referred to would be some kind of structured revision explicitly referring to the test, but conceptually it is difficult to see how one can show the 'instructional validity' of tests of generalised knowledge and skills which transcend individual subjects. Looking forward, this may make it difficult to apply the concept of 'instructional validity' to assessments of so-called 'twenty-first-century skills', such as creativity, collaboration and communication.

A parallel concern applies to the application of the Uniform Guidelines to selection tests for employment. The world of work is constantly changing and recruits to any organisation will not expect to be doing the same tasks year after year. Assessment for recruitment may therefore focus on more generalisable attributes like ability to reason, ability to work with others, clear thinking and adaptability to change. It is much more difficult to establish the construct validity of tests of such attributes than, say, to establish the validity of a test of lifting skills for a job involving lifting.

There are also practical concerns about the application of legal lenses. It is very expensive to take legal action or to defend a legal challenge. This means that access to justice may itself be unfair, in the sense that it may be denied to those lacking resources, influential contacts or the support of a pressure group (as was made available to Kim Cahill; see Case Study 4.3). Also, organisations who are challenged will want to minimise their costs and may therefore choose to settle out of court (as in the Golden Rule case) or agree to conditions to save the cost of disputing them, even if the settlement is not the fairest outcome.

Looking forward, the structured view of life taken by the courts may be challenged by the increasing diversity of life in the twenty-first century. Cumming and Dickson (2007) argue that issues such as disability and ethnicity are becoming seen as continua rather than discrete categories like those named in most (twentieth century) anti-discrimination legislation. We discuss in Chapter 7 the implications of this trend for analysing fairness in assessment.

The availability of different test delivery platforms using computers and other devices may raise questions of relational fairness, if some testing experiences are seen as easier than others (Phillips, 2016, p. 258), although it will always be important to ask whether the differences matter, either morally or educationally. Also, we may see more legal challenges by parents in the future – for example, objecting to their children being required to sit (or prevented from sitting) national tests, demanding to see the content of test items to make sure that they are religiously acceptable or objecting to modes of assessment – for example, to the use of technology (Phillips, 2016, p. 259). Some of these challenges may use the concept of fairness, though others (e.g. objections to computers) may be based on statutory laws protecting religious practices.

Conclusion

In this chapter, we have seen assessment fairness viewed through a range of legal lenses in different settings. These have particularly used concepts of relational fairness (comparing outcomes for some candidates with others), fairness of process and the 'legitimate expectations' sense of fair. Some of the cases described in the case studies presented here were brought by groups and some by individuals, and it is notable that the law may be applied at both levels. The law may conclude that an individual student was treated unfairly. It is not confined to fairness to groups or to categories of candidate.

We have seen the limitations of legal lenses and identified some conceptual problems raised by the cases described in this chapter. Some concepts – such as 'curricular/instructional validity' and 'legitimate expectations' – have influenced other lenses applied to assessment: in particular, we saw how 'curriculum/instructional validity' is now reflected in the US *Standards*. We also saw some of the controversies which have been raised, but not resolved, by the application of legal lenses, notably to cases where there are disparate assessment outcomes across ethnic groups. The question of whether the unfairness is in the test or in the 'real' differences accurately recorded by the test (or both) is a sensitive and important one.

Although it is fashionable to decry the litigiousness of modern society, in our view the statute and case law described here has had a broadly beneficial effect on good practice in educational assessment. Awareness of the risks of legal challenge and of lessons from cases in our own country and elsewhere is not a complete armoury for fairness in assessment, but it helps.

For further reflection

'Disparate impact' of end-of-school tests

Campaigners for greater fairness in school tests have heard about the 'Uniform Guidelines' applied to selection tests for employment in the USA. These prescribe a two-stage process: if the proportion of candidates from a prescribed minority group who succeed is less than 80% of the proportion of other candidates, then there is 'disparate impact' and the employer must show that there is not an alternative test, with equal or greater validity, in which the difference of outcome for the two groups would not be so great. The campaigners think that the same approach should be used for end-of-school qualifications such as high school diplomas (USA) and A levels (UK). Are they right? Would an approach similar to the 'Uniform Guidelines' make end-of-school qualifications fairer?

'Instructional validity'

A national election brings a new party into power whose election campaign included changing national exams taken by 16-year-olds to increase the content of the knowledge which students need to be able to display. They want to introduce the new exams as soon as possible, but opponents cite the requirement of 'instructional validity' established in the *Debra P.* case and say that it would be unfair to require students to sit the new exam until it can be shown that they have all been taught the new content. Supporters of the change argue that the prospect of the new exam will make teachers prepare their students for it, and waiting for the instruction to change before the test changes is a recipe for no change. Who is right? Is it fair to change the requirements for an exam without knowing that all the candidates have been taught what is going to be tested?

Notes

1. There might be subordinate forms of legislation, such as regulations, aiming to minimise bias, which go beyond protected characteristics and those could be cited in a challenge.
2. AC 562.
3. There is a fourth condition applied to UK decisions – that the loss caused by the defendant's breach of duty is recoverable – but we do not discuss that here, as it is arguably less relevant to assessment.
4. *Richardson v. Lamar County Bd. of Educ.* (1989) 729 F. Supp. 806 (M.D. Ala.), para. 823.
5. In *LB Lewisham & Others v. AQA, Edexcel, Ofqual & Others* (2013) (the case described in Case Study 4.4), this was confirmed. Private exam boards may be subject to judicial review for 'functions of a public nature'.
6. Outlined by Lord Diplock in *Council of Civil Service Unions v. Minister for the Civil Service* [1985] AC 574.
7. *Associated Provincial Picture Houses v. Wednesbury Corporation* [1948] 1KB 223.
8. *R (Peng Hu Shi) v. King's College London* (2008) EWHC 857 (Admin).
9. *Harding v. University of New South Wales* (2002) NSWSC 113.
10. In the UK, The Public Interest Disclosure Act 1998.
11. 474 F. Supp. 244 (M.D. Fla. 1979); 644 F. 2d 397 (5th Cir. 1981); 564 F. Supp. 177 (M.D. Fla. 1983); 730 F. 2d 1405 (11th Cir. 1984).
12. Some allegations were made on behalf of black students who failed the test, and some on behalf of *all* students who failed the test.

13. There were also particular allegations against Hillsborough County, which are not discussed here.
14. The 14th Amendment includes the following: 'No state shall ... deprive any person of life, liberty or property, without due process of law; nor deny to any person within its jurisdiction the equal protection of the laws.'
15. 474 F. Supp. 244 (M.D. Fla. 1979), V, C, 267.
16. Ibid., VII.
17. 644 F. 2d 397 (5th Cir. 1981), p. 4.
18. 564 F. Supp. 177 (M.D. Fla. 1983), I, 186.
19. Discussed in Phillips, 2016, p. 240.
20. The parenthesis was particularly used in the GI Forum case.
21. Age Discrimination Act 2004; Disability Discrimination Act 1992, applied to education in the Disability Standards for Education 2005 (Commonwealth); Racial Discrimination Act 1975 (Commonwealth); Sex Discrimination Act 1994 (Commonwealth).
22. In England and Wales, indirect discrimination can be lawful if it is a proportionate means of achieving a legitimate aim. Direct discrimination against people with protected characteristics will never be lawful.
23. *Bishop v. Sports Massage Training School* [2000] HREOC No H99/55 (Unreported, Commissioner Cavanough, 15 December 2000).
24. (2000) NSWSC 921.
25. (2017) IESC 29.
26. Now known as the Department of Education and Skills.
27. Irish Human Rights and Equality Commission, 'Supreme Court clarifies duties towards students in disability discrimination case', 24 May 2017, accessed November 2018 at www.ihrec.ie/supreme-court-clarifies-duties-towards-students-disability-discrimination-case.
28. The courts had also addressed the issue of whether or not the minister had a statutory duty to provide reasonable accommodations. The Supreme Court supported the conclusion that there was such a duty, although they said that the interpretation of 'reasonable' should take 'proportionality' into account.
29. (2017) IESC 29, para. 42.
30. Phillips, 2016, p. 246.
31. *Breimhorst v. Educational Testing Service* (2000) 3:99-cv-03387 (N.D. Cal.).
32. Phillips, 2016, p. 263, note 16.
33. *Walsh v. University of Technology, Sydney* (2007) FCA 1308, discussed in Kamvounias and Varnham (2010, p. 162).
34. (2013) EWHC 211.
35. Elias LJ, para. 7.
36. Ibid., para. 115.
37. Ibid., para. 84.
38. This enabled an approach called 'comparable outcomes' to be applied to achieve consistency between successive sittings.
39. Elias LJ, para. 120.
40. Ibid., para. 97.
41. Ibid., para. 157.
42. See BBC News Wales: 'GCSE English: WJEC ordered to regrade exams', 11 September 2012, accessed December 2018 at www.bbc.co.uk/news/uk-wales-19559429.

43. Elias LJ, para. 124.
44. *R v. North and East Devon Health Authority ex parte Coughlan* (2001) QB 213 and *R (Niazi) v. Home Secretary* (2008) EWCA Civ 755, para. 41.
45. Op cit., para. 94.
46. *Griggs v. Duke Power Co.* (1971) 401 U.S. 424.
47. *Golden Rule Life Insurance Co. v. Washburn* (1984) No. 419-76 (Ill. Cir. Ct. Nov 20, 1984).
48. McDaniel et al., 2001b, pp. 506–507.
49. For example, in the UK case of *R (Persaud) v. University of Cambridge* (2001) EWCA Civ 534, the university was criticised for 'reject[ing the complainant's] account of events, without first putting their doubts about its accuracy to her'.
50. *R (Gopkrishna) v. OIA (The Office of the Independent Adjudicator)* (2015) [2-15] EWHC 207, para. 143.

References

American Educational Research Association (AERA), American Psychological Association (APA) and National Council on Measurement in Education (NCME) (2014) *Standards for Educational and Psychological Testing*. Washington, DC: AERA.

Anrig, G. R. (1988) ETS replies to Golden Rule on 'Golden Rule'. *Educational Measurements: Issues and Practice*, 7(1), 20–21.

Australasian Curriculum, Assessment and Certification Authorities (ACACA) (1995) *Guidelines for Assessment Quality and Equity*. Available at: www.qcaa.qld.edu.au/downloads/approach2/acaca_equity_guidelines.pdf (accessed 01/10/18).

Brink, K. E. and Crenshaw, J. L. (2011) The affronting of the Uniform Guidelines: From propaganda to discourse. *Industrial and Organizational Psychology*, 4(4), 547–553.

Camilli, G. (2013) Ongoing issues in test fairness. *Educational Research and Evaluation*, 19(2–3), 104–120.

Council of Europe (1953) *European Convention on Human Rights (ECHR)*. As amended by Protocols Nos. 11 and 14; supplemented by Protocols Nos. 1, 4, 6, 7, 12, 13 and 16.

Cumming, J. J. and Dickson, E. A. (2007) Equity in assessment: Discrimination and disability issues from an Australian legal perspective. *Education and the Law*, 19 (3–4), 201–220.

Kamvounias, P. and Varnham, S. (2010) Legal challenges to university decisions affecting students in Australian courts and tribunals. *Melbourne University Law Review*, 34, 140–180.

Kane, M. T. (2010) Validity and fairness. *Language Testing*, 27(2), 177–182.

LB Lewisham & Others v. AQA, Edexcel, Ofqual and Others (2013) EWHC 211.

McDaniel, M. A., Kepes, S. and Banks, G. C. (2011a) The Uniform Guidelines are a detriment to the field of personnel selection. *Industrial and Organizational Psychology*, 4(4), 494–514.

McDaniel, M. A., Kepes, S. and Banks, G. C. (2011b) Encouraging debate on the Uniform Guidelines and the disparate impact theory of discrimination. *Industrial and Organizational Psychology*, 4(4), 566–570.

Mitchell, F. (2015) *The OIA and Judicial Review: Ten principles from ten years of challenges*. Office of the Independent Adjudicator. Available at: www.oiahe.org.uk/media/106876/oia-and-judicial-review-10-year-series.pdf (accessed 01/08/18).

Phillips, S. E. (2016) Legal aspects of test fairness. In N. J. Dorans and L. L. Cook (Eds.), *Fairness in Educational Assessment and Measurement*. New York and Abingdon, Oxon: Routledge. pp. 239–266.

Rhoades, K. R. and Madaus, G. M. (2003) *Errors in Standardised Tests: A systemic problem*. Boston, MA: National Board on Educational Testing and Public Policy.

Southern, J. (2018) *Black Skin, Whitehall: Race and the Foreign Office, 1945–2018*. Foreign and Commonwealth Office History Notes: 21. Available at: www.gov.uk/government/publications/black-skin-whitehall-race-and-the-foreign-office-1945-to-2018 (accessed 01/10/18).

United Nations General Assembly (UNGA) (1948) *Universal Declaration of Human Rights (UDHR)*. 10 December. General Assembly Resolution No. 217A. Paris: UNGA.

US Equal Employment Opportunity Commission (EEOC) (1973) Rehabilitation Act. Pub. L. 93–112, 87 Stat. 355. Enacted 26 September.

US Govt (1990) Individuals with Disabilities Education Act (IDEA). Pub. L. 101–476. 104 Stat.1142.

Cases cited

USA

Debra P. v. Turlington:

(1979) 474 F. Supp. 244 (M.D. Fla.1979)

(1981) 644 F. 2d 397 (5th Cir. 1981)

(1983) 564 F. Supp. 177 (M.D. Fla. 1983)

(1984) 730 F. 2d 1405 (11th Cir. 1984)

Breimhorst v. Educational Testing Service (2000) 3:99-cv-03387 (N.D. Cal.)

Doe v. Natl Bd Med Examiners (1999) No. 99-4532 (E.D. Pa. 1999); rev'd, 199 F. 3d 146 (3rd Cir. 2000); on rem., No. 99-4532 (E.D. Pa. 2005); aff'd 210 Fed. Appx. 157 (3rd Cir. 2006)

GI Forum v. Texas Education Agency (2000) 87 F. Supp. 2d 667 (W.D. Tex. 2000)

Golden Rule Life Insurance Co v. Washburn (1984) No. 419-76 (Ill. Cir. Ct. Nov 20, 1984)

Griggs v. Duke Power Co. (1971) 401 U.S. 424

Harding v. University of New South Wales (2002) NSWSC 113

Richardson v. Lamar County Bd. of Educ (1989) 729 F. Supp. 806 (M.D. Ala. 1989)

UK

Associated Provincial Picture Houses Ltd v. Wednesbury Corporation (1948) 1 KB 223

Donoghue v. Stevenson (1932) AC 562

R (Gopikrishna) v. OIA (The Office of the Independent Adjudicator) (2015) [2–15] EWHC 207

LB Lewisham & Others v. AQA, Edexcel, Ofqual & Others (2013) EWHC 211

R (Peng Hu Shi) v. King's College London (2008) EWHC 857

R (Persaud) v. University of Cambridge (2001) EWCA Civ 534

Council of Civil Service Unions v. Minister for the Civil Service (1985) AC 574

R v. North and East Devon Health Authority ex parte Coughlan (2001) QB 213

R (Niazi) v. Home Secretary (2008) EWCA Civ 755

Ireland

Cahill v. The Minister for Education and Science (2017) IESC 29

Australia

BI v. Board of Studies (2000) NSWSC 921

Bishop v. Sports Massage Training School (2000) HREOC No H99/55

Harding v. University of New South Wales (2002) NSWSC 113

Walsh v. University of Technology, Sydney (2007) FCA 1308

5
Fair assessment viewed through the lenses of philosophy

'A philosopher should be concerned about definitions in the way that a historian is concerned about putting dates in the right order.' (Priest, 2005, p. 134)

'Those with similar abilities and skills should have similar life chances.' (Rawls, 1971, p. 17)

'What the average Socialist really means when he speaks of "fair shares for all" is equal shares for all – equal shares for those who toil and those who shirk.' (Winston Churchill, 14 February 1950)[1]

Introduction

As we have seen, disputes about fair assessment arouse strong feelings, and in some countries have gone to the highest courts. If we feel that we have been treated unfairly, we may feel wronged in a morally important sense.[2] We appeal to underlying questions of right and wrong, and of how society ought to function, that have taxed philosophers for centuries. We turn in this chapter to fair assessment seen through the lenses of philosophy, in particular moral and political philosophy.

There are several reasons for including philosophical thought in this book. First, philosophical analysis may help to resolve disagreements that are based on different uses of terms, inconsistencies or arguments from different premises. Second, philosophical models may give us principles which can be applied to new, unfamiliar situations. Third, the understanding of fairness viewed through other lenses may have derived from, or been influenced by, philosophical thinking, and understanding the journey these concepts have travelled may illuminate their use by other disciplines.

Fourth, philosophical analysis may provide a vocabulary and structure for debate when values and intuitions differ. Simply appealing to intuition in judging whether an assessment is fair or not might seem attractive, but will not help much if different observers have different intuitions. For example, readers and writers from the USA (such as Anderson, 1999, 2007) may value the freedom of states from federal direction much more highly than their European counterparts. Those from a Confucian tradition may regard loyalty to family and country as more important than the interests or freedoms of individuals. Intuitions about the role of the state in a just society may be different in countries (such as post-war Britain) which have become accustomed to the notion of the welfare state. So we need a structure for our thinking that is more than a simple appeal to intuition. Lastly, the application of philosophical lenses may expose important underlying questions which are normally ignored in the busy practical world of assessment.

We have structured the discussion in this chapter using two broad headings under which philosophical thinking about fairness (and justice) can be considered. They are *conceptual analysis* and *theoretical modelling*. We discuss each of these labels in the relevant sections. They are by no means rigid categories. However, it is helpful to distinguish lenses which involve analysis – breaking things up and examining them in detail – from those which seek synthesis – bringing ideas together into theories which can inform, and be informed by, real-life situations.

We have included in each section a reference to the writing about fairness (and justice) of one philosopher in particular, and have given a brief account of their views of fairness. Of course, such short summaries of comprehensive works have to omit much that is important, but we hope that they will enable readers who are unfamiliar with the works to have a taste of what the philosopher had to say about fairness. The two we have chosen – Aristotle and John Rawls – are separated by some 20 centuries and wrote in different languages, but their insights have been highly influential and respected by those who have disagreed with them, as well as by their supporters.

We hope that this chapter will be of interest to readers from non-philosophical disciplines as well as to those more familiar with the literature. Those seeking a readable history of thought about justice and fairness will enjoy the admirable review written late in his life by David Raphael (2001). And an informative overview of modern philosophical debates about justice and equality will be found, among other places, in the writings of Jonathan Wolff (2007, 2008).

Conceptual analysis

Many moral and political philosophers from the mid-twentieth century onwards have described their work as 'conceptual analysis', which Stephen Priest (2005) describes as 'the attempt to solve philosophical problems, or exhibit them as illusory, by defining words or being clear about how concepts are used' (p. 154).[3] This often starts with a close examination of language, looking for the patterns, links or distinctions lying behind our use of words. The analytic philosopher is not (just) a lexicographer, recording linguistic usage, but will be willing to consider definitions of terms in some detail as a starting point.

And language is the first stumbling block when we consider the concept of fairness and its relation to other concepts, such as justice and equality. In French, German and Italian, the same word is normally used for 'fair' and 'just' – indeed, this prompted Amartya Sen (1980) to ask mischievously whether the French translation of John Rawls's 'justice as fairness' might be 'justice comme justice'.[4] We shall see that Aristotle's word which we translate as 'fair' – 'isos' – also meant 'equal'. The history of the English word 'fair' is distinctive, starting with the meaning of 'beautiful', implying an absence of blemishes, but being applied more widely thereafter (Raphael, 2001, p. 241). The analysis in this chapter is based on uses in the English language, but it carries the health warning that some of our conclusions based on language use may therefore be parochial.

In Chapter 1 of this book, we set out to define our terms, including 'fair', and we distinguished four senses of 'fair' and two of 'unfair' which were relevant to assessment. But what lies behind this bagful of uses? Is it just a coincidence that the same word is used in these different ways, or is there some underlying idea which links them? And if there is such a basic concept, is it positive or negative – fairness or *un*fairness? As we have observed, anger at unfairness is shown by children at a very early stage ('It's not fair') and seems much more deep-rooted in our psyche than delight in fairness (Rescher, 2002, p. xi; Ryan, 2006, p. 597). The approach of the assessment theorists described in Chapter 2 seems dependent on an account of *un*fairness in terms of construct-irrelevant bias.

If we take a negative approach, starting with 'unfair', how do we then define 'fair'? Does 'fair' denote the *absence* of unfairness or its *opposite*? The most persuasive answer, according to the negative approach, seems to be that fairness is the absence of unfairness (in whatever sense 'unfairness' is used). It is difficult to understand what might be meant by the opposite of unfair.[5]

There are two arguments in favour of the negative approach.[6] One is a theoretical argument, namely that the positive concept of 'fairness' becomes incoherent when we try to analyse it more thoroughly. We shall return to this important argument later. The second is a practical argument: instead of aiming for some unachievable/difficult-to-define ideal of absolute fairness, we can make progress by eliminating identifiable unfairnesses, such as discrimination by gender, race or sexuality, or social bias in the wording of exam questions.

At this stage, we would prefer to leave open the possibility that the concepts associated with fairness have enough coherence and distinction to indicate a positive direction of travel, if not an 'ideal', but we shall return, at the end of this section, to consider whether the negative approach wins the day.

If we retain for the moment the positive formulation of 'fairness', how does it relate to other, apparently similar, terms? Let us start with *equality*: fairness in our third sense ('relational') seems to imply a form of equality – treating like cases alike. The problem is what is meant by 'like'. In an assessment, it is highly unlikely, though not impossible, that all the candidates will have the same outcome. Even though a teacher might want all her pupils to pass a pass/fail competency test, it would not be 'unfair' if a pupil who did not reach the required standard failed the test. And if an assessment was designed to produce a rank ordering of candidates, that might seem the paradigm of an unequal outcome.

The account of equality which seems closest to home for assessment is closely linked to *impartiality*[7] – with assessors putting aside irrelevant considerations and basing their judgement on evidence relevant to the construct being assessed. This is close to the traditional depiction of justice as a (selectively) blindfolded figure. So is fairness a special type of equality? A problem with that is the received view that it can be fair to treat people differently – because of their special needs or for purposes of utility.[8] It could be argued that providing what the assessment world labels 'accommodations' – such as extra time, braille papers or special equipment – for candidates with disabilities is a form of equality: bringing them to the same level as the other candidates. The problem is defining what that level is. This is a fundamental problem for assessment, which we shall label *the counterfactual hypothesis*: is it meaningful to aim to assess what a candidate would have achieved without their disability, when that condition is not met and may never be met? If that is not the level aimed at, how else can it be described? By reference to an average attained by candidates without a disability – or to some idea of 'normality'? But what if the disabled candidate might, in another life (whatever that means), have achieved more than the average? The more the counterfactual hypothesis is explored, the more it evaporates into apparent incoherence.

A second problem is that equality implies comparing some people with others. It is difficult to apply to situations involving only one person, such as an exam with one candidate (which is by no means unknown). It seems odd to describe that person as being treated 'equally' but not to describe them as being treated 'fairly'. In reply, it might be argued that there is an implied hypothesis – that the treatment of the single person is compared with how others would be treated were they involved. But it seems strange to base such an important concept as fairness on such an imaginary scenario.

A third problem with seeing fairness as a kind of equality is that we are not always clear which comparisons create unfairness and which do not. For example, in the UK there is much indignation if access to certain kinds of health care (for example, treatment for infertility) differs in different locations. We decry this as an (unfair) 'postcode lottery'. But we would probably not be persuaded that it is 'unfair' that the authors of this book, neither of whom is Swedish nor has lived in Sweden, have not benefited from the Swedish education system. There needs to be some category of relevance established before the comparisons are made.

We shall return, in the second section, to theories of justice and equality. However, it is important to note that the concepts used in such theories need to be subjected to analysis. For example, many theories link justice (or fairness) to 'equality of opportunity', but they often omit to ask what 'opportunity' means. Does a gifted child in a poor family have an 'opportunity' to be accepted by a prestigious university? It may help to distinguish three senses of 'opportunity' which are potentially relevant to fairness. The first refers to probability: X has the opportunity to do Y if it is likely (beyond some threshold) that X will do Y.

The second sense could be described as 'intentional': X has the opportunity to do Y means that if X wants to do Y he/she can do so. The third sense refers to the absence of a negative – X has the opportunity to do Y if barriers which would have stopped X from doing Y have been removed. In this third sense, it may always be argued that, although some barriers have been removed, others remain, and readers may feel that this applies to the issue of the poor child and the prestigious university.

Our final word, at this stage, on equality and fairness: it is not always clear why treating people equally is so important. We touched on this issue in Chapter 1, in the concept of assessment. Suppose that your daughter takes the same assessment (say, in English composition) as your neighbour's daughter. Your daughter is very good at English composition, but her teacher is very strict and she gives your daughter a B grade. Your neighbour's daughter is less good at English but has a more generous teacher and is graded A. Why should this matter to your daughter – or to you as her parent? If the respective offspring were competing for a selective course and your neighbour's daughter was preferred because of her good grade, the complaint of 'unfairness' would be understandable. Or your daughter might suffer loss of esteem compared with your neighbour's daughter, because of their respective marks. But, in the absence of such contexts, the complaint of unfairness seems less worthy. It may still be appropriate to allow this situation to be described as 'unfair', perhaps in a weak sense, but the example suggests that comparisons between people in broadly similar situations may not always be at the heart of our understanding of fairness.[9] Referring to the senses of 'fair' identified in Chapter 1, the 'relational' sense in this example is not particularly important.

All the problems raised by linking fairness to equality suggest that the relationship between the two concepts is not the whole story about fairness. A more promising related term might be *equity*. There appear to be two uses of 'equity' which are relevant here: in the first, it is broadly synonymous with 'fairness'. For example, even in an exam with only one candidate, the candidate could be described as being treated 'equitably'. However, simply citing a synonym for 'fairness' does not help us understand what fairness means. In a second sense of 'equity', used in the law and familiar to the Greeks (including Aristotle, as we shall see) and Romans (Latin 'aequitas'), it can override legal justice in situations where applying the law strictly would be regarded as wrong. In the legal world, this came to be described as 'substantive' justice – and, coming round full circle, as 'fairness'.

A variant of 'impartiality' which is familiar to assessment theory is *absence of bias*, bias being seen as a paradigm of unfairness. However, further thought usually leads this to be modified as 'absence of *inappropriate* bias', which begs the question of how to decide what is appropriate. The same problem arises from an account of fairness as *absence of discrimination*. Discrimination of some kind may be seen as what assessment is about. A good assessment will discriminate between those who have achieved a standard and those who have not, or between the levels of knowledge and skill displayed by each candidate. The kinds of discrimination progressively outlawed by civil rights legislation are often labelled as 'unfair' discrimination (which does not help us to define fairness), or explicitly related to defined characteristics, such as race, gender, disability or sexuality. But this begs the question of why discrimination on these grounds is regarded as unfair. There are important answers to these questions, but without them, linking fairness with discrimination (unjustified) does not help us to understand what is meant by fairness. Another concept which is often seen as fundamental to our notions of fairness is *desert*. This appears to sit with the fourth of the senses of 'fairness' which we identified in Chapter 1 – 'retributive'. In that sense, we talk of students 'getting the grades they deserve'. 'Desert' is closely linked to 'merit' (which can be both a verb and a noun) and sometimes to 'value' or 'worth'. There is a non-moral sense of 'desert' which can be used if rules are applied correctly, even though the rule has little or no moral significance. Thus, if the rules of rugby say that a try scores five points and I score a try, my team 'deserves' the five points. Moral criticism may come into play if my team is denied five points for reasons which are not sanctioned by the rules, but the rule itself is of little or no moral significance. Some of the technical rules of a test – such as 'keep your writing within the box' – might be seen in this way.

The concepts of 'value' and 'worth' go further than the merely formal sense of 'desert'. They can imply something more important than the price that a thing can attract in the market – we criticise a person who knows 'the price of everything but the value of nothing' and we sometimes talk of 'true' value or worth reflecting important intrinsic qualities.

The position becomes more morally complex when we link desert to *merit*. We shall discuss merit more fully in the next chapter, in the context of 'meritocracy', but here we note that 'merit' is often seen as having two sources. The first is intrinsic qualities (for which the owner is probably not responsible) and the second is the result of efforts or actions by the person. As we shall see in Chapter 6, accounts of 'meritocracy' tend to proffer an equation along the lines of:

$M = A + E$ (Merit = Ability [or, more controversially, IQ] + Effort)

Satz (2007) describes and then criticises the notion of 'meritocratic equality of opportunity' as being 'desert-based'. Applied to educational opportunity, she says, the meritocractic approach would be that 'only differences in talents, abilities and motivations determine [students'] educational (and via education, their employment) outcomes' (Satz, 2007, p. 629). In the context of assessment, a fair mark or grade would match the merit of the candidate.

The ambiguity of 'merit' raises problems for fair assessment. First, it is not obvious how one distinguishes between intrinsic and extrinsic qualities in someone. Environmental factors, which are not under the person's control, may affect the amount of 'effort' which is possible for them, and so-called 'intrinsic' abilities may reflect environmental influences and prior agency by the person concerned. Indeed, the very notion of 'ability' has been questioned (Stobart, 2014). This problem becomes even more acute when applied to children, for whom the concepts of 'effort', 'decision-making' and 'responsibility' may not appear wholly appropriate. In most countries, the law has agonised over the age at which young people can be said to make competent choices,[10] but, whatever age is chosen, it will almost certainly be higher than the ages at which some educational assessments are undertaken.

Second, there is a tension when 'fairness' is used to describe a response to types of 'merit' for which the person concerned has no responsibility, such as genetically produced talents, physical attributes such as height and natural talents such as being able to run fast. We may go further and describe some of the determinants of 'merit' described in these terms as being themselves 'unfair'. This introduces us to a pair of problematic characters who will be familiar to most teachers and to whom it is difficult to apply concepts of fairness linked to desert: the *lazy but highly talented pupil* and the *hard-working but untalented pupil*. Is it fair for the former to get good grades and the latter poor ones? If the concept of desert is used in answer, we might say that the high grade is 'fair' as it matches the quality of the performance of the lazy genius, but does not have much moral weight, as he or she did not contribute greatly to the qualities displayed. The converse could apply to the hard-working poor achiever.

The last – and probably most important – of the moral concepts to which fairness is related is *justice*. This is the moment to consider what Aristotle had to say about justice and fairness.

Aristotle (384–322 BC)

Aristotle, a pupil of Plato and, later, tutor to Alexander the Great, was a polymath, writing on biology, astronomy, literary criticism, philosophy, political theory and rhetoric, with excursions into early versions of what we would now call economics and even theoretical physics. He was an observer and a systematiser. Aristotle was a moderate man – he saw virtue as a 'mean' between extremes.[11] His account of justice and fairness is largely in Book 5 of the *Nichomachean Ethics* (1955/2009), which is a series of lecture notes rather than a finished work. He starts by observing that the word 'justice' has more than one meaning, which we fail to notice because the meanings are so closely related. He first considers what we might call 'general

> justice' or justice in society (which, for Aristotle, includes lawfulness). He then distinguishes general justice from 'particular justice' – sometimes translated as 'fairness' – which, he said, comes in two forms: distributive justice and reciprocal justice (the latter including the honouring of contracts). We shall confine this summary to his account of distributive justice.
>
> For Aristotle, distributive justice/fairness is about 'the distribution of honour or money and other things that fall to be divided among those who have a share in the constitution'.[12] Although the word Aristotle uses for this sense of 'fair' – 'isos' – also means 'equal', he notes from the outset that fair shares are not necessarily equal shares. The fair share is *proportionate to the merit of the recipient*.
>
> But what is meant by 'merit'? That depends, said Aristotle, on the form of government that you favour. He distinguishes three types of society – 'oligarchy' (rule of the rich and powerful), 'democracy' (rule of the many[13]) and 'aristocracy' – the rule of those who have virtue or worth. In the *Politics* (1995), he makes it clear[14] that he prefers the last of these – rule by the virtuous.
>
> Aristotle thought it would be dangerous to adopt the 'democratic' view that it was fair to treat all citizens equally. In Richard Stalley's (1995) words, he depicted distributive justice as 'giving equal privileges to those who are equal and unequal privileges to those who are unequal'.[15]
>
> Aristotle was no modern-style egalitarian. However, he did recognise that there could be a 'domestic' (secondary) kind of justice and injustice applying to relations with a slave or a child and that there could be friendship among unequals.[16]
>
> At the end of Book 5 of the *Nichomachean Ethics* (1955/2009), Aristotle distinguishes between justice and 'equity', with 'equity' denoting what lawyers would later describe as 'substantive' or 'natural justice'. Equity 'rectifies … legal justice'[17] in instances where applying the strict letter of the law would be unfair. The just response is the one the lawgiver would have given if he had known about the particular case.

It might seem anachronistic in the extreme to include Aristotle in a section headed by the twentieth-century term 'conceptual analysis', but in many ways it is appropriate, as Aristotle was a meticulous observer and describer of the world around him and thought it was important to distinguish between the different related senses of words, including what we translate as 'justice' and 'fairness'. There are many criticisms of his account of justice and fairness,[18] but some of his insights are helpful in our analysis of fairness in assessment.

First, Aristotle's distinction between a wider concept of 'general' justice and a more particular one of 'fairness' does seem to pick up a duality in our consideration of fairness and justice in the assessment world. We may not draw the boundary in the same way as Aristotle, but our concept of 'fairness' is often more particular than our notion of 'justice', and distinguishing between the two gives us a vocabulary to describe situations in which an assessment might be seen as fair in some senses but, when considered in context, is unjust.

Second, in his account of particular justice – fairness – Aristotle's notion of 'proportional equality' helpfully brings together the two fundamental concepts which underlie fairness – equality and desert. They are combined in the sense that a fair action *matches* something. Arguably, the different senses of 'fair' which we have identified specify some of the very different things that might be 'matched' in a fair assessment, but the notion of 'matching' does seem to us to pick up what Raphael calls the 'nuance' lying behind any talk of fairness (Raphael, 2001, p. 237).

We shall consider theories of justice in more length later in this chapter, but at this point it is worth pausing to consider the concept of *justice*, particularly as it relates to fairness, and possibly to fairness in assessment. The different categories of justice are dominated by 'distributive' justice, applying to the distribution of good things in society. 'Which good things?' is, as we shall see, a question that has dominated critical discussion of Rawls's theory of justice and theories of equality in recent years (e.g. Sen, 1980; Dworkin, 1981a, b). But another line of criticism – from the left and right wings of political thought – is particularly apposite to discussion of assessment. It is that the concept of distributive justice seems to picture the state handing out resources from what Nozick (1974) calls 'a big social pot' (p. 127). Citizens are pictured as being passive recipients of goods from this pot, but, first, there is no such pot, and second, the picture ignores the role of citizens as producers of wealth and other benefits.

Is 'distributive justice' relevant to assessment at all? It is not clear what is being 'distributed' in an educational test or exam – marks? grades? qualifications? Following Nozick, it makes little sense to think of assessors doling out their conclusions from a pot in which what is given to one candidate cannot be given to another.[19] And the reference to workers as producers of wealth should prompt us to ask whether assessment is just a thing 'done' to candidates by someone – for example, by testing organisations or a public authority that commissioned the test. There is surely a sense in which candidates contribute to the assessment of their work.

Against this, wider ideas of distributive justice in society do seem more relevant to fairness of the *uses* of assessment outcomes – for example, for selection for university or entry into professions. Kai Nielsen (1985) bases his analysis of egalitarianism on the premise that we feel an instinctive sense of unfairness 'at the existence of very different life prospects of equally talented, equally energetic children from very different social backgrounds: say the children of a successful businessman and a dishwasher' (p. 8). 'If someone sees no unfairness here', he adds, 'then I do not know where to turn' (p. 8).[20]

This leads to what we believe is an important distinction in the analysis of fairness in assessment: between what we will call *situated* and *isolated* views of assessment. In the situated view, an assessment is considered as an event at a point in place and time, taking into account what else we know about what happened before and after, who the candidates were, and so on. In the isolated view, the assessment is evaluated in its own terms – whether it is valid, reliable, whether the mark scheme is technically correct, and so on. We say more about this distinction – and argue for a more 'situated' view – in Chapter 7. But here we note that the more the analysis takes a situated view, the more relevant become moral concepts applied to the world in which the assessments take place.

Another kind of fairness identified by Aristotle is about the honouring of contracts. Applying this to assessment, it might be said that those who take part in an educational assessment are implicitly or explicitly agreeing to abide by its rules. In England, schools and colleges who want to offer candidates for public examinations have to apply for 'approval' by an organisation offering the exam (an 'awarding body') and approval of the school 'signals the start of a contractual relationship which is governed by the contract between the awarding body and the centre'.[21] The schools explicitly agree to abide by the rules and regulations produced by the awarding bodies, and it might be argued that applying those rules appropriately was 'fair' in a contractual sense. Students are normally unaware of having entered into any contract, but there may be a weak sense in which they do so implicitly.

An additional category of justice which may be of assistance when considering assessment is *procedural* justice. This denotes situations where the rules governing a process are applied accurately, and it allows a distinction to be drawn between judging that a process was applied fairly and judging that the process itself – or its outcome – was fair. At the end of this chapter, we refer to the practice in some countries of using lotteries as part of the selection process for medical schools. If the lottery was done impartially and its rules applied scrupulously, a commentator might remark that the process was fair, even if some criticised the decision to use a lottery as a means of selection, but that it was unfair to the candidates for it to be applied.

Lastly, the form of justice involved in compensating people for wrongs or losses is often labelled '*restorative* justice'. This can be linked to ideas of equality, bringing the wronged person back to the position they were in before the wrong was done, or, in the language used in the English courts, to where they would have been 'but for' the loss or wrong they experienced. In an assessment context, could accommodations for candidates with disabilities be regarded as a form of restorative justice?[22] The problem with this suggestion is that of the counterfactual hypothesis, which we identified earlier: to what level are we 'restoring' the performance of the disabled candidate? In the case of congenital disabilities, there is no relevant level where the candidate was before. And it is difficult to make sense of a concept of 'where he/she would have been but for the disability'. For these reasons, we conclude that the concept of restorative justice is probably not helpful here.

Conclusion (conceptual analysis)

We have recalled the different senses of 'fairness' that were listed in Chapter 1 and considered what ideas underlie them, and how they relate to other concepts, including equality, equity, impartiality, desert and different categories of justice. We have observed Aristotle's distinction between a wider concept of justice/lawfulness and a more 'particular' concept which can be translated as 'fairness' and which he explicates in terms of 'proportionate equality', with the fair allocation of benefits *matching* the merit or value of the recipient. Earlier in the chapter, we outlined the 'negative' approach to fairness, which saw the primary concept as *un*fairness, and we saw that this had both theoretical and practical attractions. We suggested that 'equality' and 'desert' were the two moral concepts most closely linked to the positive concept of 'fairness', and although each raises problems, including when applied to assessment, we were attracted by the Aristotelian notion of a fundamental notion of 'matching' that gave the notion of fairness its distinctiveness. On balance, therefore, we favour a positive account of fairness in which the twin pillars of equality and desert are underpinned by an idea of appropriateness, or 'matching'.

Theoretical modelling

The second kind of philosophical lens which we consider in this chapter is theoretical modelling. This aims to establish a structure for our thinking – in this case about justice and fairness – which brings disparate ideas together and can provide a point of reference for judgements about the real world.

Theoretical models can involve metaphors or illustrations. For example, social contract theorists such as Hobbes, Locke and Rousseau described an imaginary contract to which individual citizens have consented and which governs social behaviour. In the words of Michael Walzer (2005),[23] 'the contract is a philosophical fiction developed … to show how political obligation rests on individual consent' (p. 174). Another 'philosophical fiction' was Adam Smith's idea that our 'moral sentiments' expressed the sympathetic feelings of an (imaginary) impartial spectator (Smith, 1790/2011). Smith did not suggest that such a spectator existed, but argued that our moral judgements reflect the feelings that the spectator would possess.

The most famous modern example of a theoretical model of justice and fairness is that expounded by John Rawls.

John Rawls (1921–2002): 'Justice as fairness'

John Rawls was a hugely influential American moral and political philosopher. His accounts of justice (1958, 1971) have been seminal in thinking about justice and fairness in the latter years of the twentieth and early twenty-first centuries.

Rawls developed an illustrative model which informed both his method of determining just societies and social arrangements and his view of the content of justice. His model was a hypothetical social contract which would be agreed on by a group of rational, self-interested people who were in an 'original position', knowing some things – including the general laws of psychology and the social sciences – but behind a 'veil of ignorance' regarding particular facts about themselves, their attributes and the society in which they lived, and who came together to agree on principles for the distribution of 'social goods', notably wealth and income.

He set out three principles in a hierarchy of 'lexical priority', meaning that only if the first is not satisfied does one proceed to the second, and so on. They are:

1. The liberty principle: 'Each person is to have an equal right to the most extensive total system of equal basic liberties compatible with a similar system of liberty for all.'

2. The fair equality of opportunity principle: 'Social and economic inequalities should be arranged so that they are ... attached to offices and positions open to all under conditions of fair equality of opportunity ...'

3. The difference principle: '... and to the greatest benefit of the least advantaged.'[24]

These principles were to be applied to determining the basic structures of society that affect people's life chances rather than to specific situations (although some critics[25] have argued that it is relevant to consider them as applied to 'micro' examples too).

In writing of 'justice as fairness' (the title of his article in 1958 and of the first chapter of his long book in 1971), Rawls was not suggesting that 'justice' and 'fairness' were synonyms. Rather, he wanted 'to show that the fundamental idea in the concept of justice is fairness',[26] and thus to remedy what he saw as a defect of classical utilitarianism in recognising the fundamental importance for Western democratic societies of securing the 'basic rights and liberties of citizens as free and equal persons'.[27]

Rawls's 'original position' was in the tradition of the earlier social contract theories and in describing what was known and not known behind the 'veil of ignorance' he was arguably fleshing out our notion of 'impartiality', as displayed by Adam Smith's imaginary spectator. The most fundamental question that is raised by all such illustrative theoretical models, including Rawls's, is why we should pay attention to such fictions at all. Why should Bill Clinton say[28] that this peculiar picture of an imaginary contract entered into by psychologically unrealistic people 'helped a whole generation of learned Americans revive their faith in democracy itself'? And what is the relevance for a book about fairness in educational assessment?

First, it is relevant to note that Rawls (1971) was clear that he was not offering a piece of conceptual analysis:

> I do not interpret this concept of right [in the sense which is closely linked to justice] as providing an analysis of the *meaning* of the term 'just' as normally used in moral contexts. ... Rather, the broader notion of rightness as fairness is to be understood as a *replacement* for existing conceptions ... So understood one may think of justice as fairness and rightness as fairness as providing a definition or explication of the concepts of justice and right. (p. 111)

What theoretical models attempt to do is to illuminate our day-to-day moral thinking by outlining a structure (which we may never have thought of or been able to articulate) which brings coherence to our thinking and gives us a framework to consider social issues in the real world. They set terms for a dialectic between theory and practice, where the theory poses questions about practice and vice versa. However, as we shall see when we consider the application to educational assessment, it is not always easy to judge what people in the 'original position' would want. And if the illustrative model appears to conflict with current received views about social policies in the real world, we need a basis on which to decide which needs to change – the model or the social policies.

Discussion of Rawls has tended to concentrate on his methodology (the 'veil of ignorance') and the third – and lowest priority – of his three principles: the 'difference' principle, whereby the right or just distribution of good things in society is that which most benefits the least advantaged. The second principle – 'fair equality of opportunity' – is less discussed.[29] However, it is arguably the most relevant to educational assessment, so we shall examine it in more detail.

Rawls's 'fair equality of opportunity' principle was intended to go beyond the principle of what he called 'careers open to talents'. 'Careers open to talents' meant simply that selection for positions should be by reference to the talent of the applicants (presumably in respects relevant to the job), and not influenced by irrelevant considerations such as race or gender. Fair equality of opportunity was, he said, a 'liberal principle' which went further: 'The thought here is that positions are to be not only open in a formal sense, but that all should have a fair chance to attain them ... [W]e might say that those with similar abilities and skills should have similar life chances' (Rawls, 1971, p. 73).

In a discussion of educational equality, Brighouse and Swift (2009) argue that 'fair equality of opportunity' on its own is not adequate to determine a 'full theory of educational justice', as it cannot do justice to the needs of children with cognitive impairments, or, more widely, to the problem of inequalities between people of different levels of talent (Brighouse and Swift, 2009, p. 119). They and others[30] feel that even the 'fair equality of opportunity' principle is too close to meritocracy for comfort. It may be a necessary condition for educational justice but it is not sufficient.

We wish to add two further criticisms of Rawls's second principle, developed with an eye to applying the principle to educational assessment. First, he does not say what he means by 'talent'. The passage quoted above refers to 'abilities and skills', but that transfers the problem to defining 'ability'. If we accept that 'abilities' are influenced both by inheritance and by environment, applying Rawls's own argument to the 'fair opportunity' principle suggests that it needs to be rolled back even further – to the principle that all should have similar chances to develop their abilities and skills. But even that does not do justice to the case of those who have inherited low talent or cognitive disabilities.

Second – and this criticism applies to much of Rawls's writing – he says very little about children. It seems strange to take their abilities and skills as given, particularly in the case of young children. This point becomes particularly relevant when we apply Rawls's models to educational assessment.

The flood of discussion that followed Rawls's publications, and which largely concentrated on the difference principle, broadly focused on two questions, both raised at length by Dworkin (Dworkin, 1981a, b; Wolff, 2008). The first was about the *currency* of theories of justice – what kinds of benefits the theory should take into consideration. This linked to discussions of equality, and in particular to the comparative claims of 'equality of resources' and 'equality of welfare'. The second was the problem that some people might deserve good things more than others. Some people are badly off because of the poor choices that they have made, whilst others are victims of ill fortune. The quotation from Winston Churchill at the beginning of this chapter criticises an approach to fairness that means 'fair shares to those who toil and those who shirk'. There was also a problem which many writers found particularly troubling, but which we shall not discuss in detail here, namely the claims of those with expensive taste compared with those with simpler preferences. It did not seem right that the state should subsidise a diet of caviar and best claret.

The biggest insight in Dworkin's commentaries on Rawls was, arguably, that Rawls's account of justice as fairness did not take sufficient account of what we saw earlier in the chapter was one of the twin pillars of the concept of fairness, namely *desert*. Perhaps the weaker version of Rawls's second principle ('careers open to talents') implies a form of desert – that those who best meet the requirements for a position deserve to be appointed. But, otherwise, the difficult examples cited in discussion of Rawls – shirkers, caviar-eaters and all – are problematic for a theory of fairness because these people do not appear to deserve the same benefits in society as those who have done all they could but remain disadvantaged. The absence of an account of desert is a particular problem in a model 'explicating' justice in terms of fairness.

What is the relevance of Rawls's principles to educational assessment? Rawls himself would probably reject this question, as he wanted his theory applied to social systems in total rather than to specific actions. However, we would join with those who have found this distinction between the macro and the micro in social policy unhelpful. As Nozick (1974) pointed out, it seems strange to talk of characteristics of the social structure as a whole that are not displayed in any part of it.[31] And anyone who has worked in social administration – for example, in government departments – knows that in real life social policy progresses by specific 'micro' decisions, for example about tax levels or changes to the rules for health services or education. These may be informed by high-scale principles (such as maximising or minimising the role of the state) but the focus of policy-makers and the public is usually – and, in our view, rightly – on the specific decisions.

We shall therefore proceed with considering how Rawls's principles might apply to assessment. We suggest that there is an important distinction to be drawn between assessments that are made before the application of Rawls's principles and those which are actions to which the principles might be applied. Turning to Rawls's second principle in its weaker form ('careers open to talents'), that raises the question of how one knows what talents the applicant for a job has. The answer must be by some sort of assessment that comes before the principle is applied. The principle (which has not yet been evoked) does not help to decide what constitutes fairness in a (prior) assessment of talent. In the second sense (applying the principle to an assessment), the principle could be used in evaluating the fairness of an assessment for appointment to a position: the weak version of the second principle ('careers open to talents') would support an account of fairness in terms of the absence of bias based on irrelevant considerations. The stronger concept of 'fair equality of opportunity' may suggest that that account of fairness is too narrow.

Turning to Rawls's second principle in its stronger form ('those who have similar abilities and skills should have similar life chances'), the same distinction is relevant. Before the principle is applied, we need to know what levels of ability and skill those concerned have. Again, that presumably requires some sort of prior assessment. But addressing the principle to the assessment itself can be more difficult, and raise important challenges for educational assessment. Assuming that we have made an assessment of ability or skill, how do we ensure that the assessment enables those with equal abilities to have equal life chances?

In addition to its intrinsic value, education has been labelled a 'positional good',[32] meaning that educational achievement can give the holder a relative advantage in terms of access to careers, professions and leadership positions in society (Anderson, 2007; Satz, 2007). Without doubt, some educational assessments, such as degree examinations in universities or entrance examinations for college or professional training, are gateways to such advantage. If the construct they assess is the same as the 'abilities and skills' referred to in Rawls's stronger principle, then it collapses into the weaker principle. But if there is a difference – for example, if not all students have the same opportunities to study the construct being assessed, or if the style of the assessment is more familiar to some candidates than to others (with the same 'abilities and skills') – then perhaps Rawls's stronger version of the second principle does provide a more substantial challenge for assessment.

It is not very easy to apply the 'difference principle' to educational assessment, partly for the reasons given in the comments earlier in this chapter about 'distributive justice' – it is not clear what, if anything, is being distributed in educational assessment. Interestingly, for students of assessment, Robert Nozick (1974) wrote about an imaginary attempt to apply the difference principle to a situation which he called 'grading', in which a group of students, who had studied for a course and sat an examination, were told that a range of marks from 1 to 100 would be allocated, and they congregated in the 'original position' to decide on the allocation of grades they would prefer. Initially, says Nozick, they would probably opt for the same grade for all; later, he imagines that a list of grades headed 'entitlements' is shown to them. He argues that rational self-interest in the original position (when they do not know how talented they are or how hard they have worked) would not necessarily lead them to adopt the 'entitlements' distribution, rather than a '"reverse entitlements" distribution, in which the highest achievers got the lowest mark, and so on' (Nozick, 1974, pp. 199–204). What Nozick's example illustrates is that the concept of desert, which is one of the central tenets of fairness, cannot be derived from the 'original position', where rationally self-interested individuals do not know how deserving they are.

Another concept which is difficult for Rawls to accommodate, but which can be included in some accounts of fairness, is luck. How would Nozick's students feel about the proposal that the grades should be pulled out of a hat? The potential low-scorers would have the same chance as the potential high-scorers of achieving a high mark, so there would be an element of relational fairness in that no candidate would be favoured. There would also be procedural fairness if the draw was done properly. However, there is no clear basis for determining whether people in the original position would prefer the chance of a high mark (the luck of the draw) to the certainty of a moderate mark (if the marks were shared equally). It would depend on what in business is called their 'risk appetite'.

In Chapter 6, we shall consider in more detail different accounts of equality in education. One question which educational writers face is whether/how to accommodate the idea of desert in an account of how education can support social justice. Elizabeth Anderson (1999) labelled as 'luck egalitarianism' the view that justice should compensate for the effects of bad luck (such as congenital disability), but not for the effects of poor choices or lack of effort. Writers have differed on their willingness to tolerate social systems where those who make bad choices are left to suffer the consequences without assistance, but most baulk at the extreme version of this approach – where the drunk driver is left to die at the side of the road. Another criticism levelled at luck egalitarianism is the intrusiveness and lack of respect involved in inquiring about the reasons for disadvantage, in order to find out whether to compensate them or not (Wolff, 1998, 2010).

A major problem in applying these concepts to educational assessment is the issue of *low talent* – what Nagel (1979) called 'the injustice of the smart and the dumb' (p. 104). However much environmental features and choices by individuals may have contributed to their abilities, most of us would accept that some people are just brighter than others. Assessment practitioners are at ease with the practice of making accommodations for students with disabilities (a form of 'luck egalitarianism') and also – though sometimes with less ease – with the idea of modifying a construct if parts of it cannot be displayed by a student with a particular disability, such as listening skills for a deaf candidate sitting a language test. But the logic of 'luck egalitarianism' would have us consider stupidity, or, perhaps, lack of ability to reason, as a disability and compensate for it in an assessment – particularly if the outcome affected the candidate's life chances. Such assessments would not satisfy Rawls's second principle, even in its stronger form. And they would not be valid. But would they be fair?

There could be utilitarian arguments against such a practice: for example, if the assessment led to entry to a more advanced course which would not benefit the low-talent candidate, then there might not be anything to gain from compensating for lack of talent in the entry test. Also, in assessments leading to professional qualifications, it could be argued that it would be unfair to users of the assessment outcome, such as future clients of the professional, if the assessment compensated for candidates' lack of talent and made them appear more competent than they were.

However, the challenge of the candidate with low talent might rightly cause those setting a test or an examination to check carefully whether the tasks set really are essential to the construct being assessed, or whether they reflect social assumptions about generic abilities which are thought relevant to all assessments, but may not always be so. Thus, for example, a student may have good practical skills and be able to demonstrate them in practice, but may have difficulty writing about them.

The injustice remains that some students, through no lack of effort on their part, do not do well in educational assessments. Although it may be possible to structure an assessment to enable students of lower ability to display what they can do,[33] at the end of the day it may be impossible to devise a 'fair' assessment which remedies this injustice. The decision on what to do in such circumstances may, however, be informed by wider considerations of justice, such as by finding other ways to maximise the life chances of the untalented candidate.

Conclusion (theoretical modelling)

We have described theoretical models developed by moral and political philosophers, and looked in more detail at John Rawls's account of 'justice as fairness', particularly his second principle (fair equality of opportunity), in both its strong and weak forms. In considering how this might be applied to assessment, we made an important distinction between assessments that come before the application of the principle and assessments which are actions to which the principles might be applied. We agreed with those critics who have argued that Rawls's second principle is not sufficient on its own, and with the arguments, started by Dworkin, that Rawls's methodology does not allow sufficiently for the concept of desert. We found it difficult to decide what people in Rawls's 'original position' would say about assessment, and we were left with the difficulty of applying the concept of fairness to Nagel's 'injustice of the smart and the dumb' (1979, p. 104).

Postscript

Why should assessments be fair? Our account of fairness has taken for granted that fairness in assessment is (normally at least) a good thing. But why? There are at least three answers to this question. The first is that it is true by definition, as 'fair' is a term of approval. However, that still leaves open the question of whether the weight of approval conveyed by 'fair' might, on occasion, be outweighed by that of another term of approval. That in turn raises the question of what our basis is for determining the comparative weights of the different terms. The second answer is instrumental – fair assessment might be a means to a desirable end. Thus, for example, providing accurate information about the extent of a student's learning could enable them to be allocated to an appropriate class. The third answer justifies fairness in assessment by reference to other concepts such as fulfilling an implied contract, delivering individual rights, or to a more fundamental underlying moral principle, such as respect to each candidate as an end (Kant), or contributing to the greatest happiness of the greatest number (utilitarianism).

In our view, almost all senses of 'fair' (perhaps excluding the purely formal sense) have some moral force, but could be outweighed by other moral principles or values, such as kindness, keeping a promise or duties to one's family. It adds clarity to the moral debate if we have terms which enable such conflicts to be explored. If fairness is not the same as 'right action', then it follows that it could be wrong to be fair. We see no reason in principle why this should not apply to assessment. In the words of R. M. Hare (1977): 'Sometimes it is impossible to be absolutely fair in this imperfect world without transgressing some even more important duty' (p. 209).

For further reflection

Assessment by lottery[34]

Medical schools have to be restricted in size and they usually face the task of selecting a small number of students from large numbers with high examination grades. Certain schools in the Netherlands and England decided to use a lottery to select a shortlist from the large number of applicants with high grades. However, public opinion was highly critical of this practice and it had to be abandoned – or, in the Dutch case, modified to 'weight' the lottery in favour of those with the highest grades. A parent of a student who was unsuccessful in a lottery complained that his daughter's dreams had been destroyed 'at the throw of a dice'. Is a lottery a fair method of selecting students for entry to a competitive course? Is the outcome of such a lottery fair?

Compensating for differences in reasoning skills

Elizabeth and Shane are teenagers taking a beginners' philosophy course at school. Elizabeth's parents are academics: she has inherited their quick minds and from an early age has been encouraged to debate current issues at the dinner table. Shane finds it difficult to construct arguments and to criticise them. He comes from a single-parent family and has often had to entertain himself at home, whilst his mother was working to support the family. The philosophy teacher is told that if the class test is to be fair, it should make 'accommodations' for those who, like Shane, find reasoning difficult, through no fault of their own. They are to be offered extra time and the pass mark for them should be lower than for others. The teacher protests that doing that would fly in the face of the central point of the assessment, and would be unfair to the other candidates. Who is right?

The talented layabout

Jeremy is a handsome, gifted university student. His magnetic personality attracts admirers and he makes the most of the social opportunities of student life. For much of his course, he does as little work as he can get away with, but as the end of the course approaches he wants to get a good class of degree. For the term before the final exams, he asks Stephen, a conscientious but shy young man in the same year, to spend time helping Jeremy to catch up on the work that he has shirked. Stephen is flattered by Jeremy's attention, lends him his lecture notes and spends a lot of time with him. Jeremy does well in the final degree exams and gains a good upper-second-class degree. To the disappointment of his tutors, Stephen does poorly, gaining only a third-class degree, and appears to have been inadequately prepared. Are the degree outcomes fair?

Notes

1. Quoted in Raphael, 1951, p. 168.
2. We accept that this may not apply to unfairness in the purely formal sense (breaching of rules).
3. Entry for 'conceptual analysis' in Honderich (Ed.), 2005.
4. In fact, the French translator used 'Justice comme équité', but 'équité' is a more specialised term than the English 'fairness'.
5. This could refer to an extremely strict or precise application of the rules, but such rigour might itself be criticised as being unfair.
6. We are grateful to Ben Colburn for raising these points.
7. Brian Barry based his entire model of justice on the concept of impartiality, and would no doubt locate fairness in that model (Barry, 1995).
8. For example, Raphael (1946) discusses the claims by some people for extra rations in wartime Britain, e.g. citizens with medical conditions requiring extra milk (need), or those in priority occupations requiring strength (utility).
9. Similar questions are raised by the New Testament parable of the 'Labourers in the Vineyard' (Matthew 20: 1–16), where those workers who started late were paid the same rate by their generous employer as those who had worked through 'the heat of the day'. Theological interpretations of this story go beyond concepts of fairness, but the story does raise questions about the importance of relational fairness.
10. In the UK, this is often referred to as 'Gillick competence', following an English court case.
11. Aristotle frequently reflected this approach in mathematical models (including mathematical illustrations of justice), which most readers now find rather obscure and which we are ignoring for the purposes of this summary.
12. Aristotle, *Nichomachean Ethics* (1955/2009) V.3.1130b.
13. For Aristotle, 'the many' applied only to citizens, and not, for example, to women, children or slaves.
14. E.g. at *Politics* 1278 a 19–20.
15. In his notes to the World's Classics edition of the *Politics*, p. 357.
16. Aristotle, *Politics* 1163 a 30ff.
17. Aristotle, *Nichomachean Ethics* (1955/2009) V.10.1137b, 12–13.

18. For example, Raphael (2001) criticises the absence of anything approaching a theory of punishment in Aristotle's account.
19. An exception to this observation might be the marking scheme for an assessment aiming for a rank ordering of candidates with no shared marks.
20. Neilson (1985), quoted and discussed in White (1994, p. 173).
21. Joint Council for Qualifications, *General Regulations for Approved Centres*, 1 September 2019 to 31 August 2020, p. 4, para. 3.1, accessed November 2019 at www.jcq.org.uk/exams-office/general-regulations/general-regulations-for-approved-centres-2019-2020.
22. We are grateful to Robin Downie for raising this question.
23. In the article on 'Social contract' in Honderich (Ed.)., 2005.
24. As stated in Rawls (1971: 302), although he reverses the order of (2) and (3) in his description. The order of lexical priority is as set out in our summary.
25. Notably Nozick (1974: 204–207).
26. Rawls (1958: 164).
27. Rawls used this formulation in an introductory essay to a French translation of his *Theory of Justice* in 1987.
28. When presenting Rawls with the National Humanities Medal in 1999.
29. But see Alexander (1986), Arneson (1999), and Brighouse and Swift (2009).
30. Including Arneson (1999: 81).
31. Nozick (1974: 205).
32. The term probably derived from Fred Hirsch, *Social Limits to Growth*, Harvard University Press, Cambridge, MA, 1976.
33. An example of this is the 'tiering' of some examinations, with a lower tier which can earn a lower range of marks but allows the student to tackle questions at the simpler end of the spectrum covered by the construct being assessed.
34. See Ryan (2006) and Stone (2007, 2013).

References

Alexander, L. A. (1986) Fair equality of opportunity: John Rawls' (best) forgotten principle. *Philosophy Research Archives*, XI, March.

Anderson, E. S. (1999) What is the point of equality? *Ethics*, 109(2), 287–337.

Anderson, E. S. (2007) Fair opportunity in education: A democratic equality perspective. *Ethics*, 117(4), 595–622.

Aristotle (1955/2009) *The Nichomachean Ethics* (trans. J. A. K. Thomson, Penguin Books, 1955; trans. D. Ross, revised and with an Introduction and Notes by L. Brown). Oxford World's Classics. Oxford: Oxford University Press.

Aristotle (1995) *Politics* (trans. E. Barker; revised and with an Introduction and Notes by R. F. Stalley). Oxford World's Classics. Oxford: Oxford University Press.

Arneson, R. (1999) Against Rawlsian equality of opportunity. *Philosophical Studies*, 93, 77–112.

Barry, B. (1995) *Justice as Impartiality*. Oxford: Clarendon Press.

Brighouse, H. and Swift, A. (2009) Educational equality versus educational adequacy: A critique of Anderson and Satz. *Journal of Applied Philosophy*, 26(2) (May), 117–128.

Churchill, W. L. S. (1950) Quoted in D. D. Raphael (1951) Justice and liberty. *Proceedings of the Aristotelian Society*, New Series, Vol. 51 (1950–1951), pp. 167–196.

Dworkin, R. (1981a) What is equality? Part 1: Equality of welfare. *Philosophy and Public Affairs*, 10(3), 185–246.

Dworkin, R. (1981b) What is equality? Part 2: Equality of resources. *Philosophy and Public Affairs*, 10(4), 283–345.

Hare, R. M. (1977) Opportunity for what? Some remarks on current disputes about equality in education. *Oxford Review of Education*, 3(3), 207–216.

Honderich, T. (Ed.) (2005) *The Oxford Companion to Philosophy* (2nd edn). Oxford: Oxford University Press.

Joint Council for Qualifications (JCQ) (2019) General Regulations for Approved Centres, 1 September 2019 to 31 August 2020, p. 4, para. 3.1, available at: www.jcq.org.uk/exams-office/general-regulations/general-regulations-for-approved-centres-2019-2020 (accessed 01/11/19).

Nagel, T. (1979) 'The Policy of Preference', in *Mortal Questions*. Cambridge: Cambridge University Press.

Nielsen, K. (1985) *Equality and Liberty: A defense of radical egalitarianism*. Totowa, NJ: Rowman & Allanheld.

Nozick, R. (1974) *Anarchy, State and Utopia*. Oxford: Basil Blackwell.

Priest, S. (2005) Conceptual analysis. In T. Honderich (Ed.), *The Oxford Companion to Philosophy* (2nd edn). Oxford: Oxford University Press. pp. 154–155.

Raphael, D. D. (1946) Equality and equity. *Philosophy*, 21(79), 118–132.

Raphael, D. D. (1951) *Justice and Liberty: Proceedings of the Aristotelian Society*. New Series, Vol. 51 (1950–1951), pp. 167–196.

Raphael, D. D. (2001) *Concepts of Justice*. Oxford: Oxford University Press.

Rawls, J. (1958) Justice as fairness. *The Philosophical Review*, 67(2) (April), 164–194.

Rawls, J. (1971) *A Theory of Justice*. Oxford: Oxford University Press.

Rescher, N. (2002) *Fairness: Theory and practice of distributive justice*. New Brunswick, NJ: Transaction Publishers.

Ryan, A. R. (2006) Fairness and philosophy. *Social Research*, 73(2) (Summer), 597–606.

Satz, D. (2007) Equality, adequacy and education for citizenship. *Ethics*, 117(4), 623–648.

Sen, A. (1980) Equality of what? In S. M. McMurrin (Ed.), *The Tanner Lectures*. Cambridge: Cambridge University Press.

Smith, A. (1790/2011) *Theory of Moral Sentiments* (London edn, 1790). London: Gutenberg Press (reprinted 2011).

Stalley, R. F. (1995) The unity of the state: Plato, Aristotle and Proclus. Polis 14, *The Politics* by Aristotle. Oxford World's Classics. Oxford: Oxford University Press. pp. 129–149.

Stobart, G. (2014) *The Expert Learner: Challenging the myth of ability*. Maidenhead: Open University Press/McGraw-Hill Education.

Stone, P. (2007) Why lotteries are just. *The Journal of Political Philosophy*, 15(3), 276–295.

Stone, P. (2013) Access to higher education by the luck of the draw. *Comparative Education Review*, 57(3), (August), 577–599.

Walzer, M. (2005) Social contract. In T. Honderich (Ed.), *The Oxford Companion to Philosophy* (2nd edn). Oxford: Oxford University Press. pp. 174–175.

White, J. (1994) The dishwasher's child: Education and the end of egalitarianism. *Journal of Philosophy of Education*, 28(2), 173–181.

Wolff, J. (1998) Fairness, respect and the egalitarian ethos. *Philosophy & Public Affairs*, 27(2) (Spring), 97–122.

Wolff, J. (2007) Equality: The recent history of an idea. Review Article. *Journal of Moral Philosophy*, 4(1), 125–136.

Wolff, J. (2008) Social justice and public policy: A view from political philosophy. In G. Craig, T. Burchardt and D. Gordon (Eds.), *Social Justice and Public Policy: Seeking fairness in diverse societies*. Bristol: Policy Press.

Wolff, J. (2010) Fairness, respect and the egalitarian 'ethos' revisited. *The Journal of Ethics*, 14(3–4), 335–350.

6
Fair assessment viewed through the lenses of social justice

'I have a dream that my four little children will one day live in a nation where they will not be judged by the color of their skin but by the content of their character.' (Martin Luther King, 1963)

'We hold these truths to be self-evident, that all men are created equal, that they are endowed by their Creator with certain inalienable rights, that among these are life, liberty, the pursuit of happiness and a high school diploma.' (Young, 1994, p. 33)[1]

'Today we ... have rule not so much by the people as by the cleverest people; not an aristocracy of birth, not a plutocracy of wealth, but a true meritocracy of talent.' (Young, 1958/1994, p. 11)

'I have been sadly disappointed by my 1958 book, *The Rise of the Meritocracy* ... the book was a satire meant to be a warning (which needless to say has not been heeded) against what might happen to Britain.' (Young, 2001)[2]

Introduction

In Chapter 5, we considered some theoretical models of fairness in society. We distinguished between approaches founded on a negative concept of *un*fairness and those which attempted to unpack and describe a positive view of fairness, linked to concepts of equality and desert. Many of these models have practical implications and there is no fixed line separating theory from practice. We now move across that spectrum to consider some accounts of how society is or ought to be organised in practice, and the implications for fairness and fair assessment.

In the English language, practical agendas for a better society tend to adopt the term 'justice' rather than 'fairness', and we have used 'social justice' in the title of this chapter in the hope that it will encourage the reader to call to mind wider social movements and debates which are certainly relevant to any discussion of education. However, that does raise the question of how the approaches we consider here relate to fairness, and in particular to fairness in assessment. As we have argued in Chapter 5, 'fairness' can be viewed as a narrower concept than 'justice', with fairness concentrating on process and/or particular aspects of an action, including those we identified in Chapter 1, such as relational fairness and meeting legitimate expectations. We therefore start this chapter by considering whether some kinds of assessment are by their very nature fairer than others. We then broaden the lens to social justice, starting with approaches targeted against injustice and moving on to more positive accounts of justice, including the 'educational adequacy' movement, as advocated by Elizabeth Anderson and others (Anderson, 2007; Satz, 2007; Anderson and White, 2019). In the final section of this chapter, we look in some detail at 'meritocracy', much loved and hated since the word came on the scene in the mid-twentieth century and often linked by its supporters with fair assessment.

Fair types of assessment?

In Chapter 3, we discuss many accounts of good practice in educational assessment which are explicitly directed at fairness, or at the elimination of identified categories of unfairness. Some focus narrowly on particular aspects, or stages of an assessment, such as the wording of tasks/questions, whilst others take what we have called a 'situated' view, asking questions of fairness about the assessment in its context, including students' preparation for it and use of the results.

Chapter 3 largely refers to guidance by the assessment industry for the assessment industry, aiming to promote the assessment values of validity, reliability – and fairness. But if we start with accounts of social justice, do these lead to a conclusion that some kinds, or modes, of assessment are inherently fairer than others?

A view of social justice linked to equality of outcomes, or to an objective of fulfilment for all (Sen's (1980) 'capability to function'), may appear to favour assessments which emphasise obtaining the fullest account of each individual rather than comparing candidates with each other. Such thinking may favour basing decisions on multiple tests rather than a single one, or the use of adaptive testing, where different routes can be taken by different individuals, rather than setting the same tasks for all. Even though the design of an adaptive test may involve comparisons with norms (based on the achievements of others),[3] information from the route chosen by an individual from a wide range of possibilities is arguably more informative about that individual than a simple comparison with others required to take identical routes.

We suggest that the persuasiveness of those views depends on the purpose of the assessment. Adaptive testing may indeed produce richer information about each student than can be obtained from a one-size-fits-all test. And this richer information may often be useful. But there are situations, such as some fitness-to-practise professional examinations, in which there are clear public good arguments for the same standard to be applied to everyone, even if candidates are allowed to display their achievement of the standard in different ways. Also, even in the most egalitarian society, there will always be some situations where individuals have to compete for a limited good, such as expensive medical school training. These instances may be fewer than is sometimes thought (as we shall argue in the final chapter). But where they do exist, there is a danger of unfairness, in the relational sense, if the information provided about each applicant is markedly different in content and quality.

A famous example of social justice being used to justify a particular type of assessment can be found in the history of 'standardised testing' in the USA.[4]

In brief, attempts to make assessment more comparable to a scientific endeavour were seen as a weapon against prejudice, inherited privilege and unfair (sic) discrimination and a means to enhance civil rights and social mobility. Claims of objectivity were made, in contrast with more judgemental forms of assessment – for example, by employers in recruitment – which were prone to injustices stemming from bias, notably against people with the characteristics enjoined by progressive civil rights legislation in the 1960s and 1970s.

The fairness of standardised testing merits a book of its own, but we shall limit ourselves to two observations. First, if a test that claims to be 'objective' is shown by analysis to be unfair, then the result can be doubly harmful – candidates and users of the test outcome may believe what they were told, namely that the test is fair, and so be less wary of the risk of bias than they should be. Stein (2017) described early IQ testing practices in the USA as being 'characterised by a multifold lack of objectivity, including a lack of even basic forms of reliability and construct validity' (p. 161), and accused the IQ testing movement of 'pretensions of objectivity' (p. 165).

Second, the outcomes of so-called-standardised tests, whether for school or college entrance or employment, distressingly seem to perpetuate – rather than reduce – differences in outcome for disadvantaged groups. For example, the SAT (formerly 'Scholastic Aptitude Test') is a standardised assessment that is widely used for university and college admissions in the USA and is seen as one of the main policy mechanisms for increasing college enrolment among all sections of the population. It is also seen to have positive effects on cognitive strategies, content knowledge and learning/behavioural techniques (Conley et al., 2011; Conley, 2012). Opponents of the SAT, however, have pointed to cultural bias as a possible explanation for the disparity in scores between the least and most well-off who sit the test (Zwick, 2006), family income as a possible explanation for variance in SAT scores (Rampell, 2009) and achievement gaps reflecting differences in the educational quality of schools attended by different racial groups (see Thernstrom and Thernstrom, 2004).

The problem of persisting inequalities of outcome has proved particularly controversial in the context of testing for recruitment to employment. In Chapter 4, we discuss the 'Uniform Guidelines', developed in the 1990s under US Civil Rights legislation, and the suggestion by some of a 'diversity/validity dilemma' – what if differences in test outcomes, for example, between ethnic groups, are 'real' and not a sign of an unfairly biased test? (McDaniel et al., 2011, p. 512).

There have also been disappointments in attempts to develop tests for children which do not have an 'adverse impact' on disadvantaged groups. In England, a minority of counties have retained 'grammar schools', state-funded, for brighter secondary school pupils, with entrance largely determined by tests historically referred to as the '11 plus'. Supporters of grammar schools have argued that they give a 'leg up' to bright children from poor families and they have sought ways of increasing the proportion of pupils from disadvantaged backgrounds who are selected. In particular, it has been seen as unfair that rich parents can afford to hire private tutors to prepare their children for the test. One education authority engaged an academic organisation to produce a 'tutor-proof test' for grammar school entry, but the differences in outcomes for children from different socio-economic groups persisted, and the education authority later reverted to its previous provider.[5] In commentary on this episode, it is important to note that the allegedly 'tutor-proof' test may have been fairer than its predecessors, or than its successors, in several of the senses of 'fair' we have identified. It may or may not have been less susceptible to the benefits of private tutoring.[6] But a lesson from the experience of employment selectors and school admission testers so far is that assessment alone cannot bear the burden of reversing social inequality. A test that is fairer than alternatives may be a good thing, and justified as enabling what Jonathan Wolff calls 'fertile functioning' (Wolff, 2008, p. 28), but it is not a silver bullet for social justice.

Slaying the giants: attacking social *in*justice

As we saw in Chapter 4, one conceptual approach to fairness is to take as its root the negative concept of *un*fairness. The parallel practical approach to social justice is to focus on eliminating or reducing identified forms of injustice or injustice to specific groups. The justification of this approach may be based on a vision of social justice and/or a view of human rights, but the practical expression is to identify and tackle injustice. The injustices identified can be particular kinds of hardship – such as the five giants (idleness, ignorance, squalor, disease and want) famously described by William Beveridge in 1942[7] – or defined groups of people seen to be particularly disadvantaged or at risk (such as minority ethnic populations, low socio-economic groups, refugees, children, women, people with a disability).

The giant-slaying approach is reflected in some of the perspectives we have described in earlier chapters. As we discuss in Chapter 4, lawmakers in many countries have developed waves of anti-discrimination legislation, forbidding discrimination on the basis of listed characteristics, such as gender, ethnicity or disability. In the world of educational assessment, many of the theoreticians and good practitioners cited in Chapters 2 and 3 are giant-slayers. Good practice in assessment design can identify and eliminate aspects of an assessment that are not essential to the construct being assessed and which can create difficulties for defined groups. The definitions of the groups can provide a structure for subsequent differential functional analysis. These approaches lie at the heart of much thinking about fair assessment.

The giant-slaying approach to injustice has many attractions. The more precisely the giant is defined, the more practicable it is to develop policies to address the injustice and to measure the effect. Selective giant-slayers will not pretend that the giant they are pursuing is the only one around, but will concentrate on making a difference where they can and argue that they can make progress in the right direction. Educational assessments which follow the good practice described in Chapter 3 are surely better – and fairer – than those which do not.

However, there are problems with this approach, both in theory and in practice. First, it is not clear what the basis is for deciding which injustices to identify and target. There seems to be an element of arbitrariness in the content of the various statutory lists of protected characteristics, and concentrating on them leaves other unfairnesses unlisted. If the giant-slayers reply that they are opposed to 'all injustices', that prompts the question of what they mean by 'injustice', removes the distinction between them and pursuers of a more positive concept of justice, and reduces the practical usefulness of their approach.

Second, there may be problems in the categories of injustice identified for attack. Viewed from the perspective of the twenty-first century, some of the language used in the anti-discrimination discussions in the 1960s and 1970s seems out of date, although the underlying social issues remain highly relevant. Ethnicity is a difficult concept in countries such as the UK and the USA with large numbers of second- and third-generation immigrant families and widespread interracial marriage. In the UK population census ethnicity is self-assessed – in England, there are 18 categories[8] for the citizen to choose from – and the results are widely regarded as unreliable. Similarly, our thinking about categories of disability needs to accommodate the increasing complexity of our map of disability, including multiple disabilities, and our increasing understanding of psychological disability. We say more about these developments in the final chapter.

This may not be too serious a problem for the giant-slayers, who may regard these trends as signs of the success of slaying earlier giants and happily re-define their targets. However, whilst they are doing so, there is a danger that injustices are missed through not being covered by categories currently in use. Also, there may be problems in attributing individuals to target groups in order to measure any possible injustice. How, for example, can assessment researchers correctly classify the ethnicity of examination candidates for the purposes of DIF analysis if the census providers tell us that individuals cannot even categorise themselves reliably?

Perhaps the most important limitation of the giant-slaying approach is that the giants tend to hunt in packs: disadvantage and inequality present as an amalgam of factors – income, health, education, housing, crime, family structure, access to culture and recreation – which cluster together. Robert Putnam describes this 'clustering' vividly in his account of families in *Our Kids* (Putnam,

2015). Concentration on particular categories does not take account of the influences of all the other clustering factors and may divert attention from the more fundamental underlying issues of social attitudes and values.

What does this mean for educational assessment? As we have seen, good practice in identifying and eliminating bias is clearly beneficial. And some of the good practice described in Chapter 3, such as clarity in the phrasing of questions and readable font sizes for printed test questions, benefits all candidates, not just those with defined disadvantages. However, the judgements involved in attributing characteristics to candidates and selecting which characteristics to target, may themselves be open to charges of bias or unfairness. The more assessments are seen as 'situated' in a context, the more they raise wider underlying issues of justice (and injustice) that giant-slaying alone cannot tackle. And the clustering of disadvantage raises the question of how to analyse – and take account of – possible unfairness to candidates who are, say, of an ethnic minority, from an unstable family, inadequately housed and with health problems linked to poor diet. There is always a danger that if one giant is slain by careful scrutiny of the assessment to be used, the others will make their presence felt to reinforce the original disadvantage.

Positive views of social justice

In contrast to targeted attacks on injustice is an approach inspired by a positive view of justice. This appeal to a vision of the good may seem intuitively more attractive than the more limited, pragmatic, giant-slaying approach. Interestingly, in English the word 'idealistic' can be a term both of approval (for someone who is motivated by high ideals) and of disapproval (for someone who is unrealistic and impractical),[9] but those motivated to pursue or achieve justice may deserve the term of approval: they want to make the world a better place and their aspirations go beyond their own fortunes and those of their own family.

In Chapter 5, we discussed different theoretical concepts of justice and the link with other values, notably equality. Competing models of distributive justice have linked it to equality of resources (inputs) and equality of welfare (outcomes) (Dworkin, 1981a, b; Wolff, 2008), with some arguing that justice requires redistribution of resources from the advantaged to the disadvantaged to compensate for the latter's bad luck in life's lottery (Arneson, 1989).

How does this debate translate into practice? And what is the relevance to educational assessment? An initial problem is that the concept of 'distributive justice' does not sit easily with some models of education. Followers of Piaget or Dewey will resist the idea of teachers 'distributing' knowledge – or other educational goods – to their pupils. They may allow that questions of distributive justice can apply to the allocation of funding to schools and colleges, teaching expertise and time available to individuals and access to other resources (buildings, laboratories, books, etc.). But it is notoriously difficult to spell out in detail what educational practices are demanded by justice – or equality. Christopher Jencks asked this question at the level of the individual teacher in a classroom, with pupils of different abilities and with different needs, and concluded that the objective of treating children in the class equally was incoherent (Jencks, 1988).

Even if we understand what is meant by all students getting the same amount or quality of educational input – or all students obtaining the same educational outcomes – we have to define the level to which all should be brought. This raises the problem of 'levelling down' – reducing the opportunities and benefits to the more advantaged for the sake of equal levels for all. It has also been seen as conflicting with the freedom of those who value education more to spend more money on it and give their children greater support (Anderson, 1999; Satz, 2007; Anderson and White, 2019). Satz (2007) describes a 'deep tension' between equality and freedom: 'We cannot secure the equal development of children's potentials while permitting a world with diverse families, parents, parenting styles, geographical locations and values' (p. 634).

Opinions may vary about the moral weight that should be given to the freedom of rich parents to give their children an educational advantage, but most people would accept that there is a prima facie tension between equality and the extent to which individuals should be free to develop and pursue in their families their concept of the good, which may include a high value being placed on education.

As we saw in Chapter 5, it is particularly difficult to apply 'distributive' language to assessment, as it is not at all clear what (if anything) is being distributed. However, the products of assessments, such as qualifications, diplomas or degrees, can be a crucial gateway to prosperity and welfare. An approach to social justice based on equality of inputs will focus on giving all candidates equal quality and quantity of support in preparation for those assessments. An approach based on equality of welfare/outputs will arguably go further than that, and require some levelling out of the results of the assessments, particularly if they determine life chances. The crucial question is how far – if at all – it is right to move in that direction without vitiating the purpose of the assessment or destroying confidence in it by users of its outcomes or by the wider public.

A different approach to social justice sees it as applying to social relationships and how people value each other. Elizabeth Anderson posed the question 'What is the point of equality?', and concluded that the equality that matters is equality of moral worth, with all competent adults having equal moral worth and the power to develop and exercise moral responsibility (Anderson, 1999, p. 312). As we shall see, this idea led her to define an 'adequacy' standard for fairness in education. But, before we consider that position, we would observe that an approach to social justice based on equality of status has implications well beyond the distribution of goods. It affects how we think of each other and how we behave towards others. It also links with the value of *respect* – a term which has become increasingly popular in the twenty-first century, even if all its users may not mean the same by it.[10]

Jonathan Wolff has argued that value of respect can conflict with some approaches to equality, notably those which involve intrusive questioning of the disadvantaged if they are to qualify for redistribution of benefits from the advantaged (Wolff, 1998, 2010). He invents the term 'respect-standing' to denote 'the degree of respect that others have for me' (Wolff, 1998, p. 107), and regards any practices in the name of equality to be 'demeaning' if they ask the potential beneficiary to do anything that might reasonably be expected to lower their respect-standing. He sees this as an argument against social policies which require 'shameful revelation' by some and where, he suggests, those who have to reveal shameful things about themselves are treated as less than equal in moral status than those who require the revelation (Wolff, 1998, p. 109). Anderson similarly criticises approaches to equality which involve making 'intrusive, moralising judgements' about others (Anderson, 1999, p. 327).

What are we to make of this approach to social justice and what are the implications for educational assessment? One of the benefits of a 'social relationships' view of justice is that it gets us off the hook of founding social justice on a model of society based on competition for limited goods, with justice concerned with distinguishing winners from losers. In a society of mutual respect, it may be possible for all to benefit. However, one problem is that it is difficult to translate this approach into practice in real situations – how does the CEO of an examination board ensure that the assessments provided by their organisation show respect for all involved as moral agents? And how can the organisation check its assessments and activities against this requirement? Arguably, this might be done by qualitative research involving interview or feedback questionnaires completed by candidates, although some candidates emerging with relief from the exam room might be nonplussed if asked 'Were you treated with respect?'.

One lesson from this debate might concern the language and behaviour used to communicate the outcomes of assessments, including the language of failure. In the US legal case of *Debra P.*, discussed in Chapter 4, one judge commented that labelling a young person who failed the test as 'functionally illiterate' was demeaning and damaging.[11] Against that, some would argue that using euphemistic terms such as 'unclassified' instead of 'failed' is itself disrespectful, as it is not treating the candidate as able to take the truth. In our view, it is pertinent, when considering an assessment in its context, to ask: 'Are all those involved in this assessment treated with respect at every stage?' Even if it is not always easy to answer the question, asking it could point up any instances of disrespect, for example, in the practicalities of administering special arrangements for candidates with a disability.

In most countries, the rules governing accommodations for candidates with disabilities or special needs involve obtaining information about them which might be regarded as intrusive. For example, claims for extra time for a candidate with dyslexia might require a report from a psychologist. Is this a 'shameful revelation' in Wolff's sense? We think not, for two reasons. First, there is no sign that parents – or candidates – are put off by these requirements, as the numbers of applications for accommodations increase year by year in many countries,[12] with anecdotal accounts of particularly large increases in applications from schools serving high socio-economic groups. We are conscious of distressing accounts of deserving claimants being too ashamed to apply for means-tested welfare benefits, but it is not clear that these considerations always apply to assessment. Second, Wolff does not acknowledge that a request which may normally be embarrassing or disrespectful may be less so if it is made by someone in a social role, such as a doctor or a teacher. On balance, an assessment system allowing accommodations for those who need them is surely fairer than one without such accommodations, even though administering them requires asking personal questions.

Adequacy – a minimum standard for social justice in education?

The perception, which we have described, of a 'deep tension' between equality and freedom has been particularly challenging for writers in the USA, concerned not only with the freedom of families to pursue their values in their input to their children's education but also with the freedom of states to decide what priority (and funding) to give to education (Anderson, 1999, 2007; Satz, 2007; Anderson and White, 2019). Approaches based on equality have been seen as raising the problem of 'levelling down', which is not only a restriction on freedom but also denies society the benefits to all from the better education of some, who might improve the experience of others as consumers and citizens (Anderson and White , 2019, p. 13).

The response of Anderson and Satz to this challenge has been a shift from an equality-based standard for justice in education to an 'adequacy' standard. Adequacy of education is a floor, not a ceiling: all must be educated to the 'adequate' standard, but inequality beyond that – for example, through the expenditure and support of parents who value education highly, or through provision for very able students whose development may benefit society as a whole – is permitted. Brighouse and Swift (2009) described this as a 'tactical retreat from equality' (p. 117).

Anderson developed this position in the context of her account of 'democratic equality', in which all should be enabled to play a full part in a democratic state. She has used this argument to justify integrated education, wider access to elite colleges and a more diverse governing elite. We shall not consider those wider arguments here, but concentrate on the idea of 'adequacy' and its relevance to educational assessment.

What level of education is 'adequate'? How much is 'enough'? Anderson said that she was setting a high bar, which would require a lot of 'levelling up' for the least advantaged: 'What counts as adequate is ... enough to relate to others as an equal in society' (Anderson and White, 2019, p. 13). Satz argued that in the US system this required 'everyone with the potential [to have] the skills needed for college' (Satz, 2007, p. 638). What do we think of this approach and what are the implications for assessment?

The most obvious criticism is that the adequacy standard still leaves room for a great deal of inequality and advantage to the rich. It is not obvious, the critic would say, that a society meeting the adequacy standard would be socially just. In reply, Anderson could appeal to her wider manifesto for integrated education, less focused on traditional academic subjects, and suggest that, in that context, the adequacy standard would create a much more just society, whilst still allowing for freedom. In our view, this debate depends on the priority given to conflicting values in our conception of the good. Arguably, the priority given to freedom, and in particular to the freedom of states in a federal country, is particularly high in American culture and history. Others might give greater priority to equality at the cost of reining back on some of the freedoms of the rich to perpetuate their advantage through their children. Green and Kynaston (2019) discuss this dilemma in the context of the role of private education (through 'public schools') in England.

Turning to the implications for educational assessment, in our view the adequacy view of fair educational opportunity leaves some important questions unasked. First, how is the adequacy of students' education to be assessed? What is a fair assessment of college readiness or for a high school diploma, if these are the rights of all, in order to participate in a democratic state? What is a fair assessment of those who do not meet the standard? Satz (2007) argues that everyone 'with the potential' should be prepared for college. But what of those who do not have the potential? Should the assessment be such that everyone meets the standard? Or should there be no assessment against a standard of college readiness, but rather a record of the work that each student has done?

As Satz (2007) herself acknowledges, there is a danger that equality of certified college readiness (or a system of college entrance for all) transfers the problem to one of equality of preparation and ability to *complete* post-school education (p. 643). Drop-out rates from US colleges seem alarmingly high to observers from inside and outside the USA.[13]

Anderson argues that widening the scope of information about applicants for college, including the elite colleges, beyond traditional academic subjects would open up opportunities for a more diverse college population, with different strengths and cultures. However, we suggest that, for reasons discussed by Putnam and others (Putnam, 2015), the clustering of disadvantage means that children from richer households have better opportunities for sport, voluntary activity in the community, music and what the Singaporeans call 'co-curricular activities', and can therefore often provide richer evidence of wider activities than are available to poorer children. There may be good reasons for widening the range of evidence considered for college entry, but that on its own will not ensure diversity.

There are other possible developments of the 'adequacy' approach that might overcome some of these difficulties.[14] For example, the emphasis on education obtained at school (and assessed at the end of school) might be relaxed to an entitlement for some to take longer to achieve the 'adequate' standard, and receive support for as long as it takes. Also, the idea of the content of the 'adequate' standard might be modified to represent what each individual requires to participate as fully in society as he or she can in a way that reflects their desires and values. The latter, pluralistic, approach to 'adequacy' comes close to 'self-realisation' models of equality, but raises the danger of teachers making stereotyped low assumptions about what some students could aspire to.

For those designing systems for national or state examinations which affect students' life chances, one lesson from the 'adequacy' movement is that the system developed should give as many students as possible the opportunity to show what they know or can do and should gather information about students that is as rich as possible. But, if the standard required is demanding (the 'high bar' that Anderson claims), that leaves the question of how to certify the adequacy of the education of those who are not able to meet it. If the standard is lowered so that all can reach it, then there is a danger of postponing unfair inequality to the next stage – for example, to college completion (as opposed to college entry).

Meritocracy: the aristocracy of the talented

The term 'meritocracy' is younger than many of the terms considered in this book. It is now thought to have been first used – as a highly critical epithet – by the socialist writer Alan Fox in 1956:

> This way lies the 'meritocracy': the society in which the gifted, the smart, the energetic, the ambitious and the ruthless are carefully sifted out and helped towards their destined positions of dominance, where they proceed not only to enjoy the fulfilment of exercising their natural endowments but also to receive a fat bonus thrown in for good measure. (Fox, 1956, p. 13)

The most celebrated source, however, is Michael Young's *The Rise of the Meritocracy*, written two years later. It is a satirical dystopian fable, in which the person of the author pretends to celebrate the development in Britain of a society in which the ruling classes are the talented, identified and recertified through batteries of intelligence tests. This is increasingly resented by the rest of the population, culminating, on May Day 2034, in the 'Battle of Peterloo' in which the populists, led by the fed-up wives of the ruling classes, defeat the meritocrats and the author is killed.

As we saw in Chapter 5, the classic statement of meritocracy was that social status and reward should depend on 'merit', defined by the equation which was initially expressed as:

M = I + E (Merit = Intelligence + Effort)

In some later versions, 'intelligence' was replaced by 'ability' but the equation was coined in the heyday of IQ testing, and Young's fable described the increasing volume and accuracy of those tests (his narrator ironically described them as 'the very instrument of social justice'[15]). The comparative contribution to 'merit' of intelligence and effort is left tantalisingly unclear by Young.

In the 60 years since Young's story was written, the term 'meritocracy' has undergone a paradigm shift, described by Littler (2018): 'from a negative, disparaging criticism of an embryonic system of state organisation … using a controversial notion of "merit" in education, to a positive, celebratory, term, one connecting competitive individuality and "talent" with a belief in the desirability and possibility of social mobility' (p. 43). When Theresa May became Prime Minister of the UK, she announced: 'I want Britain to be the world's great meritocracy – a country where everyone has a fair chance to go as far as their talent and their hard work will allow.'[16] Selection and progression by 'merit' was favourably contrasted with past times in which social status and influence depended on birth or inherited wealth – in the words of Theresa May, 'who your parents are or what your accent sounds like'.

Successive social and political systems have adopted and adapted meritocracy for their own purposes. In founding the nation state of Singapore, not long after Young's book was written, Lee Kwan Yew embraced a state-administered version of meritocracy for unashamed utilitarian reasons – in such a small country, with no natural resources and dependent entirely on human capital, talent was precious and limited, so it was essential to identify and nurture those who had the ability to run the country (Lee, 1998, 2000, 2011). It is still commonplace in Singapore to hear meritocracy described as part of the country's DNA. In the UK, 'New Labour' under Tony Blair endorsed a social democratic version of meritocracy, combined with a blanket of social welfare provision for the less successful. More recently, neo-liberal thinking influencing administrations in the UK and the USA has redescribed meritocracy not as a state-administered system, but as the availability of doors open to all with 'aspiration' to achieve, if they have the talent and put in the effort (Allen, 2011).

Terms such as 'meritocracy' can be descriptive – describing how things are, or normative, denoting what they should be. In its descriptive sense, the claim that a society is meritocratic can be countered by citing evidence that success and social status are (still) aligned with inherited privilege – for example, exhibited through attendance at expensive private schools (Green and Kynaston, 2019) – or that social mobility is not increasing.

Normative conceptions of meritocracy can apply at two levels. First, 'meritocracy' can favourably denote the criteria that should be used for selecting the elite – by merit, rather than, say, wealth or family background. Second, use of the language of meritocracy can be understood to imply approval of the underlying system of 'winners and losers', with individuals competing with each other for personal advancement. Indeed, opponents of such a capitalist culture may claim that the term 'meritocracy' is (falsely) used to legitimise capitalism as fair and offering 'equality of opportunity' (Littler, 2018). We shall return to this criticism later.

Discussions of meritocracy tend to use one of two metaphors for the mechanisms by which 'winners' are distinguished from 'losers'. One is the metaphor of a ladder, which is supposed to be open to all to ascend, although doing so requires ability and effort. The second metaphor is that of a sieve, allowing some people through and stopping others. Writing in 2001, Young attributed the 'sieve' role to education: 'A social revolution has been accomplished by harnessing schools and universities to the task of sieving people according to education's narrow band of values' (Young, 2001, in a letter to *The Guardian* newspaper).

Arguments for and against meritocracy

What arguments can be used to justify 'meritocracy' in its normative sense (something to be aimed for)? As we have seen in the thinking of Singapore's founder, one argument appeals to *efficiency*. In his preface to the 1994 edition of his book, Michael Young referred (ironically, one assumes) to a '"Social Darwinist" concern to avoid a run-down of the precious "stock of ability" which is always and everywhere so limited' (Young, 1994, p. xiv). This argument raises questions of whether there really is such a finite pool of talent, and hearkens to the view, alluded to later by Young (2001), that the proportions in the distribution of IQ, modelled on Galton's bell curve, cannot be altered. Contemporary thinking has largely questioned that view (Bell, 1972; Allen, 2011) as well as questioning what IQ tests actually measure. We cannot do justice to these arguments here. However, even if one rejects mid-twentieth-century thinking about intelligence testing, there does seem to be a plausible utilitarian argument that it benefits society if the people running it have the relevant knowledge and skills. Some of the first generation of working-class products of English (selective) grammar schools in the period after the Second World War arguably made good leaders (Hennessy, 2015).

Other justifications are moral, based on *fairness*: whatever its shortcomings, one argument goes, a system of selection for advancement based on merit is surely fairer than the alternatives – advancement based on birth, wealth or what the ancient Chinese called 'guanshi' (loosely translated as 'connections'). There must be some strength in this argument. However, the counterargument is that, in practice, the upper classes have a better chance of developing and displaying 'merit', whether it is measured in academic exams or in broader assessments of character and 'extra-curricular activities'. Access to the superb facilities of some of the leading English public (i.e. private) schools or the ability to pay for private tuition and tennis coaching in Singapore gives youngsters from wealthy families a clear advantage (Lim, 2013; Green and Kynaston, 2019).

Another moral justification is based on a conception of fairness linked to 'equality of opportunity': meritocracy, it is argued, means, in Theresa May's words, that all have 'a fair chance to go as far as their talent and their hard work will allow'.[17] Counterarguments to this justification have broadly taken two forms: the first is to question the importance of 'equality of opportunity', preferring equality at the finishing line – 'equality of result' (see, for example, Bell, 1972). The moral argument between these two approaches is not normally determined by considerations of fairness: for example, supporters of ethnic quotas in selection for college could accept that there was an element of unfairness in selecting students on the basis of race – a criterion that would fall foul of anti-discrimination law if it were a basis for rejection – but they could argue that equality of result had more moral importance than fairness.

The other counterargument, which we consider particularly strong, is the insight shown by Rawls when distinguishing between the weaker and stronger versions of his principle of equality of opportunity. As we have seen in Chapter 5, he argued that the weak version – 'careers open to talents' (selection by merit) – was not enough for a fair society:

> This [meritocratic] form of social order follows the principle of careers open to talents and uses equality of opportunity as a way of releasing man's energies in the pursuit of economic prosperity and political dominion. [But] there exists a marked disparity between the upper and lower classes in both means of life and the rights and privileges of organizational authority. (Rawls, 1971, p. 106)

Or as Littler (2018: 5) put it, 'climbing the ladder is simply much harder for some people than for others'.

These justifications of meritocracy, then, are not altogether persuasive. Let us turn to some criticisms of meritocracy as a desirable goal.

One moral criticism of meritocracy is the undesirable effect on the attitudes of 'winners' and 'losers', with the former becoming arrogant and self-righteous and the latter demoralised and resentful, 'internalising' their failure. Young (2001) suggested that those who believed that they deserved their success could be 'insufferably smug' and more arrogant than the old-fashioned aristocrats who knew that their social position was an accident of birth. And the 'losers' will resent and envy the power of the talented over them, to an extent that, paradoxically, is all the more powerful because of the apparent fairness of the inequality from which they are suffering. This is what continental philosophers[18] have labelled, using the French word *ressentiment*, hostility directed at the cause of one's disadvantage.

It is difficult to assess this criticism: if it is intended as a factual description of the attitudes of real people, then one would need to test it against some kind of representative survey of attitudes, which would not be easy to do. Perhaps it is more credible as a kind of parable, illustrating in an extreme picture the possible effects on human feelings of inequality resulting from human action rather than chance or history. And the apocalyptic conclusion of Young's book – the revolt of the populists – may strike a chord with some twenty-first-century politics in Western Europe[19] and the USA. As Daniel Bell wrote back in 1972: 'Contemporary populism ... is not for fairness but against elitism; its impulse is not justice but *ressentiment*. What the populists resent is not power ... but authority – the authority represented in the superior competence of individuals' (p. 65).

Another moral criticism of meritocracy is that it is *unfair*. Despite understandable moves in the late twentieth century away from eugenic accounts of intelligence, most people would accept that genetic inheritance has at least some effect on ability or on performance in assessments of knowledge and skill. In so far as that is so, advantage based on intelligence seems as unfair as advantage based on birth or social class. In Young's words, 'Being a member of the "lucky sperm club" confers no moral right to advantage. What one is born with, or without, is not of one's own doing' (Young, 1994, p. xvi). If, as we have argued, there is a conceptual link between fairness and desert, then advantage based on inherited ability is – at least in one sense – unfair.

A further moral criticism of meritocracy is that it is *dishonest*, disguising – or legitimising – unfairness and inequality through the appearance of, and language of, fairness and equality of opportunity. If one could show that champions of meritocracy – politicians, for example – knowingly seek to disguise regressive and unequal policies, then the charge of dishonesty would stand. But, in the absence of evidence for such a damning verdict, a more appropriate version of the criticism might be that the language of meritocracy can be misleading and draw attention away from persisting inequality. A practical objection to meritocracy is that it does not extend to second or third generations, as 'winners' pass on their advantages to their children (Bell, 1972; Littler, 2018). The English working-class youngster who becomes a famous footballer sends his children to elite schools and colleges; in Singapore, a disproportionate number of holders of the prestigious Public Service Commission Scholarships come from families with an income of over S$10,000 (US$7,300) a month (Lim and Kwek, 2006). In the words of one honest writer in the UK's *Financial Times*: 'I can think of no better use of my money than maximising my children's prospects. But I cannot pretend it is fair.'[20]

The last of this list of criticisms of meritocracy is particularly favoured by left-wing writers. It is that the selection mechanisms of meritocracy are culturally biased, implicitly valuing the cultural values of the professions and the upper/middle classes (Littler, 2018). This criticism may be voiced whether selection is made on the basis of tests of academic knowledge and skills, interviews or wider assessments of character. In response, it may be argued that it can be right for criteria for advancement, say, in the professions to reinforce the professional values of those professions. For example, those selecting future doctors in the UK explicitly refer to the professional regulator's published account of 'Good Medical Practice'.[21] However, it must be recognised that selectors and examiners probably do not realise the extent to which they value candidates who mirror their own values and behaviours.

Where does educational assessment fit in?

Where the metaphor of sieves is used to describe the infrastructure of meritocracy, it is clear that the sieves are seen as wielded by a selective education system and by the professions:

> With an amazing battery of certificates and degrees at its disposal, education has put its seal of approval on a minority, and its seal of disapproval on the many who fail to shine from the time they are relegated to the bottom streams at the age of seven or before. (Young, 2001, in a letter to *The Guardian* newspaper)

Some see the academic focus of assessments which determine progression (for example, high school diplomas in the USA and A levels in England) as an instrument of inequality (Anderson, 2007). In his book, Michael Young (1994) tantalisingly mentioned, but did not develop, a possible alternative to the meritocratic society – the 'Chelsea Manifesto'. It included the following:

> Were we to evaluate people, not only according to their intelligence and their education, their occupation and their power, but according to their kindness and their courage, their imagination and sensitivity, their sympathy and generosity, there could be no classes. (Young, 1994, p. xvii)

In response, we would cite a striking example, part of a system explicitly avowing meritocracy, which does precisely what the Chelsea Manifesto suggested. It is the extraordinarily elaborate assessment system used in Singapore to select candidates for the Public Service Commission Scholarships, which lead to top posts in government and elsewhere. The following description, by Singaporean writers in 2011, is well worth reproducing in full:

> The scrutiny begins at junior college [age 14–18], when principals and tutors observe and prepare reports on top-performing students. These are sent to the Public Service Commission (PSC) even before the 'A' level results are announced. These reports measure on a 12-point scale a range of personality traits: integrity, emotional maturity, leadership, interpersonal skills, creativity and helpfulness. The principals also rank the students. A tutor writes an evaluation, taking into account his co-curricular activities (CCAs), behaviour and weaknesses. Another report contains his achievements in CCAs and community work.
>
> The applicant then sits for a battery of multiple-choice tests that measure his ability to reason verbally, mathematically and spatially. He has to write an essay on his core beliefs and values ... He also has to take a personality test comprising nearly 2000 multiple choice questions which map his warmth, emotional stability, sensitivity, perfectionism and dominance, among other traits. A second test requires him to reflect on a stressful episode in his life. Next is an interview with a PSC psychologist on his goals, family relationships and attitudes. The psychologist submits a lengthy report, citing even observations such as eye contact. Male applicants also get a report on their national service performance.
>
> By the time an applicant appears before the PSC panel that awards the scholarships, a thick dossier on him would have been compiled. But still the questions keep coming during this final interview. The assessment continues after the scholarship winners graduate and return to serve in government. (Lee, 2011, p. 132)

Leaving aside the technical challenges of drawing valid assessment conclusions from such a diverse and voluminous collection of data, it is notable that, despite their apparently humane scope, beyond traditional academic subjects, such assessments have not proven to be an instrument of equality, contrary to the scenario alluded to in Young's Chelsea Manifesto. As Lim has observed, rich families in Singapore can afford tutors, coaches and opportunities for 'co-curricular activities' which are not open to poor families (Lim, 2013). And some of the young Singaporeans featured in these assessments will have been in the top 1% of 9-year-olds selected through the Gifted Education Programme and given additional support 'to develop intellectual rigour, humane values and creativity, to prepare them for responsible leadership and service to culture and society' (Ministry of Education Singapore, 2011). Perhaps it is not surprising that candidates with such advantages do well in the battery of assessments leading to the much-coveted scholarship.

Are meritocratic assessments fair?

It is clear that educational assessments can be essential instruments of meritocracy. We have examined the arguments for and against meritocracy and we conclude that, on balance, the criticisms outweigh the attempted justifications. Educational assessment used as a 'sieve' for meritocracy must heed Rawls's insight in distinguishing between a weak version of equality of opportunity ('careers open to talents') and a stronger version requiring a social context which makes it possible for all, including the most disadvantaged, to have a genuine opportunity to be considered. The description above of differential access to coaches and tutors in Singapore would not meet the strong version of Rawls's principle.

Tests and exams which are valid, minimise construct-irrelevant bias and are used in a meritocratic society, may be 'fair' in several of the senses which we have identified earlier in this book. They may treat like cases alike and meet the legitimate expectations of candidates. In those senses, fair assessments are better than unfair assessments. However, if assessments are considered as 'situated' in the context in which they are used – in this instance, as part of the infrastructure of a meritocratic society – they will not satisfy Rawls's stronger principle of equality of opportunity.

If the core concepts in fairness are equality and desert (as we have argued in Chapter 5), assessments considered as instruments of a meritocratic society have a lot to answer for.

Conclusion

In this chapter, we have considered the implications for educational assessment of different approaches to social justice in practice: the view that some kinds of assessment are inherently fairer than others, an approach based on eliminating injustice (slaying the giants), a range of positive accounts of justice, the 'adequacy' movement in the USA and, lastly, the chequered history of 'meritocracy'. Assessment can learn from all of them, though there are problems with them all, and on balance we side with the critics of meritocracy rather than with its champions.

When the lenses of social justice are applied to assessment, there is a fundamental choice to be made – how far should we go in the direction of equality beyond trimming away the individual unfairnesses that can be identified? In the words of Thomas Nagel:

> The main issue is whether we should regard certain human inequalities and their consequences as natural, and only be concerned not to impose further artificial ones, or whether we should base social policy on the assumption that all persons

are equally deserving of a good life, and that their society should try to make it possible for them to have it. This latter goal of positive equality will not be realised through mere equality of opportunity, since equal opportunity combined with unequal ability and luck produce very unequal results. (2005, p. 267)

For further reflection

Weighting assessment by postcode

Social research shows clearly that families who live in a particular inner-city area, with the postcode AB10, have multiple disadvantage. AB10 is known to have concentrations of poverty, poor housing, family breakdown, crime and poor health. Inspired by Rawls's second principle in its strong form ('that those with similar abilities and skills should have similar life chances'), the state authorities decide that in the public examination taken by 16-year-olds, there should be lower grade boundaries for candidates with the postcode AB10, to give them a better chance to succeed in life and to compensate for the disadvantages they have suffered. Parents of students in neighbouring districts complain that this is unfair. Are they right?

Compulsory mathematics for all?[22]

National politicians are concerned by the low aptitude in mathematics shown by many of the country's young people. They judge that quantitative skills are important for the modern economy, and are keen that all should have the opportunity to develop such skills. They therefore decide that students who do not achieve a satisfactory grade in mathematics at the age of 16 should be required to continue to study mathematics and retake the examination until they achieve a 'pass' grade, as a condition for progressing further in their education. But the outcomes for most students who resit the exam are poor, teachers find the students unmotivated and many students fail to attend class. Critics of the scheme argue that it is unfair to make students try to develop capacities for which they have little talent or liking, when they could be doing other things that would be more useful and rewarding. Are the critics right? Is it fair to require all students to retake the assessment if they fail to achieve a pass grade? Or is it unfair to allow students to abandon mathematics at a young age and thus reduce their job opportunities later? What would a fair assessment regime look like in this situation?

Donor preference schemes in admission to Ivy League universities

American Ivy League universities offer explicit donor preference schemes where those who make a big donation to the university can increase the chances of their son or daughter getting a place. Lawrence Summers, former president of Harvard, said: 'It is not realistic to expect that schools and universities dependent on charitable contributions will not be attentive to the offspring of their supporters.'[23] The English politician and writer David Willetts (2017) commented: 'It would not be acceptable to say that in England.'[24] Are such 'donor preference schemes' fair?

Notes

1. Cited by Young (1994: 33), referring to Richmond, W. K., *Education in the United States*, 1956.
2. Letter to *The Guardian* newspaper, Friday, 29 June 2001.
3. We are grateful to Lesley Wiseman for this point.
4. For a comprehensive account and discussion of this, see Stein (2017).
5. See www.theguardian.com/education/2016/sep/12/tutor-11plus-test-grammar-schools-disadvantaged-pupils.
6. The impact of private tutoring on the fairness of education (and assessment) is a world-wide issue, well-described in the writings of Mark Bray (Bray, 2003; Bray et al., 2013).
7. *Social Insurance and Allied Services* (Cmd. 6404), November 1942.
8. For a discussion of the categories used for census purposes in the UK, see www.ons.gov.uk/methodology/classificationsandstandards/measuringequality/ethnicgroupnationalidentityandreligion (accessed November 2019).
9. The same can be said of 'ideology', which can be used negatively to connote a dogma without an evidence base (Williams, 1976/1983).
10. We owe this observation to Mary Richardson.
11. 474 F. Supp. 244 (M.D. Fla. 1979), section III.C.
12. In England, Ofqual produces an annual statistical release on the uptake of access arrangements, compared with the previous year. Its report on the academic year 2017–18 can be found at https://assets.publishing.service.gov.uk/government/uploads/system/uploads/attachment_data/file/770570/Access_Arrangements_for_GCSE__AS_and_A_level_2017_to_2018_academic_year.pdf.
13. See, for example, J. J. Selingo, 'Why do so many students drop out of college? And what can be done about it?', *Washington Post*, 8 June 2018.
14. This paragraph draws on comments to the authors by Lesley Wiseman.
15. Young (1994: 84).
16. Accessed at: www.gov.uk/government/speeches/britain-the-great-meritocracy-prime-ministers-speech.

17. Ibid
18. Nietzsche, Kierkegaard and some existentialists.
19. Including the UK, where political discourse in 2016, in the context of the referendum on EU membership, included resentment of – and hostility towards – 'experts'.
20. R. Shrimsley, 'A frightfully British purge of the posh', *Financial Times*, 4 June 2016.
21. See www.gmc-uk.org/ethical-guidance/ethical-guidance-for-doctors/good-medical-practice.
22. This case is based on an educational policy debate in England: see 'Labour: We'll end compulsory GCSE maths and English resits', *The Guardian*, 20 November 2018; and Vidal Rodeiro, 'Which students benefit from retaking Mathematics and English GCSEs post-16?', *Research Matters*, Cambridge Assessment, Issue 25, Spring 2018.
23. Quoted in 'How the land of opportunity can combat inequality', *Financial Times*, 16 July 2012.
24. Willetts (2017: 172–173).

References

Allen, A. (2011) Michael Young's *The Rise of the Meritocracy*: A philosophical critique. *British Journal of Educational Studies*, 59(4), 367–382.

Anderson, E. (1999) What is the point of equality? *Ethics*, 109(2), 287–337.

Anderson, E. (2007) Fair opportunity in education: A democratic equality perspective. *Ethics*, 117(4), 595–622.

Anderson, E. and White, J. (2019) Elizabeth Anderson interviewed by John White. *Journal of Philosophy of Education*, 53(1), 5–20.

Arneson, R. (1989) Equality and equal opportunity for welfare. *Philosophical Studies*, 56(1) (May), 77–93.

Bell, D. (1972) On meritocracy and equality. *The Public Interest*, 29, 29–68.

Bray, M. (2003) Demand for private supplementary tutoring: Conceptual consideration, and socio-economic patterns in Hong Kong. *Economics of Education Review*, 22(6), 611–620.

Bray, M., Mazawi, A. E. and Sultanan, R. G. (Eds.) (2013) *Private Tutoring across the Mediterranean: Power dynamics and implications for learning and equity*. Rotterdam: Sense Publishers.

Brighouse, H. and Swift, A. (2009) Educational equality versus educational adequacy: A critique of Anderson and Satz. *Journal of Applied Philosophy*, 26(2) (May), 117–128.

Conley, D. T. (2012) College and career readiness: Same or different? *Educational Leadership*, 69(7), 29–34.

Conley, D. T., Drummond, K. V., de Gonzalez, A., Rooseboom, J. and Stout, O. (2011) *Reaching the Goal: The applicability and importance of the Common Core state standards to college and career readiness*. Portland, OR: Educational Policy Improvement Center.

Dworkin, R. (1981a) What is equality? Part 1: Equality of welfare. *Philosophy and Public Affairs*, 10(3), 185–246.

Dworkin, R. (1981b) What is equality? Part 2: Equality of resources. *Philosophy and Public Affairs*, 10(4), 283–345.

Fox, A. (1956) Class and equality. *Socialist Commentary*, May, pp. 11–13.

Green, F. G. and Kynaston, D. (2019) *Engines of Privilege: Britain's private school problem*. London: Bloomsbury Publishing.

Hennessy, P. (2015) *Establishment and Meritocracy*. Haus Curiosities series. Chicago: University of Chicago Press.

Honderich, T. (Ed.) (2005) *The Oxford Companion to Philosophy* (2nd edn). Oxford: Oxford University Press.

Jencks, C. (1988) Whom must we treat equally for educational opportunity to be equal? *Ethics*, 98(3), 518–533.

King, M. L. Jr. (1963) *'I Have a Dream' Speech*. Lincoln Memorial, Washington, DC, 28 August.

Lee, K. Y. (1998) *The Singapore Story*. Singapore: Michael Cavendish Editions.

Lee, K. Y. (2000) *From Third World to First: Singapore and the Asian economic boom*. New York: HarperCollins.

Lee, K. Y. (2011) *Hard Truths to Keep Singapore Going*. Singapore: Straits Times Press.

Lim, L. (2013) Meritocracy, elitism, and egalitarianism: A preliminary and provisional assessment of Singapore's primary education review. *Asia Pacific Journal of Education*, 33(1), 1–14.

Lim, L. and Kwek, K. (2006) Why the elite envy. *The Straits Times*, 20 June, p. 10.

Littler, J. (2018) *Against Meritocracy: Culture, power and myths of mobility*. London and New York: Routledge/Taylor & Francis Group.

McDaniel, M. A., Kepes, S. and Banks, G. C. (2011) The Uniform Guidelines are a detriment to the field of personnel selection. *Industrial and Organizational Psychology*, 4(4), 494–514.

Ministry of Education Singapore (2011) *Gifted Education Programme: Rationale and goals*. Available at: www.moe.gov.sg/education/programmes/gifted-education-programme/rationale-and-goals (accessed 01/07/19).

Nagel, T. (2005) Entry on equality. In T. Honderich (Ed.), *The Oxford Companion to Philosophy* (2nd edn). Oxford: Oxford University Press. pp. 266–267.

Putnam, R. D. (2015) *Our Kids: The American dream in crisis*. New York: Simon & Schuster.

Rampell, C. (2009) SAT scores and family income. *Economix: Explaining the Science of Everyday Life*. Available at: https://economix.blogs.nytimes.com/2009/08/27/sat-scores-and-family-income (accessed 27/08/09).

Rawls, J. (1971) *A Theory of Justice*. Oxford: Oxford University Press.

Richmond, W. K. (1956) *Education in the USA: A comparative study*. Baltimore, MD: Enoch Pratt Free Library.

Satz, D. (2007) Equality, adequacy and education for citizenship. *Ethics*, 117(4), 623–648.

Selingo, J. J. (2018) Why do so many students drop out of college? And what can be done about it? *Washington Post*, 8 June.

Sen, A. (1980) Equality of what? In S. M. McMurrin (Ed.), *The Tanner Lectures on Human Values*. Cambridge: Cambridge University Press. pp. 195–220.

Shrimsley, R. (2016) A frightfully British purge of the posh. *Financial Times*, 4 June.

Stein, Z. (2017) *Social Justice and Educational Measurement: John Rawls, the history of testing, and the future of education*. New Directions in the Philosophy of Education Series. London: Routledge.

Thernstrom, S. and Thernstrom, A. M. (2004) *No Excuses: Closing the racial gap in learning*. New York: Simon & Schuster.

Vidal Rodeiro, C. (2018) Which students benefit from retaking Mathematics and English GCSEs post-16? *Research Matters*, Cambridge Assessment, Issue 25, Spring.

Willetts, D. (2017) *A University Education*. Oxford: Oxford University Press.

Williams, R. (1976/1983) *Keywords: A vocabulary of culture and society*. London: Fontana (revised 1983).

Wolff, J. (1998) Fairness, respect and the egalitarian ethos. *Philosophy & Public Affairs*, 27(2) (Spring), 97–122.

Wolff, J. (2008) Social justice and public policy: A view from political philosophy. In G. Craig, T. Burchardt and D. Gordon (Eds.), *Social Justice and Public Policy: Seeking fairness in diverse societies*. Bristol: Policy Press.

Wolff, J. (2010) Fairness, respect and the egalitarian 'ethos' revisited. *The Journal of Ethics*, 14(3–4), 335–350.

Young, M. (1958/1994/2017) *The Rise of the Meritocracy* (first published by Thames and Hudson, 1958; published with new introduction by Transaction Publishers, 1994; published by Abingdon, Oxon/New York: Routledge, 2017).

Young, M. (2001) Letter: Down with meritocracy (The man who coined the word four decades ago wishes Tony Blair would stop using it). *The Guardian*, 29 June.

Zwick, R. (2006) Higher education admissions testing. In R. L. Brennan (Ed.), *Educational Measurement* (4th edn). Westport, CT: American Council on Education/Praeger. pp. 647–679.

7
Conclusions, challenges and a template for fairness

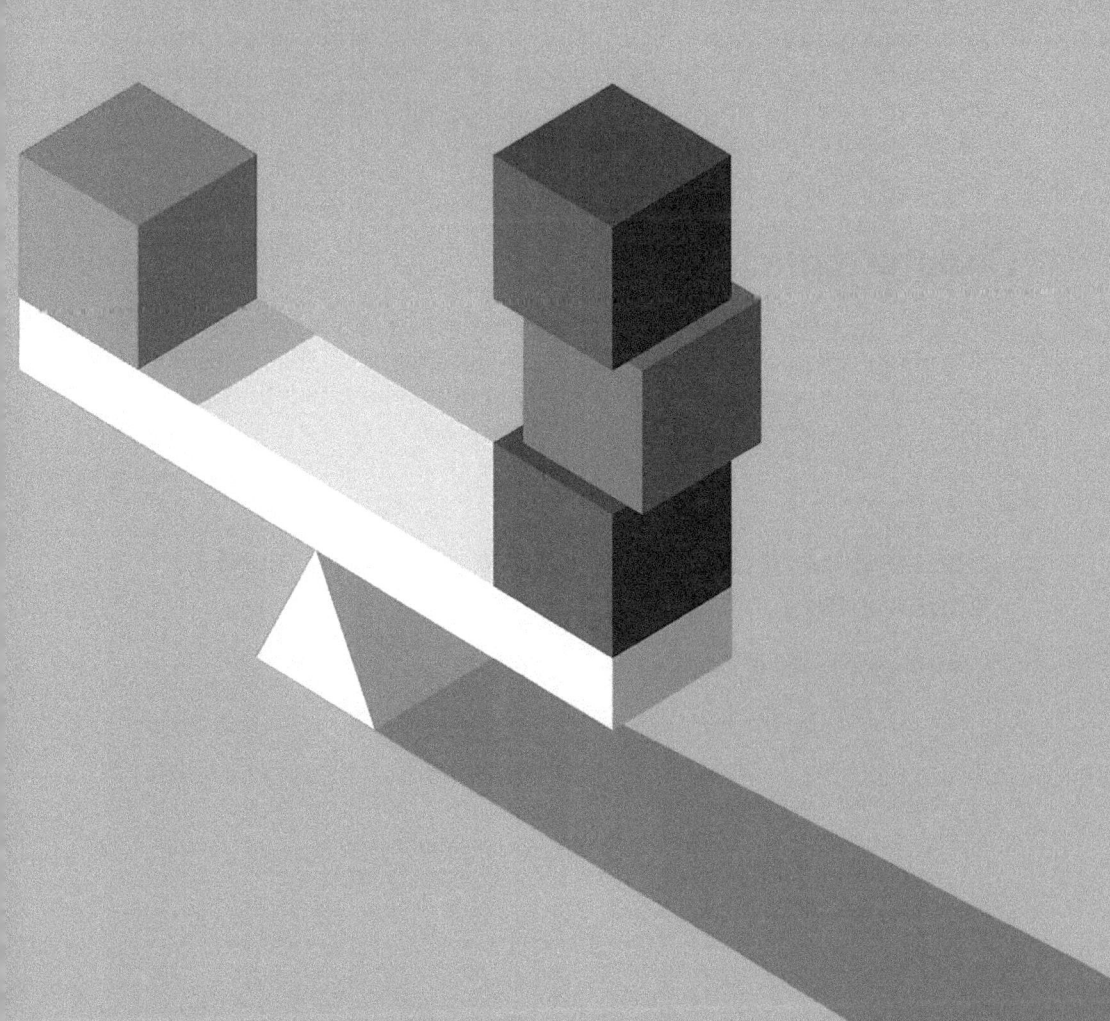

'It is philosophically naïve to assume that fair judgements can only be made if every candidate's script is judged by precisely the same set of criteria ... It is psychologically naïve to assume ... that performance is not profoundly affected by the context of the task being carried out.' (Cresswell, 2000, pp. 16–17)

Introduction

In this book, we have looked at fairness in educational assessment through different 'lenses', which influence what was seen and how it is perceived and described. The lenses apply insights and approaches from different intellectual and cultural traditions, but we saw how they have influenced each other – concepts from the courts have become enshrined in guidance for assessment professionals, and in their turn the courts have looked to assessment theorists and practitioners for authoritative professional views. And philosophy both draws from and influences real-life discourse and discussion. In this concluding chapter, we recall the main conclusions from the application of each lens, and set out some of our overarching conclusions from the whole exercise. Looking forward, we also explore some of the ethical, theoretical and practical challenges for fair assessment in the twenty-first century.

Chapter conclusions

In Chapter 1, we defined our terms and distinguished a number of senses of 'fair' (and 'unfair') which are commonly applied to assessment – often without being clear which sense is being used. We returned to this classification throughout the book and it is summarised here for ease of reference.

Six senses of 'fair' and 'unfair', when applied to assessment

The four main senses of 'fair' are as follows:

1. A *formal* sense, denoting accuracy or appropriate application of a rule or design.
2. An *implied contractual* sense, in which something is fair if it meets the *legitimate expectations* of those affected.
3. A *relational* sense – treating (relevantly) like cases alike. This is reflected in a requirement of comparability between marks/grades awarded to candidates,

> and also in the concept of impartiality, which implies disregarding irrelevant considerations, and can be applied to judgements about one person/instance, with no others immediately concerned.
>
> 4. A *retributive* sense, in which an outcome is regarded as fair if it is an appropriate reward (or penalty) for what has gone before.
>
> We also distinguished two senses which were used mainly in discussions of *un*fairness:
>
> 5. *Consequential* – in this sense, an assessment might be judged as unfair if its outcomes might be used as a basis for unfair actions in the future.
>
> 6. *Retrospective* – in this sense, an assessment might be judged as unfair if its outcomes were the consequence of unfair/socially unjust actions in the past.

Much that is written about fair assessment assumes that the only sense that matters is relational fairness – treating (relevantly) like cases alike. However, we concluded that others, such as the 'implied contractual' sense (in which a fair assessment meets legitimate expectations and an unfair one does not), can also be important. The later chapters invoke most of the senses listed above, and are not confined to relational fairness.

The question 'Fairness to whom?' is often neglected: there is an assumption that fairness only applies to candidates ('test-takers'), but we argued that fairness to others (such as users of the test outcomes) may also be relevant. Fairness can apply to individuals as well as groups, and in the world of educational assessment it can apply to assessments used for formative as well as summative purposes. Fairness is not confined to assessments that are typically classified as 'high stakes'.

Chapter 2 applied the lens(es) of measurement theory to assessment fairness. Fairness has increasingly come to share centre stage with validity and reliability in the literature. We described an emerging consensus view of fairness defined as an absence of *un*fairness, with unfairness shown by construct-irrelevant variance in assessment outcomes, which can be identified, in arrears, by 'differential functional analysis'. The relationship of fairness (so understood) to validity is difficult to describe, as it depends to some extent on how validity is construed, but we concluded that fairness, as typically portrayed by measurement theorists, was a necessary but not sufficient condition for validity.

We concluded that the measurement theoreticians' consensual view of fairness was informative but incomplete. It focuses almost entirely on relational fairness, and in particular does not do justice to the 'legitimate expectations' sense. It is wrongly confined to groups rather than covering fairness to individuals.

We considered fair assessment for candidates with a disability (itself a sensitive term) and the problem of evaluating the fairness of modifications which affect the construct being measured. We also considered fairness in the contexts of classroom assessment and assessment in higher education and concluded that more work needs to be done on fairness – and on validity and reliability – in both contexts.

In Chapter 3, we moved from theory to practice and considered a hierarchy of sources of guidance on fair assessment practice, ranging from the requirements of the law to authoritative professional guidance by national and international organisations and local guidance, such as handbooks used by organisations which provide tests. These sources are often invaluable to practitioners, as they convey advice based on years of practical experience. And much of this advice – for example, on how to use clear language in assessment tasks and provide legible diagrams – can benefit all candidates, not just sub-groups with particular difficulties. We asked for more work to be done on the practicalities of fair assessment in the classroom and the workplace, and we commented that following a set process does not guarantee fairness or a just outcome.

Chapter 4 looked at assessment fairness through legal lenses. We considered different kinds of legal challenge to assessment fairness in a range of contexts: testing requirements for graduation from high school (USA); testing accommodations for candidates with disabilities or special needs (Australia); the fairness (or unfairness) of annotating a candidate's certificate to show that they were exempt from part of the assessment because of their disability (Ireland); the setting of grade boundaries and cut scores in a national exam (UK); and selection for employment. The bar for successful legal challenge is generally very high.

The US case of *Debra P. v. Turlington*[1] brought to prominence the idea of 'instructional validity'. A test is valid in this sense if the candidates have actually been taught the material being assessed. It is not sufficient to argue that they ought to have been taught the construct in question – in the case of *Debra P.*, basic numeracy and reasoning skills. We pick up some of the thinking behind this concept later in this chapter, but in Chapter 4 we observed that it is difficult to apply the principle to the assessment of highly generic skills which underlie much teaching and learning, and where it is not possible to determine precisely when and where they were taught. We also noted that access to justice can be limited unfairly and denied to those lacking resources, influential contacts or the support of a pressure group. Our general conclusion was that the impact of the legal challenges that we described on fair assessment in practice had been beneficial, but keeping free from successful legal challenge is not sufficient for fairness.

In Chapter 5, we looked at assessment fairness through the lenses of moral and political philosophy, distinguishing two types of approach: conceptual analysis and theoretical modelling. Conceptual analysis looks for patterns, links and distinctions behind our use of language. We traced many uses of 'fair' to underlying concepts of equality and desert. However, in considering what kind of equality is relevant to fairness, we identified a major problem which had also reared its head in Chapters 2 and 4, and which we labelled 'the counterfactual hypothesis'. We talk of fair assessment as bringing people, including those with disabilities or special needs, up to the same point so that they can be fairly compared. But we had to conclude that this talk is problematic – how do we identify a level which a candidate might have achieved in different circumstances (which, by definition, were not present)? We return to this difficult question later in this chapter.

There is a choice to be made between seeing the root concept in assessment fairness as *un*fairness and trying to define or describe the linked ideas behind the positive concept of fairness. The negative approach (starting with unfairness) has attractions, not least as it supports manageable courses of action to make things better, by identifying sources of unfairness and then eliminating them. However, on balance we preferred a more positive view of fairness, linked to the idea of a 'match' between what is done and what is merited or appropriate. Although there is an element of anachronism in labelling Aristotle with the twentieth-century term 'conceptual analyst', we described his accounts of justice and fairness, and commended his depiction of fairness as a kind of proportional equality matching what is merited.

Moving on to theoretical modelling, we described the account of 'justice as fairness' by the twentieth-century American philosopher John Rawls. Rawls is best known for informing his model of a just society by a parable advocating the choices of people in the 'original position' who are unaware of their background or material advantages. However, we focused on his separate (and, he argued, superior) principle of 'equality of opportunity'. Rawls insightfully commented that the principle of 'fair equality of opportunity' went beyond the more restricted principle of 'careers open to talents'. 'Careers open to talents' meant simply that selection for positions should be by reference to the applicant's suitability for the job, and not influenced by irrelevant considerations such as race or gender. However, the principle of fair equality of opportunity saw the selection event in a broader context and required that 'those with similar abilities and skills should have similar life chances' (Rawls, 1971, p. 73). Rawls's insight in making this distinction has influenced our account of a 'situated' view of assessment, which we shall develop further in this chapter.

In Chapter 6, we moved from theory to views of social justice in practice and considered their relevance to fair educational assessment. We started with movements to minimise or eliminate identified categories of *un*fairness ('slaying the giants') which we concluded can be helpful as far as they go, but do not address unfairness with multiple sources. When one source of unfairness is identified and tackled, another tends to pop up in its place. We proceeded to consider

Elizabeth Anderson's influential account of 'adequacy' as a level for fair educational opportunity. This raises questions of how 'adequacy' is assessed and what is meant by fair assessment of those who fail to meet the adequacy standard.

Chapter 6 proceeded to discuss the much-celebrated – and much-criticised – concept of 'meritocracy', largely stemming from Michael Young's mid-twentieth-century dystopian fable *The Rise of the Meritocracy* (Young, 1958). In some quarters, the term 'meritocracy' has been transformed from the intended satirical horror story to an ideal, with educational assessment seen as a key 'sieve' used to determine who has the 'merit' to advance. We considered arguments for and against meritocracy and the implications for educational assessment. On balance, we sided with the critics of meritocracy and observed that it fails to meet the challenge of Rawls's strong version of fair equality of opportunity, which requires a social context making it possible for all, including the most disadvantaged, to have a genuine opportunity to be considered.

When standards of social justice are applied to fairness in assessment, we are left with an underlying dilemma, which we express but do not answer at the end of Chapter 6: how far should we go in trying to eliminate or take account of differences of ability and luck which apply to all societies and generations? And should fair assessment accurately reflect these differences or be modified to take account of them?

General conclusions

Our exploration of fair assessment, as perceived through these different lenses, was done in the hope that it could support more generalisable conclusions, perhaps drawing on insights from more than one tradition. We set out here some of our conclusions from this work:

Relational fairness is not the only kind of fairness that matters. From the outset, we have sought to distinguish a range of senses in which the concept of 'fairness' is applied to educational assessment. They include, but are not restricted to, the relational sense (treating like cases alike). The measurement theorists examined in Chapter 2 appeared to assume that fairness meant relational fairness between (groups of) test-takers. There are contexts in which treating candidates comparably is very important, and any signs of bias in marking, or of 'unfair' (sic) discrimination, rightly prompt accusations of unfairness. Hence, the theoretical and methodological insights described in Chapter 2 (including the use of differential functioning analysis to detect construct-irrelevant bias against identified groups) and Chapter 3 (including the 'universal design' of test items) are welcome and useful as far as they go, but they are by no means the whole story for fairness in assessment.

Underlying the measurement theorists' unquestioned focus on relational fairness is a fundamental question about the purpose(s) of assessment. In exchanges between assessment experts, it is often stated, or taken for granted, that the main – or even the only – purpose of summative assessment is differentiation between candidates. It follows from this view that tests which produce a normal distribution of scores are 'good' and those where the scores are bunched at one part of the distribution are 'bad'. In our view, this cannot be assumed. The importance of differentiation depends on the kind of assessment and its purpose. There are contexts, such as competition for a limited good like entry to a medical school, where differentiation is crucial. But, in other contexts, it may be more important to get accurate, rich and usable information about individuals, even if that is in a form which makes comparisons with others difficult.

In making this point, we can learn from the debate by social and political philosophers about 'distributional justice', which seems to see society as distributing good things, in a context where more for one person means less for another. Borrowing a metaphor from the philosopher Richard Hare (1977), this view imagines the opportunities achieved through examination scores to be like a cake, with different sizes of slice available and the assessment deciding who gets what. In Chapter 5, we saw that social philosophers have questioned the 'dividing the cake' approach to social justice. In a similar spirit, we question the assumption that the cake paradigm can always be applied to fair assessment.

A different perspective is illustrated in competency tests.[2] For example, in Singapore there is a system of Swimming Proficiency Awards,[3] graded at six levels, with detailed requirements to be met for a range of strokes at each level. The requirements for an award at Level 2 ('turtle') include completing 100 metres, using front crawl, in under 2 minutes and 30 seconds. Level 6 ('whale') requires 1,500 metres to be swum in under 40 minutes. There is scope for unfairness in the assessment of swimmers for these badges – for example, if a stopwatch was tampered with, the wrong time was entered in a report, or if the distance required to be swum was changed for some swimmers without a good reason. But that would be unfair because the information about the individuals concerned would be misleading and inaccurate. If swimmers got a reward that they did not deserve, then that would be unfair in the retributive sense. However, the prime purpose of the test is not to distinguish between the swimmers or result in a normal distribution of scores – if all the children in a school class achieved the 'whale' award, their teacher would be delighted. The point is that swimmers at all levels of ability have a chance to show what they can do, and there is motivation to do better. The assessment outcomes can also provide useful information to the public authorities about the swimming proficiency of Singaporean children.

In the UK, the licensing authority for doctors (the General Medical Council) runs performance assessments[4] of individual doctors where questions have been raised about the doctor's competence to an extent that calls the doctor's fitness to practise into question. These are individualised assessments, tailored to the nature of the individual doctor's work, and the purpose is to gain information about the individual's knowledge and skills to form the basis of a judgement on whether it is safe for that doctor to treat patients. The doctor is tested against a (negative) standard of (in)competence, below which he or she would be judged unfit to practise. The most important question that the assessment answers is whether the doctor is above or below that level – not how the doctor's competence compares to that of other doctors (most of whom will never be tested under this procedure). There are many possible issues of fairness which may arise when a doctor is assessed under the performance procedures. These may include questions about relational fairness if the doctor believes that the standard applied to them is more difficult to achieve than that set for other doctors (on other occasions), or that the criteria applied are more stringent for doctors from a particular ethnic background. But the primary purpose of the assessment is not to differentiate among candidates.

One possible response by differentiation supporters is that the underlying purpose of a competency test is to differentiate between the competent and the incompetent.[5] If all the Singaporean children were assessed as 'whales', this would distinguish them from other, hypothetical, children who were merely turtles. And the medical performance assessment compares the doctor under assessment with the standard assumed of others, even though they have not been assessed.

We are not persuaded by this response. It seems odd to argue that the main (or only) purpose of a competency assessment is to differentiate a candidate (or candidates) from a non-existent other group of candidates. The standards against which individuals are assessed will no doubt derive from, among other things, information about the performance of others in circumstances other than the particular assessment in question. But that is not the only source: in the case of medical performance assessments, the standards are based on the profession's manual of 'Good Medical Practice'. That sets out normative standards which reflect what the public can reasonably expect. They are not measurements of what other doctors do.

Many writers on assessment come from the worlds of competitive examinations and standardised tests. There will always be a need for such tests, but they need not form a paradigm for all thinking about assessment – or about fairness in assessment. An alternative paradigm is a search for the best possible information about each individual being assessed which is relevant to the purposes for which the assessment outcomes will be used. Subject to practical constraints, the more (relevant) information the better, even if the information available about one candidate is not strictly comparable with that available about others. If we reverse the order of the paradigms, making rich information about individuals the primary paradigm and competition for limited goods the exception, that may be a better start to thinking about fair assessment in our time, although, as we shall see, it brings its own challenges and problems in achieving fairness.

Fairness applies to individuals, not just groups. The idea of limiting fairness to the treatment of groups (rather than individuals) seems to belong particularly to the lenses of measurement theory. Such limitation flies in the face of ordinary language, and of the other disciplines we have considered. Although public law normally applies to a category of subjects rather than to a particular person,[6] many of the legal challenges to fairness of assessment which we considered in Chapter 4 were on behalf of named individuals. And readers of this book who work at testing organisations or exam boards may have experience of administering tests or exams with one candidate, who still has a right to be treated fairly. We accept that the use of differential functioning analysis is probably limited to groups which can be identified and their scores compared to those of other groups, but the limitations of one measurement instrument should not be allowed to limit the understanding of the object being measured.

What is the level of the level playing field? When applying the lenses of philosophical analysis and measurement theory, we have had considerable difficulty in making sense of the idea that fair assessment arrangements bring candidates to the same level – referred to by the ubiquitous sporting metaphor of the 'level playing field'. What level should candidates be brought to? This is a problem for measurement theory, conceptual analysis and practical administration of assessments – for example, in deciding what accommodations should be offered to candidates with a disability. We saw that the counterfactual hypothesis – that we are enabling all candidates to show how they would have performed without their disability – is problematic, as there is no way of verifying it: the fact is that the candidate *does* have the disability. A particularly difficult example is the calculation of extra time to be allowed for candidates requiring it. What is the comparator for equalisation – with the time required for the candidate with a disability to achieve the average mark achieved by all non-disabled test-takers? Or with the time required to achieve the average mark of test-takers with the same broad ability level as the disabled candidate? Or with the time that the test designers think is appropriate? And what is the evidence base for any of these?

It is no doubt a laudable objective to try to make the playing field more level than it would be without an intervention. But we think it is misleading to imply that there is a measurable, evidence-based level to which all candidates can be brought. It is not fair to disabled candidates – or any candidates – to make arrangements for them based on an untestable hypothesis. A more honest approach could be based on empirical research about the effects of various possible modifications on the achievements of candidates in defined circumstances, followed by a policy decision on what the arrangements should be. These might be constrained by practicalities, such as limits to the amount of extra time that is manageable. The policy decision would be informed by the view that it is fair to give the disabled candidates some assistance in having their knowledge and skill assessed despite their disability, but the level aimed for should not purport to reflect measurable or meaningful equality with others.

Fairness is a positive, but not binary, concept. A question raised by the lenses of measurement theory, philosophical analysis and social justice was whether the fundamental concept applied to fairness in assessment is the positive concept of fairness or the negative concept of *unfairness*. For reasons discussed in Chapter 5 and summarised earlier in this chapter, we favour a more positive concept of fairness, incorporating the Aristotelian idea of a 'match' between what is offered and what is deserved or appropriate. However, the positive concept of fairness is difficult to define, and it seems difficult to satisfy, as no sooner is fair assessment achieved at one level (for example, by avoiding language unfamiliar to some ethnic groups), but new unfairnesses come across the horizon, such as historical injustices affecting the quality of teaching available to those ethnic groups. This problem was illustrated in the legal case of *Debra P.*, discussed in Chapter 4.

We suggest that the positive concept of fairness should not be seen as a binary property which is or is not present, but as a *continuum*. A helpful example of such a concept is 'health'. If your doctor declares that you are healthy, that does not imply that you have achieved a level which cannot be exceeded. The doctor may be referring to the absence of some sources of unhealthiness which are particularly relevant to you at the time. For example, you may have recovered from a broken ankle or managed to reduce your excess weight. But there may remain other respects in which your health could be improved, for example by taking more exercise or a prophylactic such as a supplement of Vitamin D in the winter to strengthen your bones.

The current definition of health by the World Health Organisation, dating back to 1948, is 'a state of complete physical, mental and social well-being and not merely the absence of disease or infirmity'.[7] That was forward-looking in its day, but it has increasingly been criticised on a number of grounds, notably for the idea that 'health' depicts a 'complete' state (see, for example, Huber et al., 2011). We take a similar approach to fair assessment as do the modern critics of the WHO's (1948) definition of health. It is unrealistic and conceptually puzzling to expect any assessment to be 'completely' fair (however that is understood). But it is realistic and conceptually coherent to expect assessments to be made fair*er*, and to be moved along the continuum of fairness. It may also be helpful and appropriate to set a threshold on the fairness continuum as the cut-off point for a judgement of fairness or unfairness in a particular context and at a particular point in time. However, there may be further to go in the direction of fairness, and the cut-off point may need to be reconsidered later. This leads to our fifth conclusion.

Fairness judgements should be iterative, not once-for-always. We suggest that judgements of the fairness of assessments can and should be made at different times in the life-cycle of the assessment – and use of its outcomes – and on the basis of different sources of evidence, including evidence about what went before the test was taken and what happened afterwards. For example, DIF analysis, carried out at one time, of possible bias against defined groups may be overtaken by new understandings of categories of candidates who might be disadvantaged or advantaged, or about possible bias in the categorisations themselves. The fairness challenge should be iterative.

Fairness requires a situated view of assessment. The experience of looking at assessment through different lenses has led us to draw a distinction between two different approaches. The 'isolated' view looks at an assessment in isolation from its context and sets aside extraneous information about the situations in which it was taken and the uses to which the outcomes were put in practice. In some ways, the isolated approach resembles the approach to literary criticism adopted by the exponents of 'Practical Criticism' such as I. A. Richards in the 1920s [1929], who 'gave poems to students without any information about who wrote them or when they were written',[8] to encourage them to put aside preconceptions and look at the 'words on the page'.

In contrast to the isolated view is what we shall call the 'situated' view, which considers assessments/tests in the contexts in which they are taken and the outcomes are used. The situated view of assessment may resemble the arguments about literary criticism used by the opponents of Practical Criticism, who argued that a poem could only be fully understood if the reader knew about the context in which it was written and the author's world view.[9]

In our view, discussion of fairness in assessment needs to take a more 'situated' view. This conclusion has partly been prompted by the insight shown by the philosopher John Rawls when he remarked that the principle of fair equality of opportunity meant more than 'careers open to talents'. It has also been prompted by lessons from some of the legal challenges to fairness of assessment described in Chapter 4, where the courts considered the circumstances leading to the challenge, not just the test considered in isolation from that context. The situated view also allows for some applications of the 'retrospective' and 'consequential' senses of fairness that we identified in Chapter 1.

There are problems, however, when the situated view is used in judging the fairness of assessments or in criticising an assessment organisation for unfairness. For a start, those who commission, design or mark some assessments – national or state exams, for example – may not know the contexts in which they will be taken. All they may know is that the same exam will be taken by students in very different circumstances. Another problem is that it is common for different organisations to be responsible for different parts of the life-cycle and context of an assessment and its use. A state authority may commission the test, a testing organisation may design it, a different organisation may mark the test and a different part of the state authority may use the outcomes. How can one of these organisations be accused of 'unfairness' if the problem occurred at a stage of the process which is another organisation's responsibility? And, lastly, test outcomes can sometimes be used in ways that assessment professionals or test organisers could not be expected to anticipate – for example, as a component of performance indicators for schools or teachers.

We acknowledge the strength of those objections. However, we are convinced by Rawls's insight that the demands of genuine equality of opportunity mean that it cannot be acceptable for testing organisations to shrug off contextual unfairness and confine their attention to the part of the process for which they are responsible. It is reasonable to draw some boundary around those parts of the context which should be taken into account when judging the fairness of an assessment and the limits to the moral and professional responsibility of assessment professionals and commissioners. The US *Standards* (AERA et al., 2014) faces this problem when applying the concept of 'instructional validity' (derived from the *Debra P.* case) to standards for assessment. It takes a narrow view, suggesting that a requirement to observe instructional validity only applies if the same organisation commissions/produces the test and is responsible for overseeing curriculum and teaching (AERA et al., 2014, p. 72). In our view, that is insufficient.

In consumer law in most countries, manufacturers are accountable for the harm caused by uses of their product that are reasonably foreseeable. They have a duty to warn against harm in circumstances which a reasonable person could foresee, such as children playing with packaging or too many doses of a drug being taken. Awareness of some contexts may change with time – for example, it is now arguably reasonable to expect greater awareness of the effect of allergies than in a previous generation. In the same way, we suggest that those considering the fairness of an assessment (or stages of an assessment) in real time should take into account what can be reasonably foreseen about contexts in which the assessment is taken and future uses of its outcomes. Later in this chapter, we offer a template for use when putting that approach into practice.

Looking forward: challenges

We have seen how approaches to fairness have been influenced by historical events and circumstances – notably the Civil Rights movement in the USA, charters of human rights developed in the second half of the twentieth century, and increased understanding of issues about ourselves and society, including disability and gender. Of course, some underlying issues and principles are timeless, and we make no apology for reference in this book to thinkers such as Aristotle. However, when considering an approach to fair assessment for the future, it is necessary to take into account recent developments that may challenge the paradigms inherited from the twentieth century.

The information about people available for use in assessment is, we suggest, moving in two directions from the structures that informed much twentieth-century thinking about fairness. Information is increasingly *smaller in focus* and *bigger in volume*. The smaller focus follows from the disintegration of some of the categories familiar to anti-discrimination legislation and rules for many types of assessment. For example, thinking about disability is now highly complex, allowing for multiple disabilities, partly the happy result of the success of modern medicine in enabling babies to survive who would not have lived in times past. The International Classification of Functioning, Disability and Health, developed by the World Health Organisation in 2001, includes long lists of medical, social and environmental factors,[10] and allows for them to be combined in countless ways. Similarly, as we noted in Chapter 2, ethnicity is increasingly complex and difficult to characterise, particularly in countries with large immigrant populations of several generations. It is not always clear which category of ethnicity is appropriate for the analysis of fairness – for example, US children with parents of Asian origin may be classified as 'American' for some purposes and 'Asian' (or 'Asian-American') for others. Categories including 'Asian' may be more germane to judgements about parental influence on student learning, whilst 'American' might be more appropriate for international comparisons of school systems.

A further challenge to categories is that disadvantage tends to cluster,[11] with poverty, poor health, poor housing, low income and poor educational outcomes often coming together, notably among the most disadvantaged. This poses the theoretical problem which is sometimes colloquially labelled 'the poor black single mother' – which category should analysts use to investigate possible bias or unfairness to her? And even if three categories are used in turn (poverty, ethnicity and parental role), more can be produced (living in poor housing, being a victim of crime, having a high probability of Type 2 diabetes).

For all these reasons, when we are considering fair assessment in the future, our focus will need to be less on traditional groups or categories and steered more towards individuals. In saying this, we are not denying that unfairness and injustice to the historic groups persist and must be challenged. We are also aware that forms of prejudice, for example against particular religions or cultures, can wax and wane, reappearing after a period of apparent quiescence. We cannot be complacent about unfairness to the categories of people identified in the past, but we need to recognise that those categories are insufficient to structure thinking about fairness of assessment in the future.

The big volume of information available about individuals is a feature of what is commonly referred to, using the obligatory capital initials, as 'Big Data'.[12] The range of available data about the subjects of assessments is potentially huge – requiring a new vocabulary (such as 'petabytes') to describe it – and machinery and methodologies for collecting and analysing many millions of data items about each person are affordable and commonplace. For example, filming a student's activities each day is now practicable and affordable, using body-worn mini-cameras or the student's own devices. Popular management literature (Marr, 2017, is but one example) talks of the '5 [or sometimes more than 5] Vs' of Big Data – Velocity, Volume, Value, Variety and Veracity. Many of these, notably Volume and Variety, raise challenges for assessment, and pose new questions about validity and reliability,[13] as well as fairness. If the potential range of information about each individual is vast and varied, what criteria should be used to select the data upon which an assessment judgement can fairly be made?

We have already challenged the primacy of the paradigm of competitive examinations for discussion of fair assessment. We also challenge the primacy of the paradigm of assessment as a discrete exercise, carried out at a fixed time, and involving performance by all candidates of a similar, or identical, set of tasks, away from the normal contexts in which their teaching and learning took place. These will always have a place. But an alternative paradigm – of assessment comprising a judgement based on a selection from vast amounts of data available – will, we suggest, become more central.

The availability of Big Data as a basis for assessment brings with it a new set of challenges to fairness, in several of the senses we have identified. A challenge to relational fairness is that more interesting – or 'richer' – data may be available about some people than about others. For example, children of rich parents may have access to sports coaches, music lessons, summer camps and Scout groups that are out of the reach of children from poorer families. The wider the scope of the information informing the assessor's judgement, the wider those differences may be shown to be.

This problem is familiar to university administrators who consider 'value-added' information about candidates for admission: some students have more opportunities to add value than others. These worries may drive the administrators back, with some relief, to standardised tests. But, in the future, when many assessments may be based on large amounts of information, with scope for even more in some cases, it will be difficult to escape from the problem of fairness in making judgements based on different amounts of information about different candidates.

There are other challenges posed by a world where assessment is focused on individuals and can be based on huge data sources, which will differ for each individual. One is how to sustain public confidence in a more varied, individualised system – particularly if the parents of students assessed in these ways are expecting the more traditional tests and examinations that they experienced when they were at school or university. There may also be a risk of unconscious bias in the selection of information for assessment and in the judgements made. In professions such as medicine, the twentieth century saw a deliberate move from interviews to more structured tests for selection to prestigious roles. This was explicitly aimed at avoiding selection by the interviewers of 'people like [them]'. Arguably, a system with more scope for judgement in selection from large amounts of material may raise similar problems.

In summary, the paradigms developed in the twentieth century for thinking about fairness in assessment were based on categories of candidate, assumed that assessment should be based on limited information, assumed that a prime purpose of (all) assessment was (fair) discrimination between candidates, and gave primacy to uses of assessment to resolve competition for limited goods. The insights and good practices identified using these paradigms, such as 'universal design' and analysis for possible bias between identified groups, are valuable and useful, but they are not enough.

The challenge for fairness in the twenty-first century is to build on these insights, addressing questions of the fair assessment of individuals subject to multiple and complex categorisations, in a world with the potential to draw on vast amounts of information about each one of them.

Making assessment fairer

We see fairness as a continuum: no assessment can be 'completely' fair, but assessments can be made fair*er*. We have argued that the paradigms of fair assessment used in the past have been beneficial but are inadequate for the twenty-first century, with huge amounts of information potentially available about each learner and increasing diversity in many societies, defying traditional categories. The quest for social justice continues, with some long-standing injustices persisting or re-appearing, whilst developments in society bring new barriers to fairness and social justice. What can assessment practitioners, teachers, policy-makers and researchers do in this context, to make assessment fairer?

We conclude this book with three suggestions. First, the assessment world should put aside the assumptions that the primary purpose of all assessments is discrimination between candidates and that the primary – or only – sense of fairness that matters for assessment is relational fairness: treating like cases alike. As we have argued, these assumptions may apply in particular circumstances, and relational fairness is often very important. But they are not the only show in town. In the future, assessment will be a matter of making judgements derived from limitless information about a diverse population of people. Increasingly, the most important purpose of assessment will be to obtain rich information about each individual, suitable for its intended purpose. Relational fairness in that context will consist of ensuring that each individual has the opportunity to show what they can do (in the relevant way), and contractual fairness consists in meeting each individual's legitimate expectations.

Second, we have argued for a 'situated' view of assessment when evaluating fairness, although we have acknowledged that this presents problems for individuals and organisations who are responsible for only one part of an assessment process – for example, for designing a national examination. We go further than the US *Standards* in suggesting that all assessment organisations and professionals should evaluate the fairness of their work in the context of what they are reasonably aware of that has gone before and what they can reasonably foresee in the way their product will be used, even if these stages are the responsibility of another organisation or individual. Those responsible for assessments should be expected to use their moral peripheral vision to scan the context of their work. They should also have a means of recording any suggestions about how the work that they are doing may contribute to greater fairness and any concerns about foreseeable unfair uses. This leads to our third suggestion.

We have argued that judgements of fair assessments should be iterative, not once-and-for-all. In many areas of public life, it is now commonplace to expect policy-makers or project managers to carry out 'impact analyses'. These involve addressing a checklist of questions, evaluating a particular aspect of a proposal or project, such as the impact on the economy or on the privacy of data subjects.[14] Completion of these impact analyses may involve some speculation, as future possible threats to privacy or future economic trends are by no means certain, and there may be disagreement about them. They may also have to be revised if and when more relevant information becomes available. However, completing an impact analysis requires those involved in policy development or programme delivery to think about the purpose of what they are doing and to consider what threats or harm they may reasonably foresee. The requirement to publish these analyses means that those involved in later stages of the development are aware of the benefits and risks identified at the earlier stages, and they need to be able to justify taking a different approach. The analyses can also prompt informed public debate and questioning.

We suggest that a similar approach should be used by organisations involved in assessments such as national or state examinations and assessments for professional qualifications. A *fairness impact analysis* would involve considering some of the questions about fairness raised in this book, including those already familiar through consensus thinking in the assessment world, but also involving the exercise of peripheral vision on the context in which the assessment will be used.

As fairness judgements should be iterative, such impact assessments may be required more than once in the life-cycle of an assessment. As an example, we set out here a possible checklist for fairness impact assessment of an assessment at the *design* stage.

A checklist for evaluating the fairness of assessments at the design stage

Understanding of the purpose(s) of the assessment

- What is/are the purpose(s) of this assessment?
- What contribution will this assessment make to:
    o the private good of the candidates?
    o the good of others/the public?

Knowledge of the construct the assessment is designed to measure

- What is the construct being assessed?
- Does the assessment provide opportunities for all candidates to show their knowledge and/or skill in relation to the construct?
- Are there any categories of candidate whom you expect to have difficulties in showing their construct-relevant knowledge/skill through taking this assessment?
- Are there any identifiable areas of knowledge or skill relevant to the construct which you expect that all or some candidates will not have opportunities to show through taking this assessment?
- What kinds of generic knowledge and skill are required by the assessment (e.g. language skills, writing skills)? Are they all essential for the construct being assessed?

Intended test-takers (including sub-groups who may raise accessibility issues)

- What do you know about the people whom you expect to take the assessment?
- What assumptions are you making about the teaching and learning experienced by the candidates:
    o in preparation for the assessment?
    o in earlier times (for example, at an earlier stage of their education)?
- Is it reasonable for you to expect those assumptions to have been realised?

(Continued)

- If not, are there particular problems that you can reasonably foresee, either for all or for a sub-set of candidates?
- Is there any aspect of this assessment which you think will be a surprise to candidates or to those who have prepared them for this assessment?
- If so, does the assessment conflict with what they have a right to expect?
- Are any candidates likely to be disadvantaged by:
  - how the construct being assessed is interpreted?
  - the mode of assessment?
  - the practical circumstances of the assessment?
- Is any action possible to reduce these disadvantages? Has that action been taken or are there arrangements in place to do so?

Uses/consequences of test outcomes

- What uses can you reasonably foresee being made of the assessment outcomes?
- Are there any possible uses which you can reasonably foresee and which you think would be *un*fair?

We recognise that it would not be practicable to use checklists like this for all assessments – such as daily classroom feedback – though the ideas behind it may also be applicable in these contexts. We also recognise that the content and wording of our template for the design stage of assessments can be improved and refined; and that different words may be appropriate at later stages of the life-cycle of an assessment. This example is offered as a starting point for further work, and as an illustration of the importance of regular analysis by the assessment industry of the fairness of their assessments, taking a 'situated' view considering the contexts in which the assessments will be taken, what went before and uses/abuses of the outcomes that may reasonably be foreseen.

The recent focus on fairness by measurement theorists and the assessment profession has clearly been beneficial, and assessments which follow the current guidance on good practice will be much better – and much fairer – than those which do not. The experience of considering fairness through different lenses has deepened and broadened our approach and led to the conclusions in this chapter, which build on the thinking that has gone before. To evaluate the fairness of an assessment, we need to see it as situated in its context and take into account all the aspects of fairness that we have identified. However, doing so draws attention to the persisting injustice lying behind the constructs of most educational assessments. In Nagel's words, we are 'left with the great injustice of the smart and the dumb' (Nagel, 1979, p. 104). This book has not resolved that injustice, although fairer assessment may enable richer and more nuanced information to be available about the knowledge and skill of each individual, not just the 'smart' ones.

Is assessment fair? Where sources of unfairness have been identified and eliminated, that is progress in the direction of fairness, but there will always be further to go. The challenge is to make assessment fair*er* in the twenty-first-century world of diversity and Big Data about each individual, and to secure and retain public confidence whilst doing so. Further work is required on assessment fairness in the new contexts we have described, moving beyond the conventional concentration on relational fairness and comparability. It will also be important to maintain a dialogue between thinking about fair assessment and thinking about social justice. The result should be fairer educational assessment, benefiting students, informing and supporting social progress and commanding public confidence.

Notes

1. 474 F. Supp. 244 (M.D. Fla. 1979); 644 F. 2d 397 (5th Cir. 1981); 564 F. Supp. 177 (M.D. Fla.1983); 730 F.2d 1405 (11th Cir. 1984).
2. In developing this argument, we have learned particularly from the writings of Jonathan Wolff on social justice.
3. See www.swimminglessons.com.sg/sspa.htm.
4. The assessment process is described at www.gmc-uk.org/concerns/information-for-doctors-under-investigation/performance-assessments/investigation-and-tribunal-directed/what-will-your-assessment-consist-of.
5. We are grateful to Paul Newton for this discussion.
6. Statutory references to people exercising a role, e.g. that of prime minister or chair of a statutory body, apply to the role-holder, not to a named individual.
7. WHO, *Constitution of the World Health Organization*, 2006. www.who.int/governance/eb/who_constitution_en.pdf.
8. See 'Introduction to practical criticism (the virtual classroom)' at www.english.cam.ac.uk/classroom/pracrit.htm.
9. Arguments famously conveyed in the 1941 lectures by C. S. Lewis recorded in *A Preface to Paradise Lost*, Atlantic Publishers & Dist (2005).
10. The template for classification can be seen at www.who.int/classifications/icf/icfchecklist.pdf?ua=1 (accessed November 2019).
11. See discussion in Chapter 6 and Putnam (2015).
12. See, for example, Raikes, N. (2019) 'Data, data everywhere? Opportunities and challenges in a data-rich world'. *Research Matters*, Cambridge Assessment, 27, 16–19.
13. Some of these issues were identified and discussed at the 2018 conference, held at St Catherine's College, Oxford, of the International Association of Educational

Assessment. See https://iaea.info/conference-proceedings/44th-annual-confer ence-2018; see also Cope & Kalntzis (2015).
14. A UK example is the guidance on Data Protection Impact Analyses, provided by the Information Commissioner's Office (see https://ico.org.uk/for-organisations/guide-to-data-protection/guide-to-the-general-data-protection-regulation-gdpr/accountability-and-governance/data-protection-impact-assessments).

References

American Educational Research Association (AERA), American Psychological Association (APA) and National Council on Measurement in Education (NCME) (2014) *Standards for Educational and Psychological Testing*. Washington, DC: AERA.

Cope, B. and Kalntzis, M. (2015) Sources of evidence-of-learning: Learning and assessment in the era of Big Data. *Open Review of Educational Research*, 2(1), 194–217.

Cresswell, M. J. (2000) *Research Studies in Public Examining*. Guildford: Associated Examining Board.

Hare, R. M. (1977) Opportunity for what? Some remarks on current disputes about equality in education. *Oxford Review of Education*, 3(3), 207–216.

Huber, M., Green, L. W., Jadad, A., Leonard, B., Loureiro, M. I., Schnabel, P., van Weel, C., Knottnerus, J. A., van der Horst, H. E., Kromhout, D., Lorig, K. R., van der Meer, J., W. M., Smith, R. and Smid, H. (2011) How should we define health? *British Medical Journal*, 343(7817). Available at: www.bmj.com/content/343/bmj.d4163 (accessed 30/03/20).

Marr, B. (2017) Data strategy: How to profit from a world of Big Data, analytics and the internet of things. *Kogan Page*, 3 April.

Nagel, T. (1979) The policy of preference. In *Mortal Questions*. Cambridge: Cambridge University Press. pp. 91–105.

Putnam, R. D. (2015) *Our Kids: The American dream in crisis*. New York: Simon & Schuster.

Raikes, N. (2019) Data, data everywhere? Opportunities and challenges in a data-rich world. *Research Matters*, Cambridge Assessment, 27, 16–19.

Rawls, R. J. (1971) *A Theory of Justice*. Oxford: Oxford University Press.

Richards, I. A. (1929) *Practical Criticism: A study of literary judgement*. London: Kegan Paul.

World Health Organisation (WHO) (1948) Preamble to the Constitution of WHO as adopted by the International Health Conference, New York, 19 June – 22 July 1946; signed on 22 July 1946 by the representatives of 61 states (Official Records of WHO, no. 2, p. 100) and entered into force on 7 April 1948.

Young, M. (1958/1994/2017) *The Rise of the Meritocracy* (first published by Thames and Hudson, 1958; published with new introduction by Transaction Publishers, 1994; published by Abingdon, Oxon/New York: Routledge, 2017).

Index

ableism, 44n17
absence of bias, 102–103
absence of discrimination, 102–103
access arrangements, 32–33
accessibility, 59–60
accommodations
  construct-irrelevant variance and, 32–33, 34–35
  equality and, 101
  for further reflection, 116
  law and, 80–83, 89
  social justice and, 129–130
adequacy, 128–129, 130–132, 149–150
American Educational Research Association (AERA), 57. See also *Standards for Educational and Psychological Testing* (AERA, APA and NCME)
American Psychological Association (APA), 57. See also *Standards for Educational and Psychological Testing* (AERA, APA and NCME)
Anastasi, A., 38
Anderson, E., 113–114, 122, 128–129, 130–132, 149–150
Angoff, W., 21, 22
anonymous marking, 40
anti-discrimination legislation, 31, 75, 80, 125–126
Apprenticeship, Skills, Children and Learning Act (2009), 55
Aristotle, 99, 104–106, 107, 108, 149, 154
assessment, 7–10. See also classroom assessment; fairness in testing and assessment
assessment for accountability, 9
assessment for learning, 9, 37
assessment for targeted intervention, 9
assessment of learning, 9, 37
assessment practices, 36–37
attainment, 39–40
attention deficit disorder (ADD), 81–82
audi alteram partem, 6–7
Australasian Curriculum, Assessment and Certification Authorities (ACACA), 80
Australia, 80–82, 83–84

Baker, E. L., 18
Bakke v. The Regents of the University of California (1978), 55
Barkley, R. A., 31–32
Bell, D., 136
Beveridge, W., 125
BI v. Board of Studies (2000), 81–82, 88, 89
bias, 20–22, 27, 102–103
Big Data, 157–158

Bishop v. Sports Massage Training School (2000), 80
Blair, T., 133
Borsboom, D., 44n11
Boud, D., 41
Breimhorst v. ETS (2000), 83
Brighouse, H., 110–111, 130

Cahill v. Minister for Education (2017), 4–5
Cahill v. the Minister for Education and Science (2017), 82–83
Camilli, G., 37
Carless, D., 65
certificate indications (certificate annotations), 45n22
cheating, 2
Chelsea Manifesto, 137–138
China, 2, 17
Churchill, W., 111
civil law systems, 74
civil rights, 75
Civil Rights Act (USA, 1964), 54–55, 75, 86
Civil Rights Act (USA, 1991), 86
Civil Rights Movement, 54–55
Civil Service, 17
Cizek, G. J., 60–61
Classical Test Theory, 44n11
classroom assessment, 36–38, 42, 61–63
Clinton, B., 109–110
common law, 74, 75–77, 88
comparability, 28
competency tests, 151
conceptual analysis, 99–108, 148–149
consequential sense of fairness, 4, 5, 147, 155
construct-irrelevant variance, 29–35, 41, 52, 66
contracts, 107
counterfactual hypothesis, 101, 107, 149
Cronbach, L. J., 23
Cumming, J. J, 80, 82, 89, 90

Debra P. v. Turlington (1979–1984)
  overview of, 77–80, 154
  consequential sense of fairness and, 5
  instructional validity and, 78–80, 90, 92, 148, 156
  LB Lewisham case and, 85–86
  retrospective sense of fairness and, 79
  social justice and, 129–130
  test score use and, 23
democratic equality, 131
desert, 103, 106, 111–113, 149
Dickson, E. A., 80, 82, 89, 90

difference principle, 109–114
differential item functioning (DIF), 20–22, 43, 154–155
disability, 30–32, 42, 75. *See also* accommodations
discrimination, 4, 102–103, 125–127
dishonesty, 136
distributional justice, 151
distributive justice, 106–107, 127–128
Doe v. National Board of Medical Examiners (1999), 82, 83
Donoghue v. Stevenson (1932), 76
donor preference schemes, 141
due process, 64–66, 88
Duke Power Company, 54–55
Dworkin, R., 111, 115

educational measurement theory
    classroom assessment and, 36–38, 42
    concept of fairness and, 16, 18–28, 41–42
    construct-irrelevant variance and, 29–35, 41
    development of, 17–18
    for further reflection, 42–43
    higher education and, 39–41
    perceptions of fairness and, 35–36, 41, 42
Educational Testing Service (ETS), 86
efficiency, 134–135
entry requirements, 42–43
Equal Employment Opportunity Commission (EEOC)
equality
    concept of, 2
    conceptual analysis and, 99–102, 106, 149
    social justice and, 127–129, 130–132, 139–140
    theoretical modelling and, 111
equality of esteem, 5
equality of opportunity
    conceptual analysis and, 101–102, 103
    meritocracy and, 134, 136
    Rawls on, 25, 39, 135, 139, 150, 156
    theoretical modelling and, 109–114, 149
equality of result, 135
equity, 102, 105
ethics of teaching, 36–37
ETS Standards for Quality and Fairness (ETS), 20, 43n7
Eugenics movement, 18
European Convention on Human Rights (1953), 65, 75

Fair Access by Design (Qualifications Wales and CCEA Regulation), 56–57
fair equality of opportunity principle, 109–114
fairness impact analysis, 160
fairness in testing and assessment
    concept and senses of, 2, 3–7, 146–147
    for further reflection, 12–13
    future challenges and, 156–159
    general conclusions on, 150–156
    'lenses' for, 10–11
    meritocracy and, 135
    perceptions of, 7, 35–36, 41, 42
    as positive concept, 154
    public profile of, 2–3
    suggestions for, 159–163
    See also educational measurement theory; guidance on good practice; law; philosophical analysis; social justice
FairTest (National Center for Fair & Open Testing), 2
five giants (idleness, ignorance, squalor, disease and want), 125–127
Flint, N. R., 35
formative assessment, 37–38
Fox, A., 132

Garner, B., 64
General Medical Council, 8, 151–152
generalisability, 28
GI Forum v. Texas Education Agency (2000), 79
Giron, J., 38
grade drift, 40
Graduate Management Admissions Test (GMAT), 83
grammar schools, 124–125
Green, F. G., 131
Green, S. K., 63
Griggs v. Duke Power Co. (1971), 54–55, 86–87
guidance on good practice
    classroom assessment and, 61–63
    for further reflection, 66–67
    hierarchy of sources of, 52–54, 66
    local guidance and, 63–64
    procedural fairness and, 64–66
    professional associations and, 53, 57–61
    rules or guidance authorised by law and, 53, 54–57
    See also law
Guidelines on Sex Bias and Sex Fairness in Career Interest Inventories (NIE), 58

Haertel, E. H., 26–27
Hare, R. M., 116, 151
Harlen, W., 8, 9, 10
Harvard University, 17
health, 154
high-stakes assessments, 9–10, 17–18
higher education, 39–41, 42–43
human rights, 75

impartiality, 100–102
indigenous populations, 43
Individuals with Disabilities Education Act (USA, 1990), 75
instructional validity, 78–80, 90, 92, 148, 156
International Guidelines for Test Use (ITC), 61
International Test Commission (ITC), 61
Interpretation/Use Argument (IUA), 34
IQ testing, 18, 124, 133, 134–135
Ireland. *See Cahill v. the Minister for Education and Science* (2017)
isolated view of assessment, 106–107

Jencks, C., 128
Johnson, B., 35

Joint Advisory Committee, 62
Joint Committee on Standards for Educational Evaluation (JCSEE), 62–63
Joint Committee on Testing Practices (JCTP), 61
Joint Council on Qualifications (JCQ), 67n4
judicial review, 76–77
justice
  concept of, 2
  conceptual analysis and, 99–102, 104–108, 149
  theoretical modelling and, 108–115
  use of term, 122
  See also social justice

Kamvounias, P., 88
Kane, M., 34, 88
Kynaston, D., 131

language proficiency, 29
Larry P. v. Riles (1979), 55
law
  overview of, 74–75, 91
  case studies, 77–87
  common themes and challenges in, 87–89
  conceptual questions on, 89–91
  for further reflection, 91–92
  marking methodology and, 83–86
  rules or guidance authorised by, 53, 54–57
  as source of guidance, 53–54
  See also anti-discrimination legislation
LB Lewisham & Others v. AQA, Edexcel, Ofqual & Others (2013), 3–4, 84–86
Lee, K. Y., 133
Leitch, J., 66
liberty principle, 109–114
Lim, L., 138
Littler, J., 133, 135
local guidance, 63–64
lottery, 116
low talent, 114–115
luck, 113–114
luck egalitarianism, 113–114

Mann, H., 17–18
marking methodology, 83–86. *See also* anonymous marking
Martiniello, M., 29
mathematics, 140
May, T., 133, 135
McArthur, J., 16, 18–19, 65, 66
McMillan, J. H., 38
Mellenbergh, G. J., 44n11
merit, 17, 103–104
meritocracy, 103, 122–123, 132–139, 150
Messick, S., 24, 28, 29, 52
Mitchell, F., 88
modifications, 33–35
Moss, P. A., 37

Nagel, T., 114, 139–140, 163
National Center for Fair & Open Testing (FairTest), 2

National Council on Measurement in Education (NCME), 57. *See also Standards for Educational and Psychological Testing* (AERA, APA and NCME)
National Curriculum and Assessment Authority (NCAA), 80
National Institute of Education (NIE), 58
National Student Survey (NSS), 35–36
negligence, 76
neo-liberalism, 133–134
neurodiversity, 31–32
Newton, P. E., 60–61
Nichomachean Ethics (Aristotle), 104–105
Nielsen, K., 106
Nozick, R., 106, 112, 113

Office for Students, 39–40
Office of the Independent Adjudicator, 77
Ofqual, 33, 55–56. *See also LB Lewisham & Others v. AQA, Edexcel, Ofqual & Others* (2013)
O'Neil Jr, H. F., 18

Parkes, J., 38
Pase v. Hannon (1980), 55
Phillips, S. E., 82, 83
philosophical analysis
  conceptual analysis and, 99–108, 148–149
  for further reflection, 116–117
  importance of, 98–99
  reasons for fairness and, 115–116
  theoretical modelling and, 99, 108–115, 148–149
Pitt, E., 40
Plake, B. S., 61–62
Politics (Aristotle), 105
Priest, S., 99
Principles for Fair Assessment Practices for Education in Canada (Joint Advisory Committee), 62
procedural fairness, 64–66
procedural justice, 107
professional associations, 53, 57–61
Programme for International Student Assessment (PISA), 10
proportional equality, 106
protected characteristics, 75
psychometric concepts, 20–22
Public Service Commission Scholarships (Singapore), 137, 138
Putnam, R., 126–127, 132

Quality Assurance Agency for Higher Education (QAA), 39

Raphael, D. D., 99, 106
Rawls, J.
  on equality of opportunity, 25, 39, 135, 139, 150, 156
  on justice as fairness, 99, 108–115, 149
regulatory bodies, 53, 55–57
The Regulatory Framework for National Assessments (Ofqual), 56
Rehabilitation Act (USA, 1973), 75

relational fairness
  Big Data and, 158
  concept of, 4, 5–6, 146–147
  Debra P. case and, 79
  due process and, 88
  LB Lewisham case and, 85
  role of, 150–153
reliability, 26–28, 37–38
respect, 5, 129
ressentiment, 136
restorative justice, 107
retrospective sense of (un)fairness, 5, 79, 147, 155
Richards, I. A., 155
Richardson, R., 31

Santrock, J. W., 37
SAT (standardized test), 124
Satz, D., 103, 128, 130, 131
Sen, A., 99, 123
Singapore, 137, 138, 151, 152
situated view of assessment
  concept of, 106–107, 123, 155, 159–160
  Rawls and, 149
  test score use and, 23
Smarter Balanced Assessment Consortium, 61
Smith, A., 108, 109
social contract, 108
social justice
  adequacy and, 128–129, 130–132, 149–150
  concept of, 122–123, 149
  educational measurement theory and, 18–19
  equality and, 139–140
  for further reflection, 140–141
  injustice and, 125–127
  meritocracy and, 122–123, 132–139
  positive views of, 127–129
  theoretical modelling and, 113–114
  types of assessment and, 123–125
social relationships, 128–129
Southern, J., 87
special consideration, 32–33
special needs. *See* accommodations
Stalley, R. F., 105
standard error of measurement, 27
standardised testing, 2, 17–18, 123–124
Standards for Educational and Psychological Testing (AERA, APA and NCME)
  overview of, 57–61
  on accommodations, 32
  classroom assessment and, 61–62
  construct-irrelevant variance and, 29
  on fairness, 16, 18, 24–25
  on group differences in outcomes, 79
  instructional validity and, 156
  on modifications, 33–34
  on 'opportunity to learn,' 80
  on reliability/precision, 27–28
  on test-users, 19–20
Stein, Z., 124
Stobart, G., 18
Stowell, M., 65
substantive due process, 88
Summers, L., 141
Swift, A., 110–111, 130

Tanzer, N. K., 27
Taras, M., 35
Task Group on Assessment and Testing, 8
test score use, 23
test-users, 19–20
theoretical modelling, 99, 108–115, 148–149
Tierney, R. D., 36–37

unfairness in testing and assessment
  concept and senses of, 2, 4–5, 147
  conceptual analysis and, 100, 108
  meritocracy and, 136
  perceptions of, 7
Uniform Guidelines on Employee Selection Procedures (EEOC), 55, 87, 90, 91–92, 124
United Nations (UN), 75
Universal Declaration of Human Rights (1948), 75
universal design, 60
USA
  accommodations in, 82, 83
  donor preference schemes in, 141
  due process in, 64–65
  standardised testing in, 2, 17–18, 123–124
  Uniform Guidelines in, 55, 87, 90, 91–92, 124
  See also *Debra P. v. Turlington* (1979–1984)

validity, 19, 24–26, 37–38, 41–42
value, 103
Van de Vijver, F., 27
Varnham, S., 88
voice, 41

Walsh v. University of Sydney (2007), 83–84
Walzer, M., 108
Wiliam, D., 21
Willetts, D., 141
Winstone, N., 40
Wise, L. L., 61–62
Wittgenstein, L., 5
Wolff, J., 99, 125, 129, 130
World Health Organization (WHO), 154, 157
worth, 103
Wu, A. D., 20

Young, M., 133, 134, 136, 137–138, 150

Zieky, M. J., 63–64, 67n1

BA'AL
MOLOCH
DEMIURGE
CODEX GIGAS
RESZO SERESS
LEVITATION ?
CHARLES FORT
EUSAPIA PALLADINO
HARRY HOUDINI
LEY LINES
ECTOPLASM
MYSTERY
MV-JOYITA
FLYING DUTCHMAN

FRANCIS LEAVY

GHOST T-REX, TEXAS

TULPA

ARG

DEMONOLOGY

M.I.B.

GHOST

SATURN CURSED?

LAVEY

666

MORAL PANIC

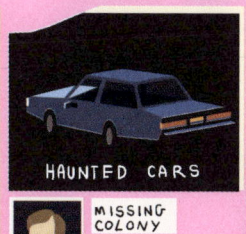

ELIZA BATTLE

STICK MEN

BLACK-EYED KIDS

SHIRTWOOD

LADY BE GOOD

OMENAINEN

ALCATRAZ ISLAND

HAUNTED CARS

EVER DREAM THIS MAN?

ISLAND OF DEATH

ZOLTAR

MISSING COLONY

BEN

For the ghosts.

Thank you to David Clarke, Hayley Stevens and Philippe Baudouin for their occult expertise. Tremendous gratitude to the Flying Eye elves for their wisdom and hard work.

Also in the series:

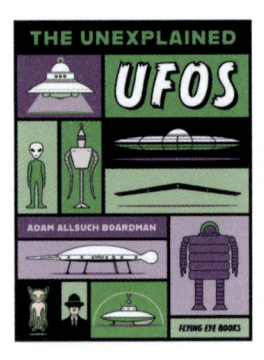

This edition first published by Flying Eye Books in 2025 from material originally published in *An Illustrated History of Ghosts* by Adam Allsuch Boardman (Nobrow press, 2022) by Flying Eye Books Ltd. 27 Westgate Street, London E3 3RL.
www.flyingeyebooks.com

Represented by: Authorised Rep Compliance Ltd.
Ground Floor, 71 Lower Baggot Street, Dublin, D02 P593, Ireland.
www.arccompliance.com

Text and illustrations © Adam Allsuch Boardman 2020

Original Content Consultant: Hayley Stevens

Adam Allsuch Boardman has asserted his right under the Copyright, Designs and Patents Act, 1988, to be identified as the Author and Illustrator of this Work.

All rights reserved. No part of this publication may be reproduced or transmitted in any form or by any means, electronic or mechanical, including photocopying, recording or by any information and storage retrieval system, without prior written consent from the publisher.

1 3 5 7 9 10 8 6 4 2

ISBN: 978-1-83874-291-1

Published in the USA by Flying Eye Books Ltd.
Printed in China on FSC® certified paper.

MIX
Paper | Supporting responsible forestry
FSC® C137217

THE UNEXPLAINED
GHOSTS

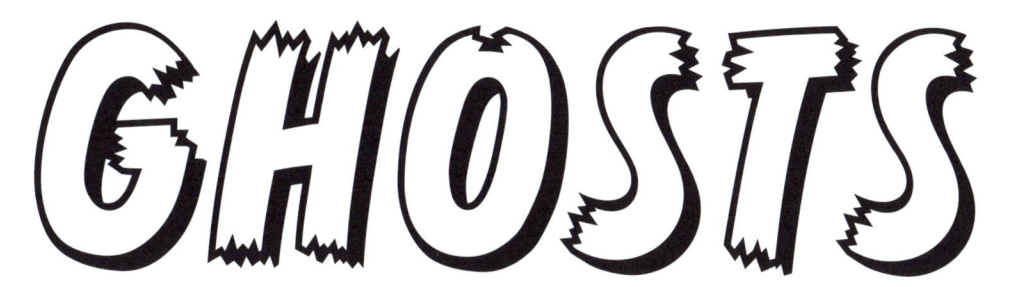

ADAM ALLSUCH BOARDMAN

FLYING EYE BOOKS

CONTENTS

Introduction   8
What is a Ghost?
What is a Haunting?
Skeptical Inquiry

Premodernity   16
Afterlife
Hantu
Duppy
Ghostly Guests
Seasonal Celebrations
Historic Hauntings
Demons
Spirit Communication
Haunted Ruins
Haunted Castles
Spiritual Protection
Knock. Knock. Who's There?

The 19th Century   36
Mediumship
Yūrei
North American Ghost Legends
Talking Boards
Infamous Isolation
Spirit Photography
Brick by Brick

The 20th Century   50
Debunkery
Ghost Hunters
Tools of the Trade
Most Haunted
Liminal Space
Simulated Hauntings
Timeslips
Doppelgängers

The Midcentury   64
Phantom Vehicles
Haunted Institutions
Vile Vortices
Phantom Animals

The Postmodern Era   72
Possessed Possessions
Ghost Towns
Ghost Hunters in Media

The 21st Century   80
Modern Hauntings
Enduring Legends
Ghosts Through Time
Ghosts Today

Glossary   90

Index   92

INTRODUCTION

Ever since humans started writing, ghost stories have been recorded and shared. They come in all shapes and sizes, such as gloomy grey ladies and creeping nightmares.

They haunt our stories, from *Casper the Friendly Ghost* (1945) to Peter Venkman's messy encounter with Slimer in *Ghostbusters* (1984).

But why do people believe in ghosts? For some it is part of tradition as ghosts have emerged from myths and legends. For others, belief is sparked by inexplicable occurrences, like eerie noises and strange sights.

This fascination with ghosts has led to the creation of ghost-hunting gadgets, theories and popular tourist locations. Ghost hunters and mediums have investigated places that many fear to visit such as haunted castles, graveyards and creepy forests, searching for evidence of ghosts.

This book has collected many myths, legends and curiosities surrounding the phenomena of ghosts. Are you ready to discover if there really is anything beyond the world of the living?

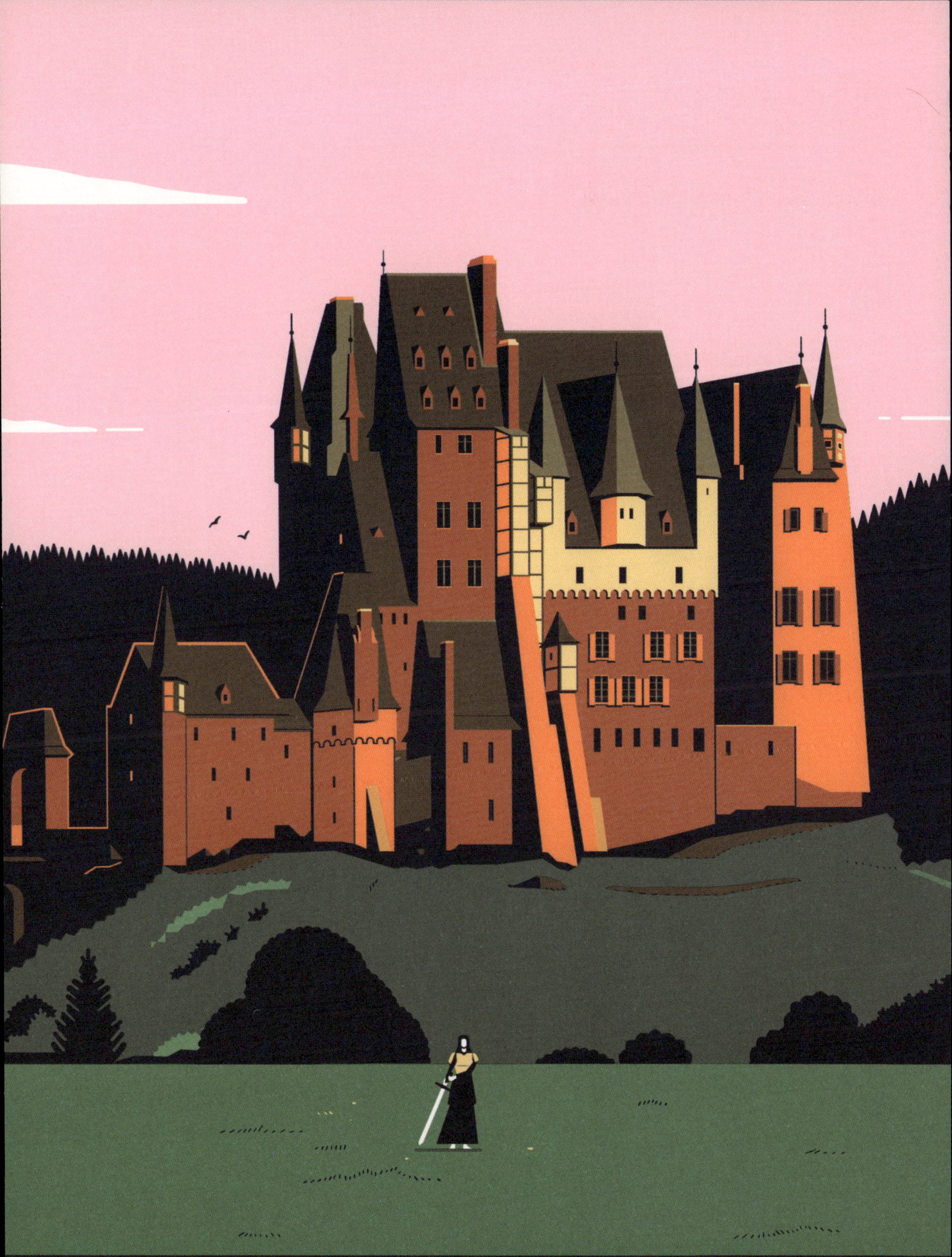

WHAT IS A GHOST?

Ghosts are thought to be spirits of the dead that often lurk near places important to their former lives. The word ghost comes from the Germanic word *gást* meaning 'soul' or 'spirit'.

Throughout time, many people have reported ghost sightings. Encounters range from fleeting glimpses of glowing ghouls to spectral ships on stormy seas. People also share ghost stories from myths and legends passed down through time.

Legend
Legends are stories about people and places that may or may not be true, but people still believe in them.

Myth
Myths are stories tied strongly to a belief system, such as the Bible or ancient Greek mythos. Myths can take thousands of years to develop and are often used to explain mysterious phenomena.

Types of Ghosts
The exact characteristics of ghosts can be confusing due to many cultural interpretations and definitions. English researcher, Peter Underwood, organised ghosts and related spirits into neat groups:

Elementals
A broad spectrum of nature spirits, such as færies, goblins and demons.

Poltergeists
In German this word means 'noisy ghost'. These ghosts are theatrical in nature and enjoy throwing objects around.

Traditional Ghosts
Spirits of the dead that are restless and sometimes talkative.

Mental Imprints
Apparitions left in the material world by historic events.

Crisis and Death-Survival Apparitions
Apparitions seen by the friends and family of someone who is close to death.

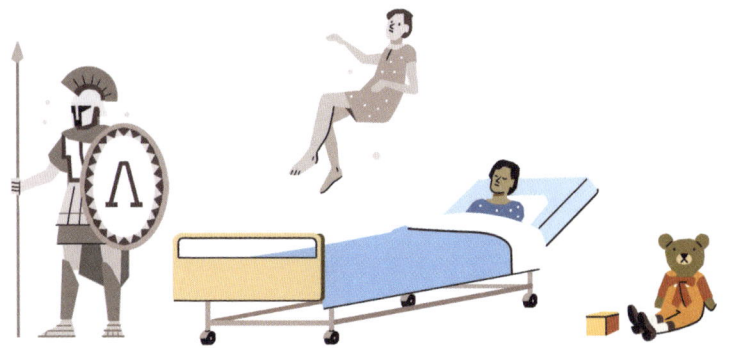

Time Slips
Localised time travel ghosts, such as the sudden appearance of an historic scene.

Ghosts of the Living
Mental projections by psychic people.

Haunted Inanimate Objects
Objects and vehicles that exhibit ghostly activity.

WHAT IS A HAUNTING?

When ghosts are believed to dwell in a fixed place it is called a 'haunting'. Traditionally, it is thought ghosts haunt the sites of their deaths, or places that were important during their lives.

People have witnessed many strange phenomena which they have attributed to a haunting.

1. **Apparition**
   A full or partial ghostly figure is seen.
2. **Apporting**
   The sudden appearance of objects.
3. **Electrical Interference**
   Lights dimming, and appliances acting oddly.
4. **Ghost Writing**
   Written messages on walls and mirrors.

5. **Knocking and Footsteps**
   Everyday sounds with unknown origins.

6. **Peculiar Pets**
   The odd behaviour of animals, such as a dog barking at an empty corner.

7. **Phantom Music**
   The sound of music from an unseen source.

8. **Voices from the Void**
   Indistinct whisperings and voices that seem to come from nowhere.

9. **Cold Spots**
   The unusual coldness of a room.

10. **Phantom Stains**
    The appearance of stains or marks.

11. **Mysterious Injuries**
    Bumps, bruises and scratches have been reported as poltergeist activity.

12. **Levitation**
    Objects that seem to float or move on their own.

13. **Possession**
    A person or object inhabited by an invasive sprit.

14. **High Strangeness**
    Dreamlike encounters.

13

SKEPTICAL INQUIRY

When paranormal claims are carefully investigated instead of being believed without question, it is called 'skeptical inquiry'. Throughout history, skeptics have investigated alleged hauntings to provide scientific explanations.

Wonky Foundations
Buildings with foundational damage can shake and make strange noises.

Plumbing
Pipes and boilers are known to make all manner of odd sounds, just like a ghost.

Hoaxing
People fake hauntings for various reasons. These can range from amusement to attempting to make money.

Hallucinations
These may be caused by head injuries and mental illnesses.

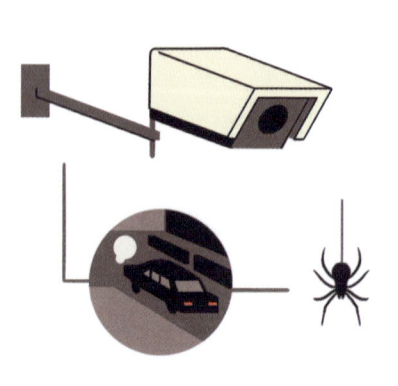

Creepy-Crawlies
Spiders, flies and other small creatures are sometimes mistaken for ghosts when they crawl over camera equipment.

Optical Illusions
Tricks of light and shadow that appear as ghosts.

Infrasound
Some studies have shown that low frequency sounds can lead to unease, dizziness and nausea.

Pareidolia
When a person sees random patterns in unrelated objects and assigns them with meaning.

Sleep Paralysis
A dreamlike awakening during sleep. A person can feel a weight on their chest and experience hallucinations.

Confirmation Bias
A pre-existing belief in the paranormal may lead witnesses to ignore other explanations.

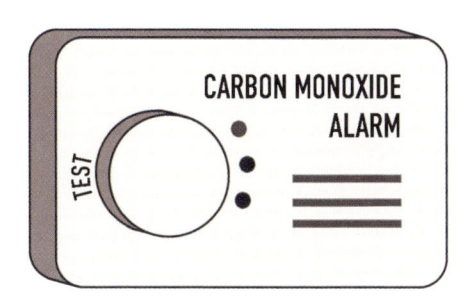

Carbon Monoxide (CO)
Exposure to this poisonous gas can cause dizziness and hallucinations.

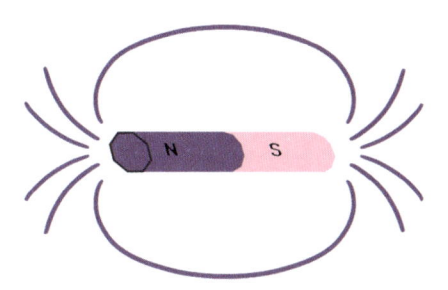

Electromagnetic Field (EMF)
Some believe high levels of EMF create feelings of unease and confusion.

15

PREMODERNITY

Oldest picture of a ghost, Babylonian clay tablet (circa 1500 BCE)

AFTERLIFE

In many ancient mythologies, ghosts were believed to be souls of the dead which have avoided or escaped the afterlife. Tradition taught that careful burial practices aided souls on their afterlife journey. The oldest burial sites discovered are over 10,000 years old. Here ancient people entombed dead bodies in caves with personal items and food.

Wrapped Up

To ancient Egyptians, the body and soul remained linked after death. To aid afterlife activities, they stocked tombs with food and tools. Rich Egyptians preserved their dead through mummification. This process involved the removal of internal organs and the use of ointments and wrappings to delay decomposition.

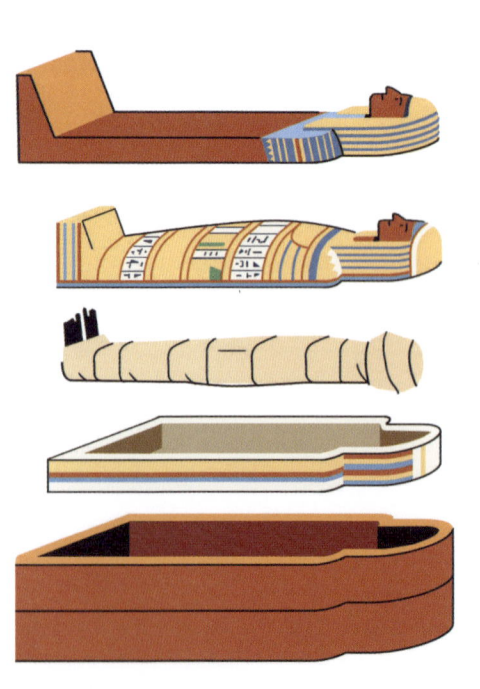

Mummy of the Theban priest Usirmose

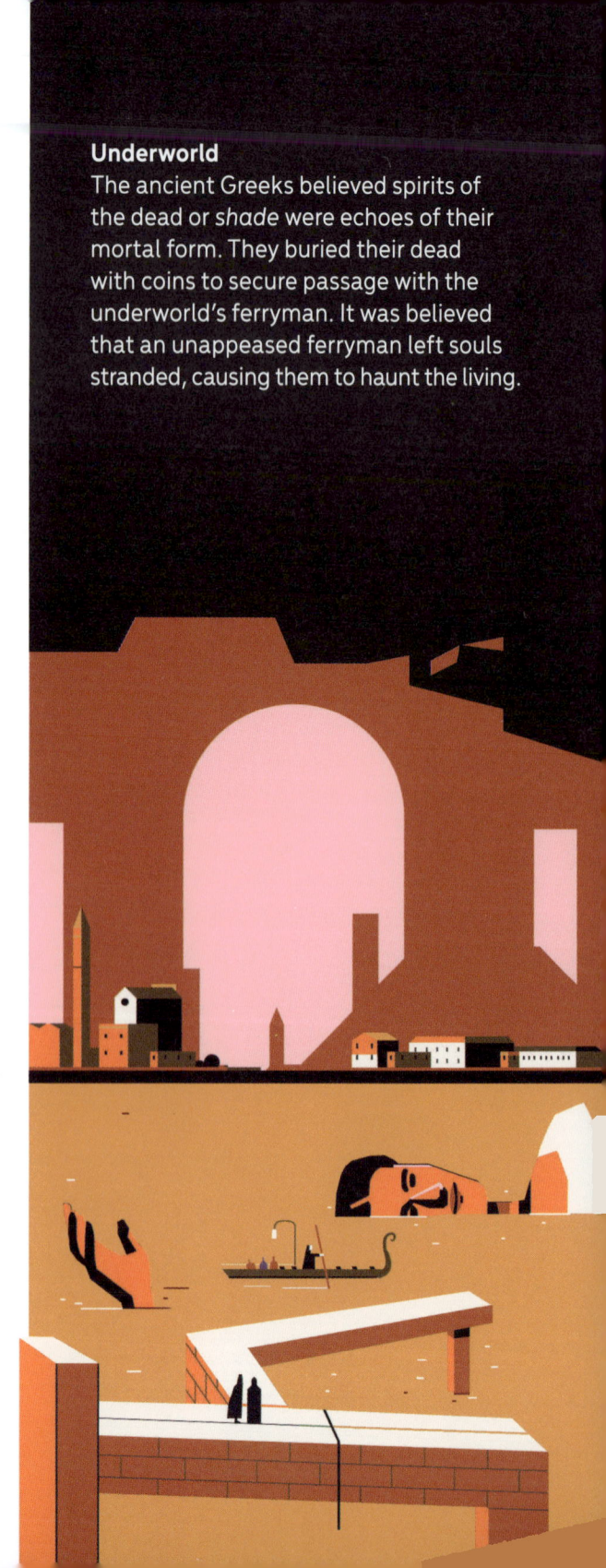

Underworld

The ancient Greeks believed spirits of the dead or *shade* were echoes of their mortal form. They buried their dead with coins to secure passage with the underworld's ferryman. It was believed that an unappeased ferryman left souls stranded, causing them to haunt the living.

Psychopomps
In Aztec mythology, the god Xolotl helped lead ghosts to one of several underworlds. A figure that performs this task is called a psychopomp (Greek for spirit conductor). Aztecs associated Xolotl with the ancient dog breed xoloitzcuintli. Sacrificial dogs and sculptures were buried alongside owners to aid in their afterlife journeys.

Sections of Soul
In ancient China, it was believed the soul was composed of two parts, the *hun* (cloud soul) and *po* (white-soul). The hun was believed to leave the body upon death, while the po remained in the corpse. During the Han Dynasty (circa 202 BCE–220 CE) nobles were buried in jade suits in effort to preserve their po soul.

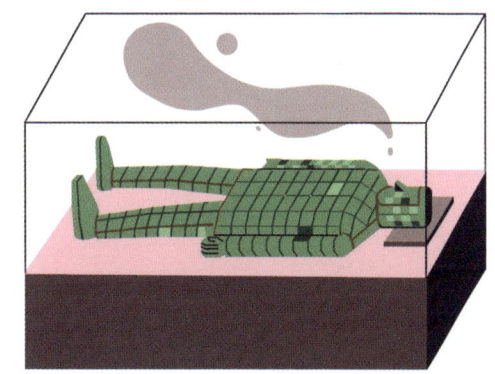

Limbo
In Catholic theology, limbo (from the medieval Latin for 'border') is home to dead sinners. It was believed souls could freely wander out of limbo and appear on earth as ghosts. In medieval Europe, the Church sold coupons to those who wanted to avoid assignment to limbo.

HANTU

The Malay peoples in Indonesia, Malaysia and neighbouring regions have developed many myths about ghosts, which they call *Hantu*. Hantu are believed to be open to negotiation through rituals and offerings. In some cases, a ghost's services may even be bought.

Bomoh
For a fee, spirit experts called *Bomoh* specialise in negotiating with ghosts in order to cure or inflict sickness.

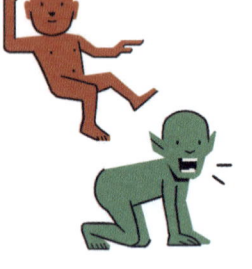

Pontianak
The ghost of a woman who has died in childbirth.

Toyol
The spirit of an infant child. It was believed that *toyol* could be commissioned to commit petty theft.

Hantu Jamuan
Party-crashing ghosts that are mischievous until fed with a meal.

Hantu Kembung
Ghosts that cause headaches and stomach pains associated with rainy weather.

DUPPY

In the Caribbean, restless ghosts are called *duppy*. The belief in duppy traces from West Africa, and they are thought to take many forms, both human and animal-like. According to legend, duppy are tricksters. There are several traditional methods that are thought to defeat the duppy, including wearing clothes inside out and eating salt.

Rollin' Calf
The large ghost of a wicked person, commonly described to be cow-like with smoking nostrils and red eyes.

Whooping Boy
A red-eyed child duppy with lethally hot breath.

Birds, Snakes and Lizards
In some cases, duppy take the form of familiar animals.

River Mumma
An aquatic duppy that lures people into dangerous waters.

GHOSTLY GUESTS

In some cultures, groups of ghosts make frequent visits to the living world. This is considered a bad omen by some cultures while others welcome their ghostly guests through festivals.

La Santa Compaña

Since ancient times, people in Portugal and Spain have witnessed a legendary procession of ghosts known as *La Santa Compaña* (The Holy Company). The company wear white hoods to conceal their skeletal features and are led by an entranced mortal from the local area. This mortal is said to awake the next day with no memory of their march.

Tradition states that there are a few ways to avoid being selected to join the procession, including the drawing of protective symbols or the offering of a black cat (no cats are harmed, thankfully).

Wild Hunt

The apparition known as the Wild Hunt or Ghost Riders appear in legends around the world. These gangs of airborne ghosts are said to ride spectral or flaming horses.

Ghost Festivals

Ghost festivals have been celebrated in countries such as China, Malaysia and Vietnam since the distant past. In Taoism, the event is called the *Zhongyuan Festival* and takes place on the 15th day of the seventh lunar month. The festival has origins in the ancient Buddhist belief that ancestral ghosts rise from the underworld every year. During this period, believers welcome the dead with many rituals.

Ghost King
A large image of the King of Ghosts is important to many observances. The effigy is traditionally set alight following the presentation of offerings, the lighting of candles and the burning of incense.

Front Row Seats
During the festivities seats are reserved at live events for the invisible dead to occupy. It is considered very unlucky for living attendees to sit on the seats.

Joss Paper
Special paper called joss paper is burned as an offering to the dead. Joss paper is often decorated with seals, stamps or made to resemble money.

Sights, Sounds and Smells
Incense, lanterns and singing are used in an effort to guide ghosts along streets and rivers.

SEASONAL CELEBRATIONS

Two of the most famous celebrations of the dead, Halloween and *Día de los Muertos*, take place at a similar time of the year. Each festival has unique traditions.

Día de los Muertos
The Mexican Day of the Dead or *Día de los Muertos* is celebrated on the 1st and 2nd of November. Some also believe it might have developed from old Aztec celebrations. The intent of the festival is to honour the dead with happiness, food and attractive decorations.

Look of the Dead
Calavera are decorative depictions of skulls. They appear in sugary snacks, face-paint and as the décor for altars. Today, designs are highly influenced by the work of 19th century Mexican illustrator José Guadalupe Posada Aguilar.

Ofrenda
Altars called *ofrenda* are decorated with food and bright petals to attract wandering ghosts. It is thought that pleasant and familiar odours attract souls from their graves and into the homes of their friends and families.

Halloween

Halloween was originally a European festival preceding All Saints Day or All Hallows Day on the 1st of November. Over time, All Hallows Eve became Halloween. Some believe it replaced an ancient pagan Celtic festival called *Samhain* (Scottish Gaelic for summer's end) that marked the start of winter and was associated, in Ireland, with the supernatural.

Trick or Treat!

This involves visiting neighbours in costume for some free sweets and chocolate! The tradition is thought to originate in Samhain practices, where people wore animal skins to ward off unwanted spirits. Halloween is also celebrated with spooky decorations, carving pumpkins and watching scary movies.

Halloween costumes

A carved Halloween pumpkin or jack o'lantern

HISTORIC HAUNTINGS

Besides ancient myths and legends, people have also recorded personal encounters with ghosts. While the oldest surviving report of a haunting came from ancient Greece, it is likely many experiences have been lost or passed into legend through speech.

Athenian Apparition
Athens, Greece, 1st Century BCE

The oldest recorded haunting comes from a letter dated around 100 CE. The ancient Roman author Pliny the Younger wrote the letter to a friend, describing an old haunting. According to the letter, tenants fled a house in Athens due to strange noises and the apparition of a ghost. Luckily the philosopher Athenodorus Cananites took over the house and appeased the ghost by giving its long-forgotten corpse a proper burial.

Drummer Of Tedworth
Tedworth, England, Circa 1661-1663

In 1661, landowner John Mompesson experienced one of the first reported poltergeist hauntings in England. The event was characterised by phantom drumming sounds and the movement of objects around his home. The haunting drew visitors from all around the country, including Christopher Wren (architect of St. Paul's Cathedral) and clergyman Joseph Glanvill.

Claw-like marks were discovered in soot.

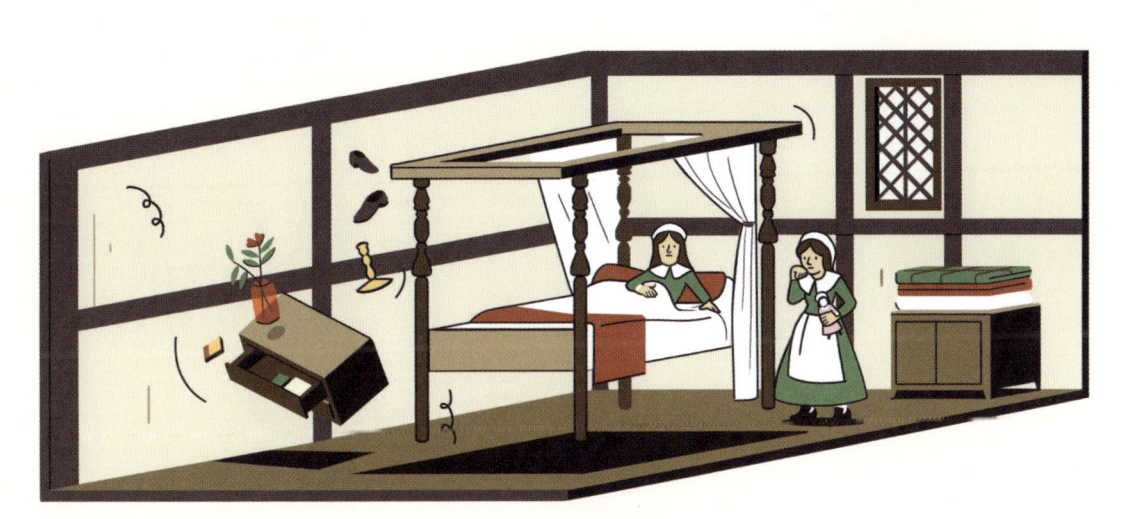

The Ghost Hunter
Glanvill organised a careful investigation of the property, making him one of the first ghost hunters. Later skeptics suggested Mompesson's daughter was responsible for faking the activity. Whether this accusation is fair or not, the blaming of children for paranormal activity is common in skeptic literature.

Despite all the activity, no one actually saw a ghost.

Joseph Glanvill

DEMONS

In myth and legend, demons are inhuman spirits often associated with mischief or evil. Despite being different from traditional ghosts, demon hauntings can be very similar. For example, they are believed to move objects, make strange sounds and be a nuisance.

Ancient Gods
Christian mythologies have many different demons, each believed to be a fallen angel. Many of their names come from beliefs that existed before the Bible. For example, Moloch was a bull-headed god or a type of sacrifice.

Japanese theatrical demon mask

Tricksters
Jinn refers to a group of paranormal forces, often associated with trickster and wish-granting spirits. A famous lamp-dwelling Jinn or Genie appears in the ancient tale *Aladdin*.

Demon Disguise
In the 16th century, many Protestants stopped believing in limbo and ghosts, which were part of Catholic teachings. Instead, they said that hauntings were the work of the devil and his demons. However, some people continued to believe in ghosts.

Mesopotamian demon statuette

Thai Yaksha temple guardian

SPIRITUAL COMMUNICATION

For thousands of years, people have tried to summon ghosts through ritual magic. Practitioners distinguish two types of summoning called 'invocation' and 'evocation'. Invocation invites a spirit to possess someone, while evocation encourages a spirit to appear in a convenient place, such as a secret dungeon.

Summoners believe ghosts can help heal sickness, pass on knowledge or even attack enemies.

Noaidi
To the Sami peoples of Nordic Europe, those who talked to the spirit world were called *noaidi*. Noaidi asked the spirits for successful hunting trips and good weather.

Jhākri
In Nepal, practitioners are called *Jhākri*. Traditionally they brandish a drum called a *dhyāngro*, which is used during rituals. Besides blessings and magical cures, they are used to call on ancestral ghosts.

Mu
In Korean cultures, those who commune with spirits are often called *Mu*. Their rituals typically involve bright costumes and dancing.

Plastic Shaman
Sometimes, people from outside a culture take and misuse traditional practices in the wrong way. Native American activists call these people 'plastic shamans'.

HAUNTED RUINS

The skeletal ruins of houses stand as eerie reminders of those who once lived there. When these buildings were abandoned under tragic circumstances, they often gave rise to ghost stories. In the 20th century, cars and planes made it easier for people to visit these supposedly haunted places.

Kinarut Mansion, Malaysia, abandoned circa 1920s
An abandoned manor house found in a forested area of eastern Malaysia. Today, the mansion is kept as a historic attraction and legends have spread that it is home to a variety of spirits.

Lui Family Mansion, abandoned circa 1950s
Known as the *Minxiong Ghost House*, this grand property has been completely covered in foliage. The property is supposedly haunted by the ghost of a maid who drowned in the property's well.

La Casa Embrujada, abandoned in 2013
Directly translated, *The Haunted House* entered local legend in 2013 after a supposed death on the property. To discourage ghost hunting trespassers a large sign reads 'This is Not a Haunted House'.

HAUNTED CASTLES

Castles are commonly identified as the sites of ghost legends. Their battles, deadly dungeons and historical figures make them perfect vessels for storytelling.

Zvíkov Castle
Zvíkovské Podhradí, Czechia, circa 13th century
Haunted by a ghost that preys on electronics and animals.

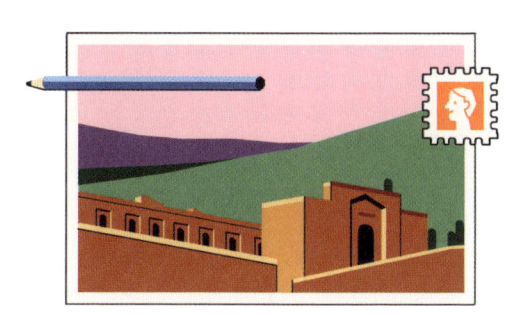

Bhangarh Fort
Rajasthan, India, circa 16th century
Legend suggests this castle is haunted after being cursed by an angry wizard.

Predjama Castle
Predjama, Slovenia, circa 13th century
Legend says that the Knight Erasmus, supposedy haunts the castle after he was murdered on the toilet.

Edinburgh Castle
Edinburgh, Scotland, UK, circa 12th century
Often attributed the title of the UK's 'most haunted' castle in tourism materials.

Kinnitty Castle
Kinnitty, Ireland, circa 19th century
The latest castle to sit on a plot occupied for over a millennium. Believed to be haunted by all types of ghosts.

SPIRITUAL PROTECTION

Belief in ghosts and evil spirits have prompted many cultures to develop protective measures. Practices come in many shapes and sizes, from amulets to magic rituals. The practice of averting evil is called 'apotropaic magic' (from the Greek for 'ward off').

Ifrit
In ancient Egypt and neighbouring Middle Eastern regions, some believed the scenes of murders were haunted by vengeful spirits called *Ifrit*. In some practices, nails were driven into the murder location to appease the spirit.

Lemures
The ancient Romans called vengeful ghosts *Lemures*. During the festival of Lemuria, Romans banished Lemures by hosting loud parties, and ritualistically throwing beans.

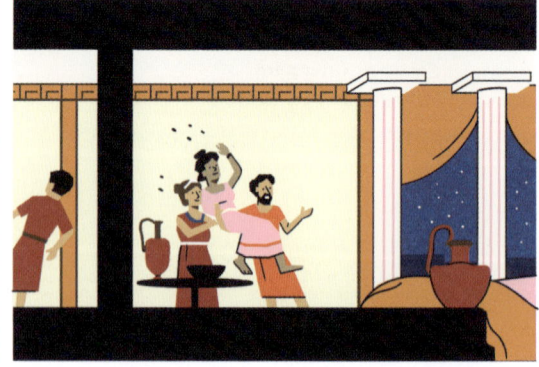

Gorgoneion
Ancient Greek architecture often features imagery associated with the gorgons (monsters in Greek mythology) to frighten away evil spirits. They are often represented in carvings, reliefs and mosaics.

Spiderweb Charm
The Ojibwe people in North America have an ancient tradition of making spiderweb-like charms to capture evil spirits and nightmares. Today, the charm is most often called a 'dreamcatcher'.

Grotesqueries
From the Middle Ages, European churches and castles featured monstrous stone carvings. They were thought to prevent the entry of evil spirits and the Devil. Grotesqueries are also used on roofs to redirect rainwater and are called 'gargoyles'.

Horseshoes
An ancient practice with origins in the Middle East saw iron horseshoes mounted above doorways to ward off evil spirits. In Europe, the practice became associated with Christianity due to a 10th century legend in which the English Bishop Dunstan thwarted the Devil with a horseshoe.

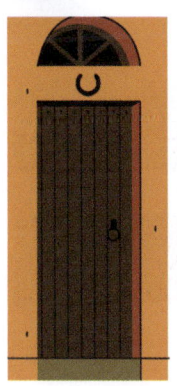

Evil Eye
One of the most common practices of apotropaic magic is the use of amulets to protect against the Evil Eye. Originating in ancient Mediterranean and Middle East cultures, the Evil Eye is believed to be a sort of directed curse. In many cases Evil Eye amulets are also used to protect against ghosts and inhuman spirits.

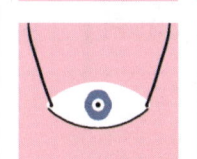

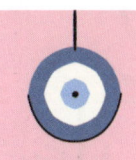

KNOCK, KNOCK, WHO'S THERE?

Cock Lane
London, UK, 1762

One of the most famous hauntings in the UK took place in an 18th century London house. Following the death of Fanny Lynes, her ghost (known as Scratching Fanny) was thought to communicate by knocking and scratching around her former house.

The boasts of landlord Richard Parsons encouraged vast crowds of sightseers to visit. Famous figures included the Prince of York.

Street chaos and news reportage led a group of intellectuals to investigate. Samuel Johnson (creator of the dictionary) attended and decided that Parsons' daughter had faked the haunting.

This was was confirmed when a piece of wood was found on her, which she used to make the scratching noises and knockings of the ghost. Later, Richard Parsons was put on trial and found guilty, resulting in a two-year prison sentence.

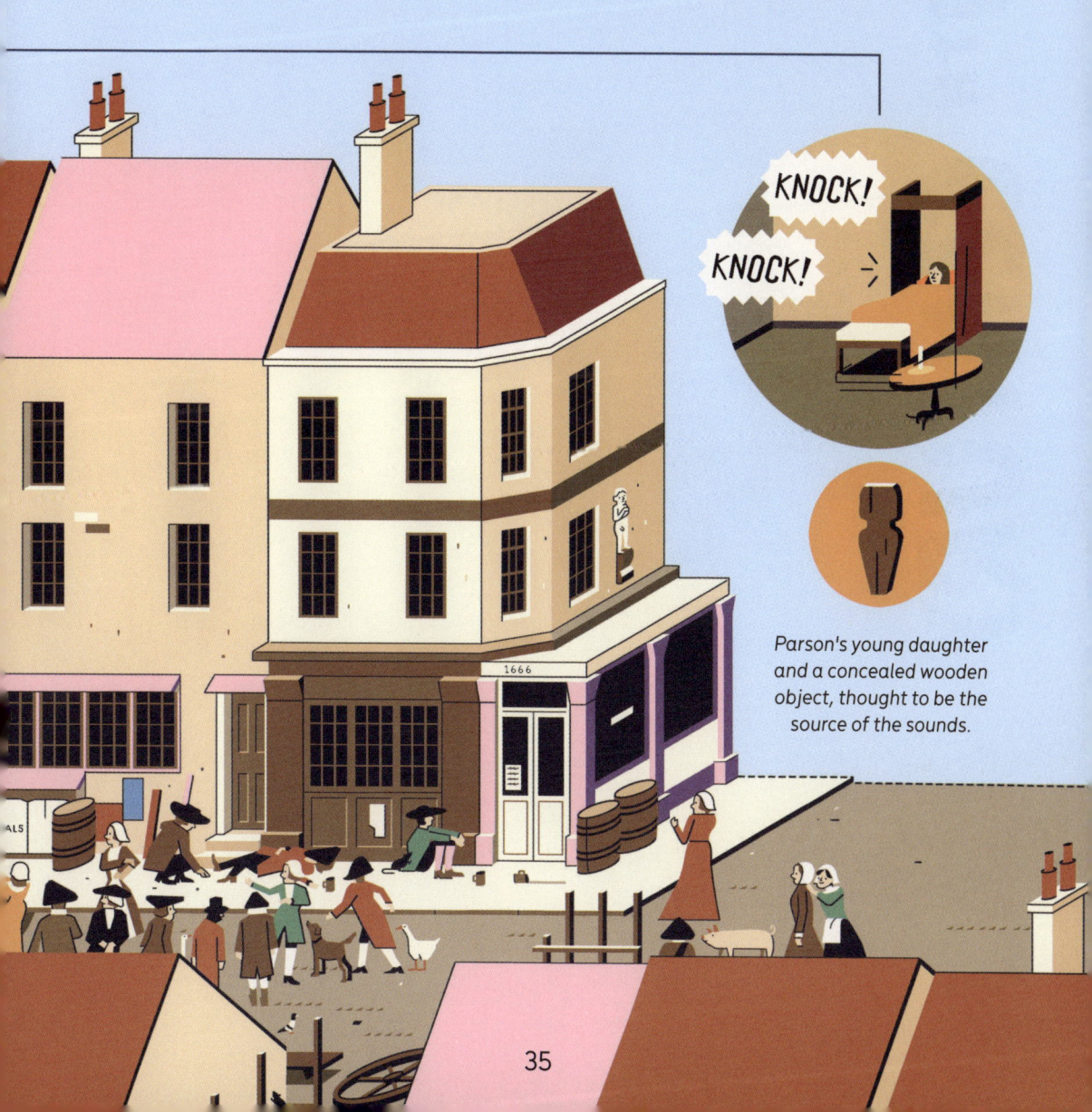

KNOCK!
KNOCK!

Parson's young daughter and a concealed wooden object, thought to be the source of the sounds.

THE 19TH CENTURY

Yūrei woodblock print (circa 1850)

MEDIUMSHIP

Spiritualism is the belief that people can contact ghosts through ritual séances (from the French word for 'session'). It became a successful business for mediums and it gave comfort to people who had lost loved ones.

Séance
In the most popular form of séances, participants sat around a table with hands touching in a dark room. Mediums led sessions and passed on messages from ghosts.

Spirit Cabinet
Some mediums conducted their séances from a small booth or cabinet.

Thrilling Theatrics
Many mediums wore theatrical costumes or involved unique gimmicks to make their performances more exciting.

Ectoplasm
A white goo ejected from the mouth. Many believed ectoplasm to be spiritual energy. Hoaxers were often caught using cloth to produce the effect.

During the heights of Spiritualism, mediums were a popular booking for private events and public theatres. Performances were made in the dark as mediums claimed that ghosts hated light. Skeptics suggested the only purpose of dim lighting was to conceal fakery.

The Davenport Brothers' Spirit Cabinet
During performances the brothers were tied up inside a cabinet filled with instruments. Once the doors closed the instruments would sound as if played by ghosts.

Houdini's Margery Box
A box built to test the truthfulness of mediums by limiting their movement.

Spirit Writing
Some mediums claimed to deliver messages from spirits by writing them on paper. During these performances, they often wore blindfolds to make it seem more believable and to reduce suspicion that they were faking the messages.

YŪREI

Eerie Art
In Japanese mythology, ghosts are called *Yūrei* (meaning 'faint' or 'dim spirit'). In the 19th century, Yūrei were popular subjects in theatre and on woodblock prints. There are many types of Yūrei, each said to haunt the earth for different grievances endured in life.

1. **Onryō**
   Ghosts that lust for revenge against those who wronged them.

2. **Funayūrei**
   A type of vengeful *Onryō* that died at sea. They are sometimes fish-like in appearance.

3. **Fuyūrei**
   Floating, aimless spirits.

4. **Goryō**
   Vengeful aristocrats, capable of summoning natural disasters.

5. **Jibakurei**
   Similar to the aimless *Fuyūrei*, except restricted to one specific place.

6. **Zashiki-warashi**
   The mischievous ghosts of children.

7. **Ubume**
   The ghost of a mother who died in childbirth. They are said to provide gifts to any surviving children.

8. **Woeful Women**
   In art, Yūrei are commonly depicted as white-clad women with sickly expressions and tangled hair, similar to depictions of ghosts in modern cinema.

NORTH AMERICAN GHOST LEGENDS

North America has many ghost legends, some of which come from the mythologies of Native Americans. Other legends are influenced by settlers from Europe.

The Bell Witch
Bell Ranch, TN, USA, circa 1817–1821

According to legend, Bell Ranch was haunted by a talkative ghost, who locals identified as Kate Batts, a local witch. The ghost enjoyed insulting the ranchers and using supernatural powers. The ghost supposedly turned a man into a mule, moved objects and injured the ranch's residents.

Bell Ranch

Monstrous apparitions

Head rancher John Bell's attempt to throw the witch ghost into the fireplace

42

Great Dismal Swamp
*Virginia and North Carolina, USA,
circa 18th century*

These sprawling alligator-filled marshes has been home to Native American communities for over 13,000 years. European explorers in the 18th century found it gloomy and named it the Great Dismal Swamp and French speakers called it the *Marais Maudit*, or 'cursed swamp'.

With thick fog, damp earth and the groans of amphibians, birds and reptiles, it is easy to understand why the swamp might have attracted so many ghost legends.

The ghost named *The Lady of the Lake* is said to paddle her canoe through the mists, lit only by fireflies. There are also tales of phantom figures, ships and lights supposedly haunting the green waters.

TALKING BOARDS

Planchette
In the 1850s, European product designers began selling a pencil-wielding wooden pallet on wheels called a *planchette* (French for 'little plank'). It was believed that participants could place their hands on the planchette, and spirits would guide their hands to make it draw shapes and letters.

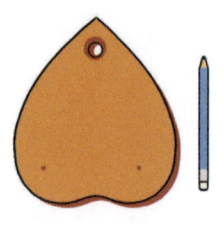

GW Cottrell (1859)

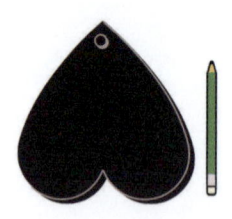

Kirkby & Co (1869)

Ouija Board (1890)

Espirito Talking Board (1891)

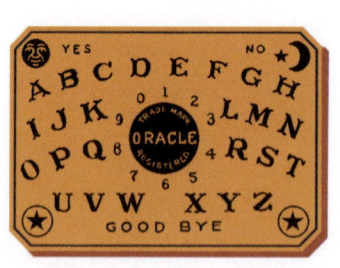

Mystifying Oracle (1915)

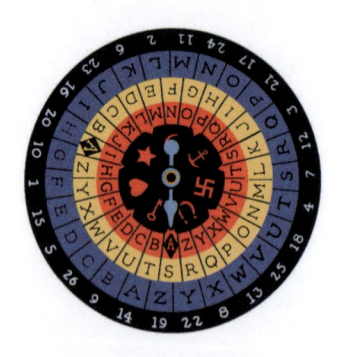

Mystiscope Fortune Teller (1925)

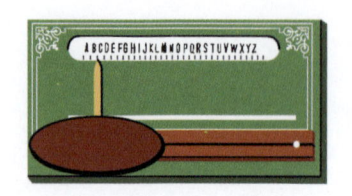

Telepathic Spirit Communicator (1936)

Hasko Mystic Board (1940)

Mystic Answer Board (1944)

Spirit Boards

A more popular design called a 'spirit board' used a small planchette which, when held correctly, would seemingly point to letters and numbers on a large board. The most famous example called *Ouija* was developed by American inventor Elijah Bond. Skeptics believe that planchette and similar devices are not guided by ghosts, but rather the ideomotor effect (the involuntary twitching made by people using the board).

Ouija Board – Deluxe Edition (1967)

Transogram (1967)

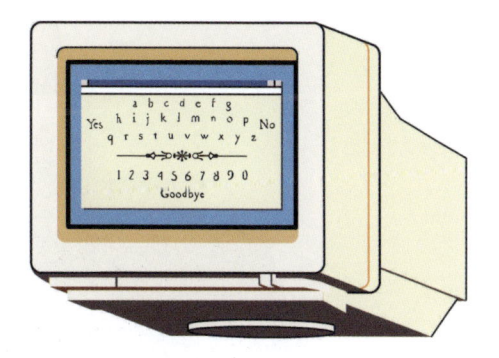

Kokkuri-San (1970s)

Ouija for Windows (1993)

Charmed Spirit Board (2006)

Ouija Board (2008)

Talking Board (2015)

INFAMOUS ISOLATION

Phare De Tévennec
The coast of France, 19th century

Besides places with strong historical connections, remote structures often gather ghost legends. Built in 1875, the French lighthouse *Phare De Tévennec* has become the subject of many ghost stories. In its early years, the lighthouse was manned by solitary lightkeepers. According to legend, the first caretaker Henri Guezennec was driven mad by the voices of dead sailors that plagued the area. The newspaper *Le Télégramme* reported that crucifixes were placed on the surrounding rocks to try and exorcise the spirits. However, over time, the tides have washed them away.

SPIRIT PHOTOGRAPHY

In the 19th century it became popular for photographers to sell 'real' ghost pictures made in a studio or at a séance.

Stereoscopic Spectres
The London Stereoscopic Company specialised in selling photos with a 3D effect. In the 1850s they sold staged pictures featuring ghosts.

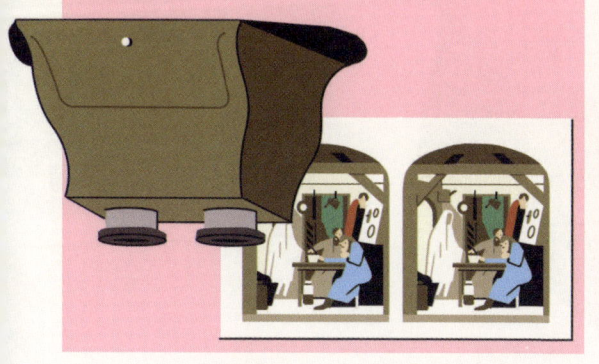

Deathly Dolls
In the 1870s, French medium Édouard Isidore Buguet created miniature dolls to model as ghosts in his double-exposed photographs. However, he was jailed for fraud.

Double Exposure

Used photo plate inserted in camera | Portrait taken | Photograph developed with overlapping images | Mysterious 'ghost' appears on photo

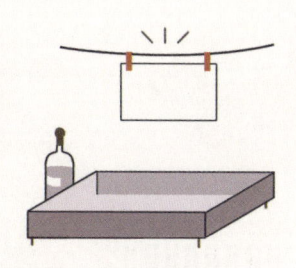

Mumler's Memorabilia
William Mumler discovered, in the 1860s, that mixing photographic negatives could create ghost-like figures. With his wife, Hannah, they sold photographs starring the deceased family members of clients. After the American Civil War, many grieving families wanted these services. One famous client was Mary Todd Lincoln, the widow of President Abraham Lincoln. During a trial, Mumler was accused of fraud but found not guilty. However, his reputation was forever damaged.

BRICK BY BRICK

Winchester Mystery House
San Jose, CA, USA

In 1884, Sarah Winchester, wife and heiress of the late William Winchester, started turning a farmhouse in San Jose into a huge, confusing labyrinth. Winchester had a strong creative vision and made the architectural plans herself. After an earthquake in 1906, she continued to redesign the house, adding strange features like doors in odd places, stairs leading to nowhere and uneven floors, all of which created a spooky and unsettling atmosphere.

Sarah Winchester

Unusual interiors

Doors to nowhere

Ghost Gossip
During her lifetime, there was persistent gossip that a spiritualist medium had told Sarah to keep building the house nonstop. The idea was that the constant construction would calm the spirits of people who had been killed by Winchester guns. This gossip became legend and today it is shared by tour guides and ghost hunters.

THE 20TH CENTURY

Houdini promotional poster (1909)

DEBUNKERY

In the 20th century, skeptics continued to challenge belief in ghosts, viewing it as a sign of superstitions or medium trickery. American magician Harry Houdini was appalled to see some mediums use stage magic to perform tricks he felt were deceptive. Rose 'Mac' Mackenberg was the lead investigator for Houdini's campaign. To gather evidence, Mac worked undercover whilst wearing imaginative disguises.

A spirit trumpet.

Mac's many disguises.

Spirit trumpets were typically used to amplify the voice of a spirit that had allegedly inhabited a medium.

Magic Tricks

Basic Tricks were exposed in pamphlets, books and during stage performances, such as those by Houdini. Tricks were engineered by mediums and their stooges (assistants). Children made good stooges as their smaller size made them harder to spot, especially in the dark during séances.

Special hooks attached to mediums' clothing could move tables without need of their hands.

Information could be conveyed to mediums through hidden Morse Code devices.

Glowing objects hung from a string were used to make ghostly lights.

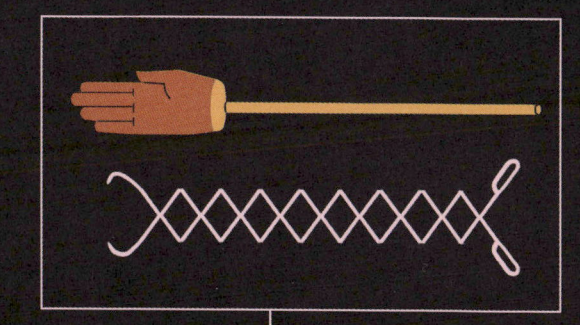

Extending arms were used to poke sitters remotely.

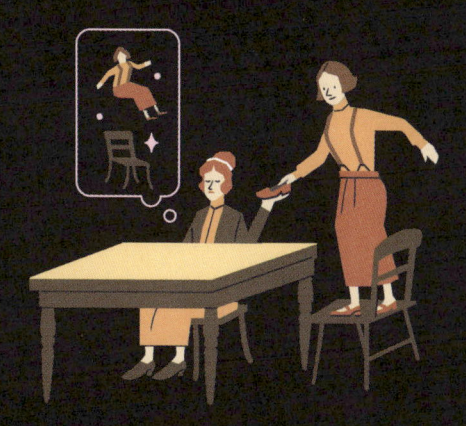

POKE!

Under the cover of darkness, levitation could be faked with various props.

ROSABELLE, BELIEVE!

Special pads were engineered to reveal spirit writing.

GHOST HUNTERS

Ghost hunting is the practice of investigating places that are believed to be haunted, with the goal of finding proof of ghosts or a rational, scientific explanation. There isn't one set way to conduct ghost hunts, but they usually involve carefully planned investigations of locations said to be haunted.

1. Interview
A witness or property owner is interviewed by the investigators.

2. Planning and Research
The place of a haunting is examined in daylight to familiarise the layout. Additional background information about the location is uncovered in libraries and online.

3. Site Investigation
Ghost hunting is typically a night-time activity dating back to the era of mediumship. However, some modern ghost hunters choose to break from this tradition and prefer to investigate during the day.

4. Vigil
Ghost hunters remain in the place until the early hours.

5. Debrief
Data collected from the site is studied and discussed.

6. Hypothesis
The investigators try to explain paranormal experiences.

7. Feedback
Investigators report back to the client and make suggestions. For example, if carbon monoxide is discovered they will suggest asking a gas engineer to resolve the problem.

TOOLS OF THE TRADE

Paranormal investigators use a range of tools to discover supposed evidence of the ghosts, or rational explanations for hauntings.

Pen and Paper
An investigator records witness statements, weather conditions and draws intricate floor plans.

Flour
Flour, chalk and other powders have been used to reveal footprints of frauds.

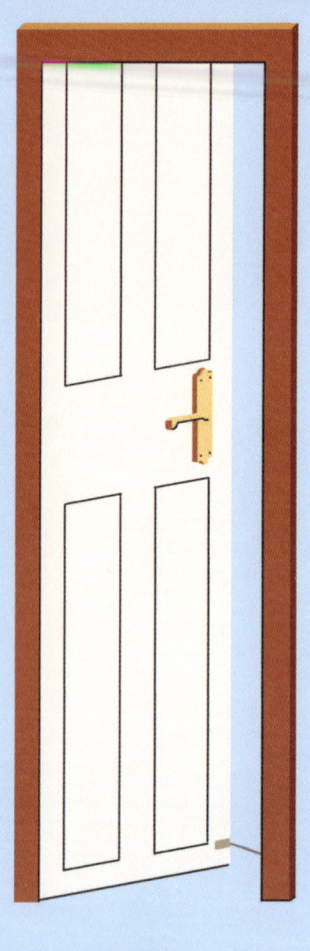

Map and Survey
Surveying a property can reveal blind spots, strange shadows and other architectural oddities that may cause bizarre experiences.

Cameras
Used in attempt to capture a picture of a ghost.

Trip Wires
Thread has been used to catch frauds sneaking through hallways and doors.

Laser Thermometers
Some use laser thermometers to detect 'cold spots' made by ghosts. These devices only measure surface temperature, and are not always accurate.

Sound Recorders
Used in attempt to capture the voices of ghosts, known as electronic voice phenomena (EVP).

Dogs
Ghost hunters have been known to bring along faithful companions to detect ghosts. Critics of the practice suggest leading a dog around in a dark building filled with anxious ghost hunters is a silly idea.

Carbon Monoxide Detector
Carbon monoxide poisoning can cause a range of symptoms associated with hauntings and is very dangerous. Detecting its presence can help prevent illness and death.

Electromagnetic Field Meter (EMF)
Some believe they can detect ghosts in the fluctuations of EMF. EMF meters are actually designed to monitor wiring and appliances.

Air Ion Counter
Atmospheres with high ion counts may cause a range of mild symptoms associated with hauntings, such as unusual fatigue.

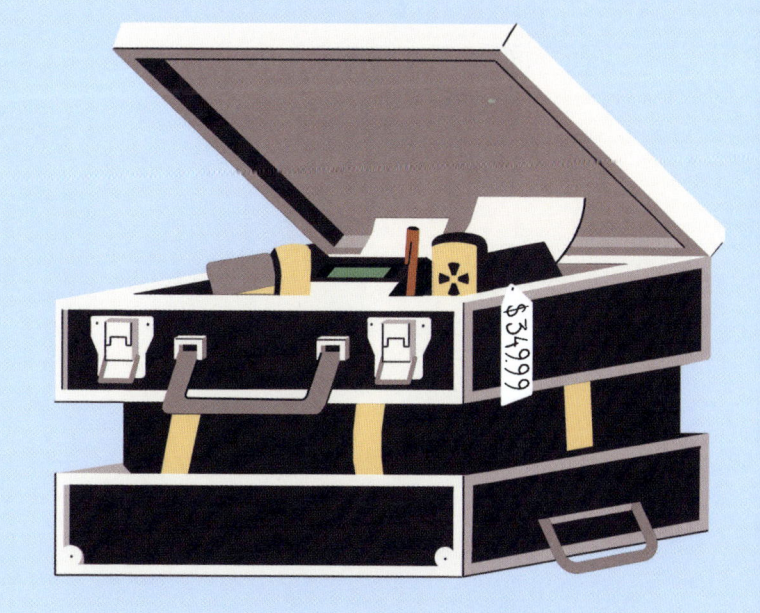

Commercial Ghost Hunting Kits
Pre-packaged sets of equipment can be very expensive.

Infrared (IR) Camera
Invisible to the human eye, IR radiation is emitted by all objects. IR cameras are deployed as night vision by teams to record goings on in the dark.

MOST HAUNTED

Borley Rectory
Borley, Essex, United Kingdom, 1927–1938

Described as the 'Most Haunted House in Britain' by ghost hunter Harry Price, Borley Rectory was home to many ghostly disturbances and investigations over several decades. Since there's no scientific way to measure how haunted a place is, the title 'most haunted' was based largely on its reputation and the many stories associated with it.

Skull

Harry Price, ghost hunter

Ghostly writing

'Ghost nun' reputedly seen at property

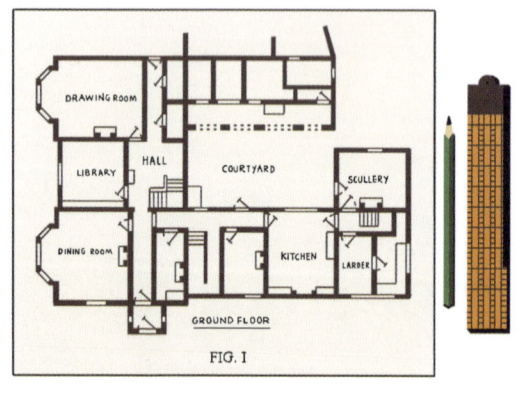

A map of Borley Rectory

'Trigger objects' were placed around the house to encourage poltergeist activity.

In 1927, Reverend Guy Eric Smith and wife Mabel moved into the Borley Rectory, finding it to be cold, drafty and old fashioned. To make matters worse, the couple found a human skull and saw a ghost in the garden.

Harry Price briefly investigated in 1929 and recorded all sorts of paranormal activity, including the throwing of objects. After his reports to newspapers, the rectory became a popular destination for paranormal tourists. In 1937, Price recruited 48 volunteers to observe the property, on the condition they follow a set of rules. Caretakers took notes, drew maps and entertained themselves with planchette but were unable to find any conclusive evidence of haunting.

LIMINAL SPACE

Some locations gain their haunted reputation because of their spooky appearance. Tunnels are passages between light and dark, making them liminal spaces, or in-between areas. Many tunnels around the world are thought to be haunted and carry legends of ghosts.

Kiyotaki Tunnel
Kyoto, Japan, 1929

The Kiyotaki Tunnel in Japan is popular amongst paranormal tourists. However, warning signs remind visitors of the dangers of walking into an active tunnel. Built in 1929, the narrow tunnel is surrounded by dark woods and traffic lights. Many ghost legends include specific conditions, such as the right time, weather condition or date best suited for the sighting of a ghost. In this case, the nearby traffic light is said to suddenly light green when a ghost is present. After an earthquake in 1968, repair workers discovered aged bones and a shattered skull amongst the rubble, likely belonging to a those who died during the original construction.

SIMULATED HAUNTINGS

In the absence of real hauntings, 20th century engineers built simulated attractions. The most popular attractions, the *Haunted House* and *Ghost Train* may still be found in theme parks and fun fairs to this day.

Ghost Train

The first ghost train ride opened in 1930 on Blackpool Pleasure Beach in England. Imported from America as a Pretzel Ride (named due to the knotted corridors within), the ride was renamed in reference to the popular play *The Ghost Train* (1923).

Actors and crew at simulated attractions

Ghost Train cars

60

Haunted Houses
The simulated haunted house involves customers wandering around a structure filled with frightful decor and actors. These haunted houses became popular in 1920s America and were often put on by magicians. Since then, they have become more advanced and realistic with the help of animatronics, optical illusions and set-dressing making them as convincing as Hollywood film productions.

Phantasmagoria
Phantasmagorias were theatrical performances of the supernatural with the help of magic lanterns (lamp-lit projectors), sets and actors. Likely first established in 17th century Germany, phantasmagorias were used to delight audiences and aid in fake séances.

TIMESLIPS

Some people have reported coming across people and places from another time period. British poet and psychical researcher Frederic W. H. Myers called this 'retrocognition'. It is more commonly known as 'timeslips', where experiences are characterised by ghost-like figures and visions.

Palace of Versailles, France
In 1901, English academics Charlotte Anne Moberly and Eleanor Jourdain apparently wandered into an 18th century version of the Palace of Versailles. One skeptical theory suggests the pair crashed an avant-garde LGBTQ+ party, as poet Robert de Montesquiou was known for hosting fancy dress parties in the area.

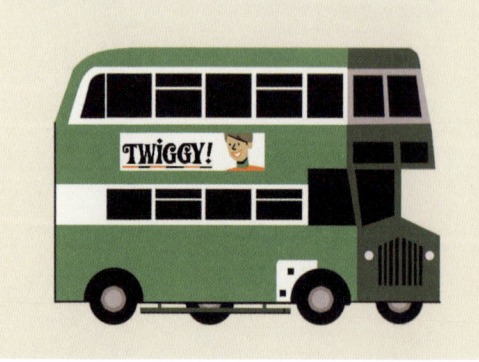

Bold Street, Liverpool, UK
There are several accounts of supposed time travel in the area of Bold Street. In one case a police officer briefly found himself surrounded by 1950s fashion and shops. In a newspaper report one man described his surprise to find himself specifically in 1967.

Mokele-Mbembe, Congo River Basin
Mokele-Mbembe is a supposed sauropod dinosaur sighted in Central Africa. Some believe the sauropod has miraculously survived extinction. Others believe the creature stumbled upon its own dramatic timeslip.

DOPPELGÄNGERS

Doppelgängers (German for double-goer) are ghostly doubles of living people. Their behaviours can range from eerie to ordinary. In her influential ghost compendium *Night Side of Nature* (1848), Catherine Crowe noted that doppelgängers were most often seen when people were ill or asleep. Psychologists explain this phenomenon as a hallucination called 'autoscopy' (from the Greek for 'self watcher').

THE MIDCENTURY

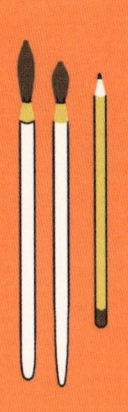

The Innocents film poster (1961)

PHANTOM VEHICLES

As cars became more common in the 20th century, phantom vehicles became a popular theme in urban legends. There were reports of ghostly cars appearing on land, in the air and even on the sea. Some believe these vehicles are haunted by their former owners or carry a dreadful curse.

1. **The Number 7 Bus (London, UK, 1934)**
   A ghostly bus that ran drivers off the road.

2. **Vauxhall Astra (A3, Surrey, UK, 2003)**
   The sighting of a phantom car led police to find a wreck that had gone unnoticed for five months.

3. **Yellow Beetle (Kuala Lumpur, Malaysia 1990s)**
   A VW Beetle believed to haunt roads.

4. **The Flying Dutchman (Atlantic Ocean, 16th Century)**
   A large ship crewed by ghosts.

5. **Silverpilen (Stockholm, Sweden, 1980s)**
   Swedish for Silver Arrow, the Silverpilen is a ghost train believed to haunt the Stockholm Metro.

6. **Flight 401 (Florida, USA, 1971)**
   Following a crash in which over one hundred people died, parts of the Eastern Air Lines plane were salvaged and used in other craft. Rumours soon

spread that planes equipped with parts from plane flight 401 were haunted.

7. **USS Zaca (Monaco, 1959)**
A yacht once owned by Australian actor Errol Flynn. Following his death, the yacht was thought to be haunted and received the attention of Catholic exorcists in 1979.

8. **Death Coach (Europe, 18th Century)**
A legendary ghost-driven carriage.

9. **Phantom Phaeton (Present, Military History Museum, Vienna, Austria)**
The car in which Archduke Franz Ferdinand of Austria was assassinated. Legends of the car being haunted first circulated in the 1950s.

10. **SM-UB-65 (Atlantic Ocean, 1918)**
According to legend this German submarine was plagued with crew deaths and ghosts.

HAUNTED INSTITUTIONS

Island of Poveglia
Venice, Italy, circa 1960s

The island of Poveglia in the Venetian lagoon was turned into a quarantine island in the 18th century. Quarantined for over 100 years, many bubonic plague victims died. In 1922, the island's buildings were converted into an asylum for the mentally ill until closure and later abandonment in the 60s. In 2016, five American tourists were rescued from the island after their ghost hunt was abandoned in fright.

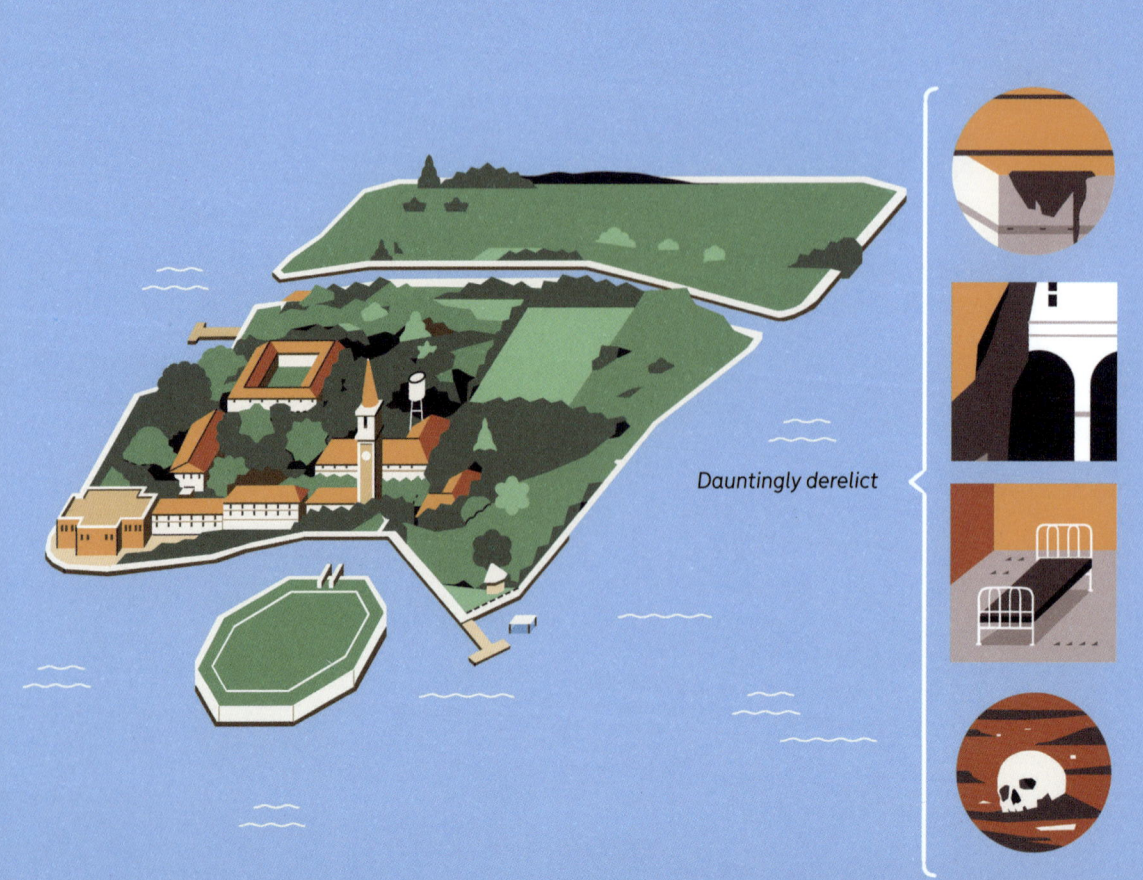

Dauntingly derelict

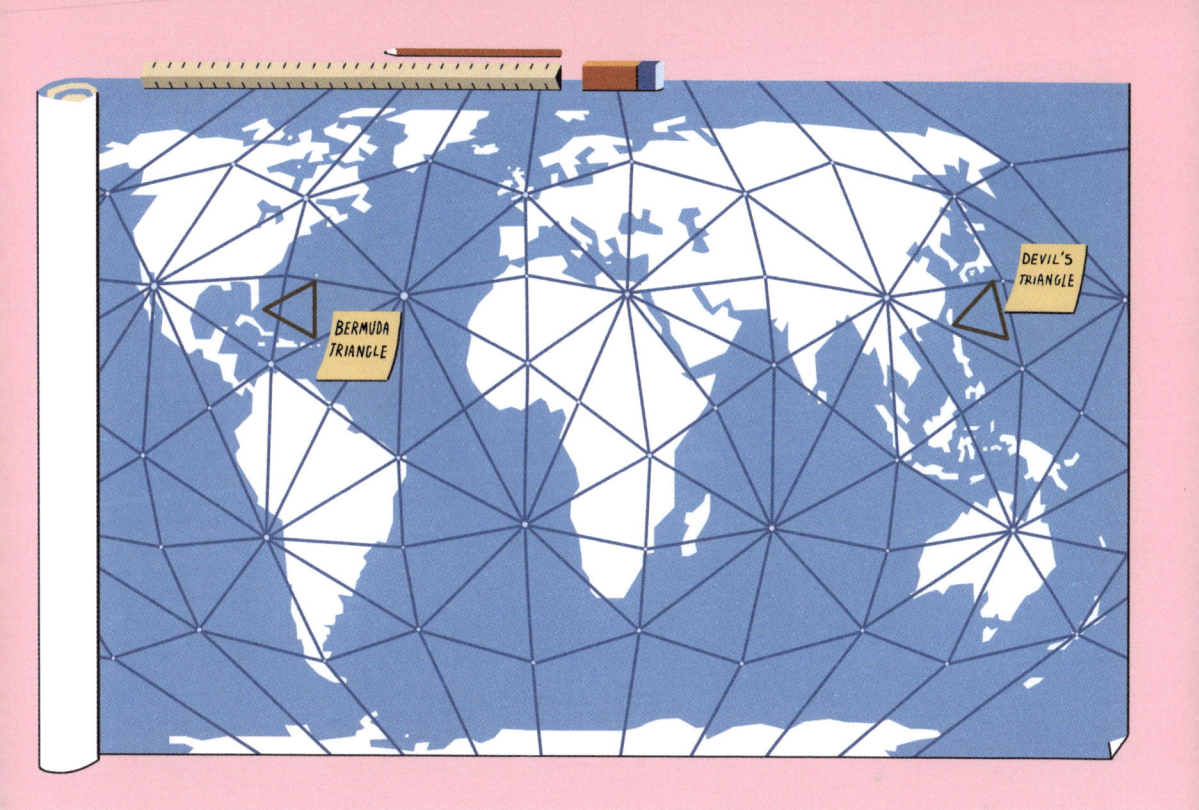

VILE VORTICES

According to some paranormal experts, strange phenomena can be mapped out to identify specific hotspots where paranormal activities are more likely to happen.

Ley Lines
In the 1920s, British archaeologist Alfred Watkins suggested that ancient landmarks were deliberately aligned. Watkins called the connections 'leys' (from the old English for clearing). While many experts rejected his theory at the time, it gained popularity among paranormal enthusiasts in the 1960s. They believed that ley lines were filled with magical energy, which could cause hauntings and even attract UFOs.

Bermuda Triangle
This loose zone in the North Atlantic Ocean is known for its many strange disappearances. Most famously in 1945, the US Navy's *Flight 19*, composed of five planes all disappeared at the same time. According to some believers to the theory, the Bermuda Triangle is one of the largest haunted areas in the world or is plagued by aliens.

Devil's Sea
This oceanic triangle is found south of Japan and has been host to several ship disappearances. Authors writing on the subject have defined the triangle's size and shape differently.

PHANTOM ANIMALS

Some ghosts have been reported to appear in animal-like forms. Cryptozoology (the study of paranormal creatures) refer to these cryptids. However, the line between ghosts, monsters and animals is often blurry as different cultures interpret these phenomena in various ways.

1. The Red Ghost (Eagle Creek, USA, 1883)
2. Martyn's Ape, also referred to as a monkey (UK, circa 16th century)
3. Ghost Deer (Mt. Eddy, USA, 20th century)
4. Old Martin (UK, 1816)
5. Nightmare (Europe, 13th century)
6. Alien Big Cat (UK, 20th century)
7. Phantom Dog (Leeds Castle, UK, 19th century)
8. Black Shuck (UK, 16th century)
9. Black Cat (Oxenby, UK, 19th century)
10. Cherry the Dog (Tapiola, Finland, 1974)
11. Gef The Talking Mongoose (Isle of Man, UK, 1931)
12. Materialised Guinea Pig (UK, 19th century)

13. Ghost Goose (Melsonby, UK, circa 19th century)
14. Ghost Owl (Eastern Russia, 19th century)
15. Útburður (Iceland, prior to 11th century)
16. Materialised Golden Eagle (Warsaw, Poland, 1919)
17. White Bird (Salisbury Plain, UK, 1885)
18. El Demonio Negro (Pacific Ocean, 20th century)
19. Loch Ness Monster (Loch Ness, UK, circa 6th century)

The Exorcism of Loch Ness
Some cryptozoologists believe the Loch Ness Monster is an ancient creature that miraculously survived extinction. However, in 1975, an English Vicar attempted to exorcise it, believing it to be an evil spirit.

71

THE POSTMODERN ERA

Pacman arcade cabinet (1980)

POSSESSED POSSESSIONS

Many legends describe the haunting of objects by an invasive ghost, demon or curse. Haunted items are typically old in nature, as though their age invites spirits to inhabit them.

In 1952, ghost hunters Ed and Lorraine Warren opened one of the first haunted museums called The Warren Occult Museum. Built in the back of their house, the museum held a collection of dolls, masks and other accursed objects.

1. 0888 88888, the haunted phone number
2. *The Legendary Painting of Glamis Castle*, a window is said to light itself
3. Haunted Mirror, Myrtles Plantation, LA, USA
4. Haunted Chest, a common item in legends
5. Haunted Phone Booth in Mizumoto Park, Japan
6. The Screaming Skull, Burton Agnes Hall, UK
7. *The Hands Resist Him*, a reputedly haunted painting by Bill Stoneham
8. Busby's Stoop Chair, Thirsk Museum, UK
9. La Pascualita, the mannequin, Chihuahua, Mexico

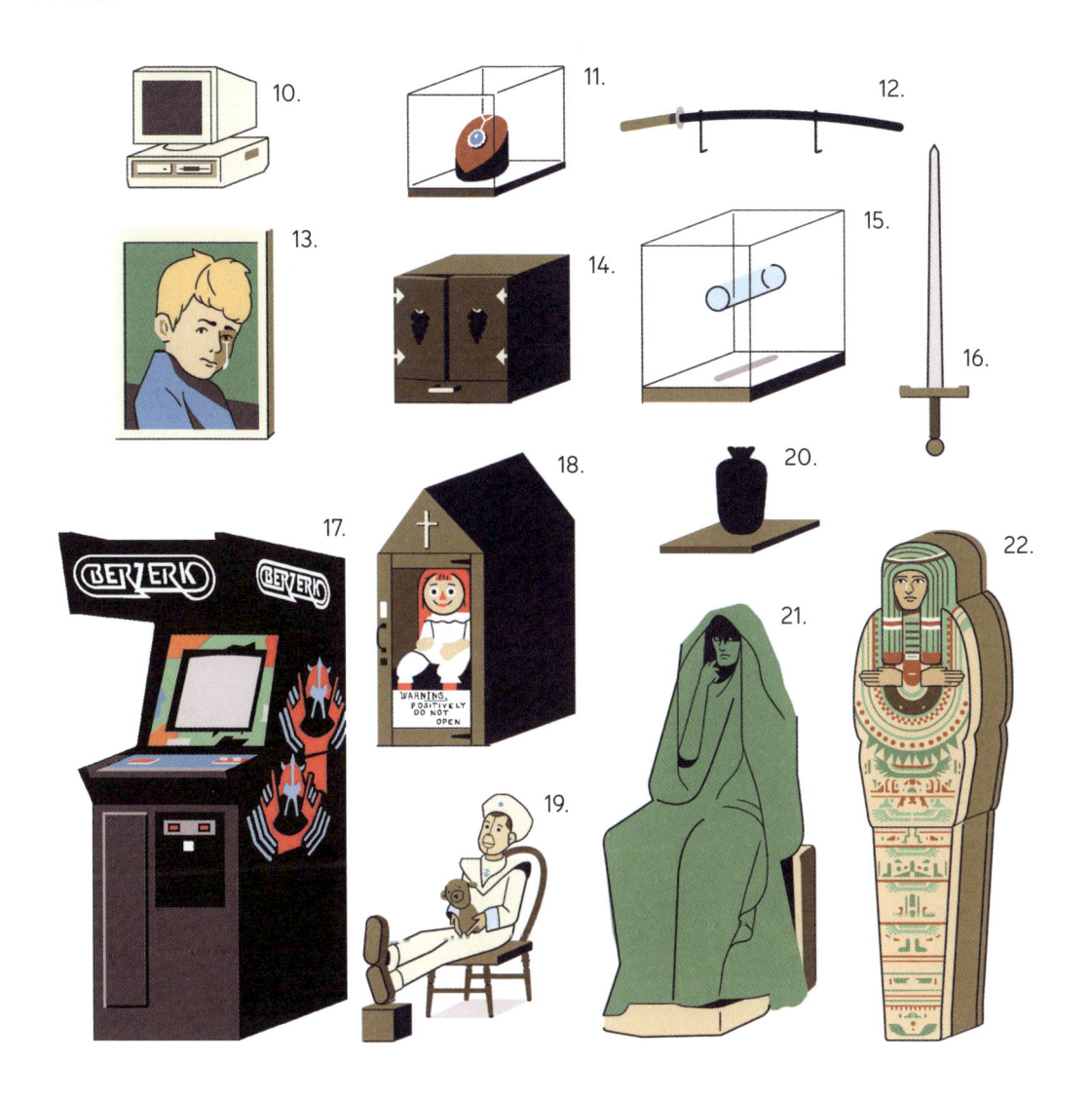

10. Haunted Amstrad PC1512, Stockport, UK
11. The Hope Diamond, National Museum of Natural History, Washington DC, USA
12. Muramasa Swords, Japan
13. *The Crying Boy*, several paintings featuring crying children are said to be haunted
14. The Dybbuk Box, reputedly a demon trapped in a box
15. The Phantom Cylinder, the Tower of London, UK
16. Haunted Sword, many antique weapons carry legendary curses
17. Bezserk Video game Cabinet, USA
18. Annabelle Doll, Warren's Occult Museum, Monroe, CT, USA
19. Robert Doll, East Martello Museum, FL, USA
20. The Basano Vase, buried in Italy
21. Black Aggie Statue, Washington DC, USA
22. The Unlucky Mummy, The British Museum, UK

GHOST TOWNS

Abandoned settlements attract the name ghost town. Settlements can be abandoned for a variety of reasons, such as pressures of economy, environment and war. Ghost towns often gain the reputation for being haunted, even when few ghost experiences are recorded. The lack of people and the damage from flora and weather leave the towns lonely and unsettling spaces.

Calico Ghost Town, CA, USA
From the 1950s, this abandoned Old West mining town was turned into a tourist spot. People worked on restoring the town for visitors who can take ghost tours and hear stories of local hauntings

Jazirat Al Hamra, United Arab Emirates
For some centuries Jazirat Al Hamra was home to people who fished for pearls but was largely abandoned in 1968 after they left to live in bigger towns. Even though it is rumoured to be occupied by Jinn, the abandoned town is now used as an outdoor art gallery.

Sanzhi UFO houses, Taiwan
A collection of incomplete houses. Construction stopped in 1980 after financial issues. The site attracted a haunted reputation due to nearby fatal road incidents. According to some, the houses were built on a Dutch burial ground. The site was demolished in 2010.

GHOST HUNTERS IN MEDIA

Literature and films show ghost hunters in different ways, from brave heroes to young vampires. One of the most famous examples is the film *Ghostbusters (1984)*, where a group of jumpsuit-wearing scientists use gadgets to battle ghosts and strange creatures from other dimensions.

The Gateway of the Monster (1910)
1. Thomas Carnacki

The Haunting of Hill House (1959)
2. Dr. John Montague

Scooby-Doo Where Are You? (1996)
3. Scooby-Doo
4. Shaggy Rogers
5. Velma Dinkley
6. Daphne Blake
7. Fred Jones
8. The Mystery Machine

78

The Ghost Busters (1975)
9. Kong
10. Eddie Spencer
11. Tracy

Pac-Man (1980)
12. Pac-Man

Poltergeist (1982)
13. Dr. Martha Lesh
14. Dr. Ryan Mitchell

Ghostbusters (1984)
15. Proton Pack
16. Ray Stantz
17. Winston Zeddemore
18. Peter Venkman
19. Egon Spengler
20. Janine Melnitz
21. Ghost Trap
22. Ecto-1

Dirk Gently's Holistic Detective Agency (1987)
23. Dirk Gently

The X-Files (1993)
24. Dana Scully
25. Fox Mulder

Mona the Vampire (1999)
26. Mona

Luigi's Mansion (2001)
27. Luigi

Wellington Paranormal (2018)
28. Sergeant Ruawai Maaka
29. Officer O'Leary

THE 21ST CENTURY

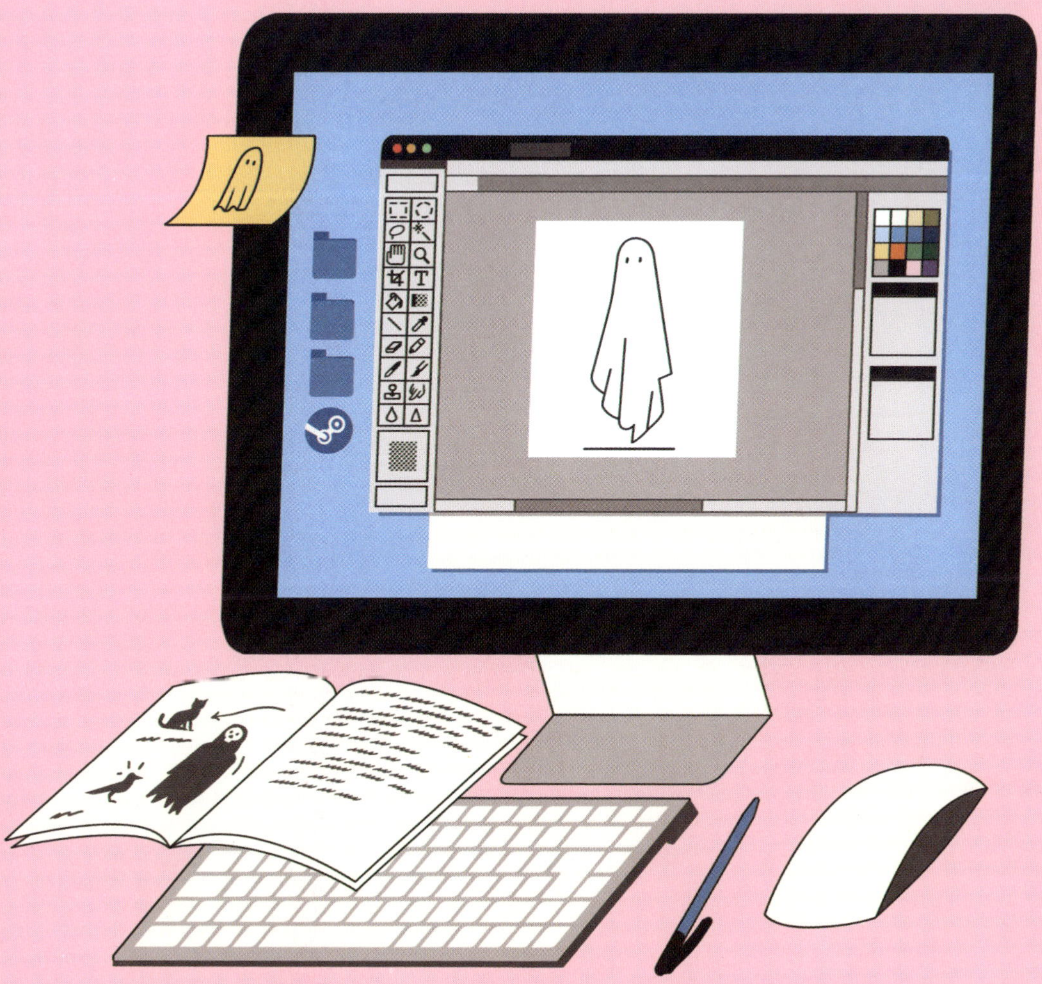

MODERN HAUNTINGS

Sherman Ranch
UT, USA

Sherman Ranch is known for unusual events, including ghosts, UFOs and cryptids. In 1996, businessman Robert Bigelow asked researchers to study any signs of paranormal. After 20 years of no clear answers, the ranch was sold multiple times. Today, it's called Skinwalker Ranch, named after a creature from Navajo mythology.

Spirit and Stories
Even though there's no clear evidence of paranormal activity, the rumours have led to documentaries, a loose fictional movie adaptation and even merchandise being made about the ranch.

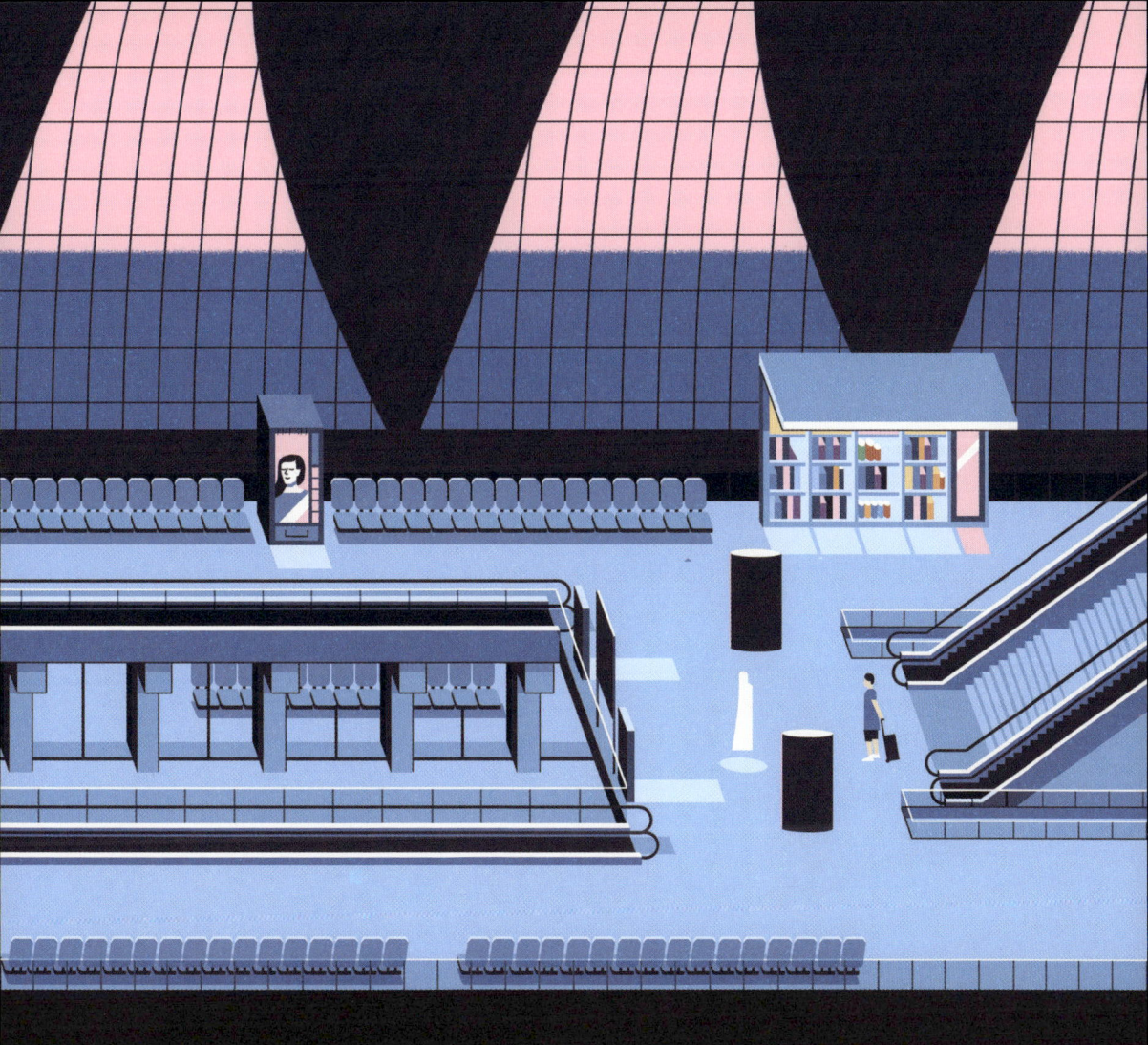

Suvarnabhumi Airport
Bangkok, Thailand

Since its development in 2006, the Suvarnabhumi airport has received a haunted reputation due to its alleged location above an ancient burial ground. During construction, builders experienced phantom wailing and strange incidents. Things worsened when 99 Buddhist monks came to perform a nine-week exorcism ritual. During the final hours, one man appeared to become possessed by a blue-faced ghost who called himself Poo Ming, the guardian of the buried cemetery.

Some visitors and staff have continued to see Poo Ming watching over the burial ground. The airport even has a Buddhist shrine where people can pray to calm the spirits.

ENDURING LEGENDS

Many of the hauntings in this book are bound to a specific locus (such as a building or period of time). Yet, some ghost legends are found all over the world with new sightings or tellings reported to this day.

Phantom Hitchhiker
The phantom hitchhiker is a common urban legend that became well-known in the 20th century. In the 1940s, folklorists Richard Beardsley and Rosalie Hankey collected over 70 different versions of the ghost story.

In most common accounts, kind-hearted drivers collect the hitchhiker at night. The passenger acts oddly and dramatically disappears during the journey. Later, the confused driver interviews locals and discovers their passenger was a ghost.

Bloody Mary

One of the most famous ghost stories is about Bloody Mary, which began as a form of fortune telling, called 'catoptromancy' (from the Greek for 'mirror divination'). Traditionally, Bloody Mary is called upon during ritual when the participant stares into a mirror, lit only by a candle and says "Bloody Mary" three times. Then, an apparition is supposed to appear, either of a future romantic partner or the ghost of Mary covered in blood.

While catoptromancy has been around for a long time, no one knows exactly where the Bloody Mary story started. In the UK, some people think she is connected to Queen Mary the First.

GHOSTS THROUGH TIME

1. Silbón Ghost, Venezuela
2. Nurse Ghosts, Cambridge, UK
3. Blackbeard's Ghost, Ocracoke, USA
4. Yakshi, India
5. Submarine Lieutenant, Atlantic Ocean
6. RAF Pilot, Croydon, UK
7. The Headless Horseman, Europe
8. Krahang, Thailand
9. Trapper Ghost, Labrador, Canada
10. Limping Woman, Pyecombe, UK
11. Black Knight, Fort Manoel, Malta
12. Myling, Scandinavia
13. Nang Takian, Thailand
14. Knights of Ålleberg, Sweden
15. Pharaoh, Valley of Kings, Egypt
16. Gwisin, Korea

17. Mae Nak, Thailand
18. Hitodama, Japan
19. Mononoke, Japan
20. Preta, Thailand
21. Wraith, UK
22. Pocong, Indonesia
23. Ma Phae Wah, Myanmar
24. Phonegyi Thaye, Myanmar

25. The Headless Nun, Canada
26. The Sandown Clown, Isle of Wight, UK
27. Spadebeard, Great Dismal Swamp, USA
28. Viking, York, UK

GHOSTS TODAY

Nowadays, one can still hear ghost stories from friends, family, books and the news. Do you, reader, have a tale to tell?

Ghosts are central to religious festivals, reminding us to honour the dead and beware the dark. They dwell in the depths of fiction to delight, appearing in stories, films and video games. While scientific explanations grow, many still enjoy the thrill of a shared chilling story.

At the very least, the power of ghosts is to inspire thrill and fear, leaving us to reach for a light with nervous hands.

I hope you will join me in asking the eternal question...

...Is anyone there?

GLOSSARY

Afterlife
A religious belief about what happens to souls after death.

Apport
The appearance of objects out of thin air.

Astral Projection
The claimed ability of individuals to separate their soul and body.

Doppelgänger
The paranormal double of a living person, often seen as a bad omen.

Ectoplasm
A substance that some people believe mediums spit out when talking to spirits.

Exorcism
The act of making spirits leave a person or place by a religious leader, like a Catholic priest.

Electronic Voice Phenomena (EVP)
The supposed recordings of ghostly voices on recording devices.

Ghost Hunter
Investigators of hauntings, with the aim to provide an explanation.

Gothic
An art style that uses dark and spooky themes, often found in old castles and churches.

Haunting
An area, person or object associated with frequent or repeated paranormal activity.

Medium
A person who believes they have the ability to communicate with the spirits of the dead.

Occult
The study of magic, mysticism and the paranormal.

Pareidolia
Seeing patterns in random data — for example, a menacing figure in a shadow.

Possession
When an evil spirit takes control of a person, object or animal.

Postmodernism
A time in the late 20th century when people started questioning traditional ideas about art, culture and knowledge. Instead of believing there is just one 'right' way to see or do things, postmodernism suggests that many perspectives can be true.

Premodernity
A time before the 1500s without modern inventions or technology like cars or electricity and people lived in simpler ways.

Psychic
A person who believes they can obtain knowledge through paranormal means.

Séance
The French for 'session'; a formalised meeting between a medium and spirits.

Skeptic
A person who trusts science and likes to ask questions to find out if something is really true.

Sleep Paralysis
An experience in which people awake unable to move. Often accompanied with hallucinations and the feeling of being weighed down.

Soul
The idea that living things contain a spirit.

Trigger Object
Some ghost hunters plant objects at suspected hauntings in attempt to provoke ghosts.

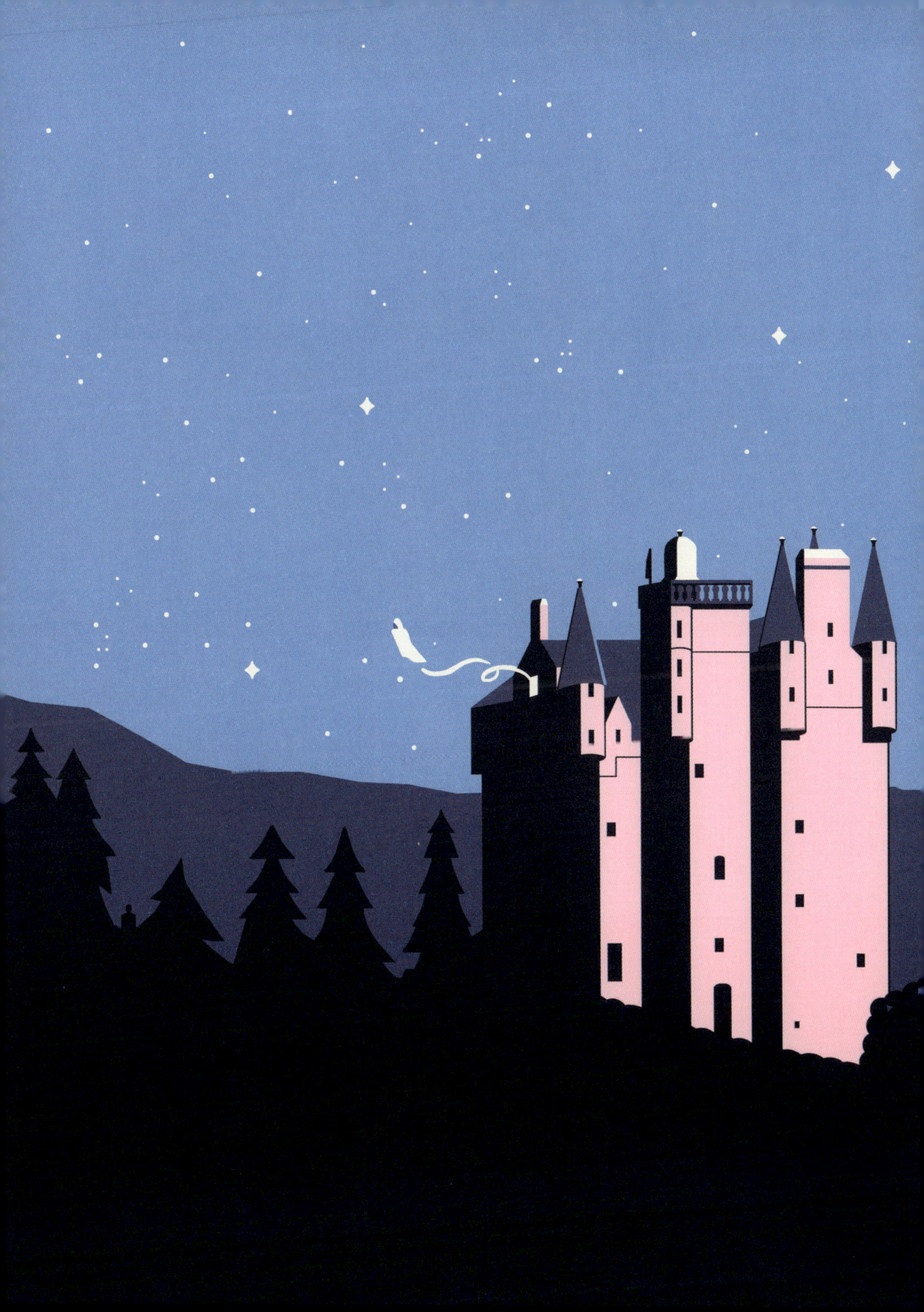

INDEX

A

afterlife 18–9
All Saints and All Souls Day 24–5
animals, phantom 80–1
apotropaic magic 32–3
apparitions 11, 44
apporting 12
Athenian apparition 26
autoscopy 65
Aztecs 19

B

Batts, Kate 44
Beardsley, Richard 94
Bell Witch 44
Bermuda Triangle 71
Bhangarh Fort 31
Bigelow, Robert 92
Bloody Mary 95
Bold Street 64
Borley Rectory 60
Buguet, Édouard Isidore 49

C

calavera 24
Calico Ghost Town 86
Caribbean 21
castles 31
catoptromancy 95
China 19, 23
Christianity 33
cold spots 13, 58
communication, spiritual 29
Crowe, Catherine 65
cryptozoology 80–1

D

Davenport brothers 39
debunkery 54–5
demons 28–9
Día de los Muertos 24
doppelgängers 65

dreamcatchers 33
drummer of Tedworth 27
duppy 21

E

ectoplasm 38
Edinburgh Castle 31
Egypt, ancient 18, 32
electrical interference 12
elementals 11
Evil Eye 33

F

festivals, ghost 22–5, 32
footsteps 13
France 48, 64

G

Germany 63
ghost hunters 27–9, 84
  in the media 88–9
Ghost Riders 22
ghost towns 86–7
ghost train 68
Ghostbusters (film) 88
ghosts
  definition of and types 10–11
  ghosts through time 96–7
Glanvill, Joseph 27
gods, ancient 28
gorgons 32
Great Dismal Swamp 45, 97
Greece, ancient 26
grotesqueries 33
guests, ghostly 22–3
Guezennec, Henri 48

H

Halloween 24, 25
hallucinations 14–5, 65
Hankey, Rosalie 94
Hantu 20
hauntings
  definition of 12–13
  demon 11, 28, 84
high strangeness 13
hitchhiker, phantom 94
horseshoes 33
Houdini, Harry 54–5
houses
  haunted 26, 34–5, 50–1
  haunted ruins 30

I

Ifrit 32
inanimate objects, haunted 11, 84–5
Indonesia 20, 97
institutions, haunted 70

J

Japan 42, 61, 71, 84–5, 97
Jazirat Al Hamra 87
Jhākri 29
Jinn 28, 87

K

Kinarut Mansion 30
Kinnitty Castle 31
Kiyotaki Tunnel 61
knocking 13, 34–5
Korean cultures 29

L

La Casa Embrujada 30
La Santa Compaña 22
The Lady of the Lake 45
legends 10, 94–5
Lemures 32
levitation 13, 55
ley lines 71
lighthouses 48
limbo 19, 28
liminal spaces 61
living, ghosts of the 11
Loch Ness Monster 81
London 13, 34
Lui Family Mansion 30

M

Mackenberg, Rose 'Mac' 54
Malay peoples 20
Malaysia 23, 30, 68
media
  ghost hunters in the 88–9
mediumship 38–9
mental imprints 11
Mexico 24, 84
Middle East 32–3
modern hauntings 92–3
Mokele Mbembe 64
Mompesson, John 27
Mumler, William 49
mummification 18
music, phantom 13
myths 10

N

Native Americans 44–5
Navajo mythology 92
Nepal 29
North America 33, 44–5

O

ofrendas 24
Ojibwe people 33
Ouija boards 46–7

P

Palace of Versailles 64
pets, peculiar 13
phantasmagoria 63
Phare De Tévennec 48
photography, spirit 49
planchettes 46–7, 60
Pliny the Younger 26
poltergeists 11, 13, 27, 60, 89
Poo Ming 93
Portugal 22
possession 13
Poveglia 70
Predjama Castle 31
protection, spirit 32–3
psychopomps 19

R

ritual magic 29
Romans, ancient 32
ruins, haunted 30

S

Samhain 25
Sami people 29
Sanzhi UFO houses 87
skeptical inquiry 14–15
séances 38–9, 63
seasonal celebrations 24–5
Sherman Ranch 92–3
simulated hauntings 62–3
Skinwalker Ranch 92
soul, sections of the 19
Spain 22
spiderweb charm 33
spirit boards 46–7
spirit cabinets 38–9
spirit protection 32–3
spiritual communication 29
Spiritualism 38–9
Suvarnabhumi Airport 93

T

talking boards 46–7
Taoism 23
timeslips 64
towns, ghost 86–7
trickster spirits 21, 28
tunnels 61
TV ghost hunting 88–9

U

UK 31, 34–5, 64, 68–9, 80–1
underworlds 18–8
USA 44, 50–1, 86

V

vehicles, phantom 68–9
voices from the void 13

W

Warren Occult Museum 84–5
Watkins, Alfred 71
Wild Hunt 22
Winchester, Sarah 50–1
Winchester Mystery House 50–1
writing, ghost 12, 39, 55

X

Xolotl 19

Y

Yūrei 42–3

Z

Zhongyuan Festival 23
Zvíkov Castle 31

Supposedly haunted New Amsterdam Theatre, USA

ELEANOR SIDGWICK

WORLD OF THE LIVING | SUMMERLAND
THE BEREAVED | THE STRANGERS

SOCIETY FOR PSYCHICAL RESEARCH Est. 1882

YES OUIJA NO
ABCDEFGHIJKLM
NOPQRSTUVWXYZ
1234567890
GOOD BYE

'I SPOKE TO YOU BY THE GLASS'

MATERIAL HANDS

SPIRIT CABINET

'TABLE TIPPING'
TABLE MOVING,
A MAGIC

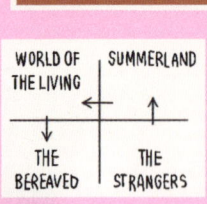

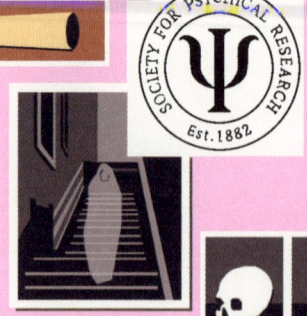

STAGECRAFT

↑↑↓↓←→←→BA

APPORT

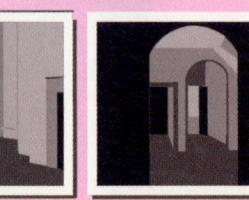

MANIFEST-ATION

BORLEY RECTORY

33

ST AUGUSTINE LIGHTHOUSE

ZENNER CARDS

SÉANCE ROBE

UFOS = GHOSTS?

VENUSIAN SPACE BROTHERS

LOST BOY LARRY

'ROSABELLE BELIEVE'

PHANTOM ISLANDS

47

PEPPER'S GHOST

1518 = ERGOT

FATE

STONE TAPE

ABOREAL ABOMINATION

WARRENS

KRAHANG

דיבוק מרוח רעה

KRASUE

GATE TO HELL

Polaroid's OneStep.
The world's simplest camera.

SHADOW PEOPLE

HAT MAN